Effective Voice and Articulation

Joseph C. Stemple
*Institute for Voice Analysis
and Rehabilitation,
St. Elizabeth Medical Center, Dayton*

Barbara Holcomb
University of Cincinnati

Merrill Publishing Company
A Bell & Howell Information Company
Columbus   Toronto   London   Melbourne

Now that this project is completed, we promise to improve our own communication skills with our strongest and most dedicated supporters. Thank you Candy and Gary for your patience.

Joe and Barbara

Cover Illustration: Jolie Muren

Published by Merrill Publishing Company
A Bell & Howell Information Company
Columbus, Ohio 43216

This book was set in Palatino.

Administrative Editor: Vicki Knight
Production Coordinator and Text Designer: Jeffrey Putnam
Art Coordinator: James Hubbard
Cover Designer: Jolie Muren

Copyright © 1988 by Merrill Publishing Company. All rights reserved. No part of this book may be reproduced in any form, electronic or mechanical, including photocopy, recording, or any information storage and retrieval system, without permission in writing from the publisher. "Merrill Publishing Company" and "Merrill" are registered trademarks of Merrill Publishing Company.

Library of Congress Catalog Card Number: 87-63487
International Standard Book Number: 0-675-20839-4
Printed in the United States of America
1 2 3 4 5 6 7 8 9 — 92 91 90 89 88

Contents

PART ONE INTRODUCTION 1

1. The Importance of Effective Communication 3

PART TWO BASES OF ORAL COMMUNICATION 9

2. Your Communication, Language, and Speech 11

   Communication, 11
   Language, 15
   Speech, 21

3. Basic Speech Processes 27

   Cerebration, 27
   Respiration, 30
   Phonation, 34
   Resonation, 35
   Articulation, 36

CONTENTS

iv

PART THREE   VOICE   39

4. The Nature of Voice   41

Anatomy of the Larynx, 41
Basic Physiology of the Larynx, 48
Voice Production, 50
Voice and Personality, 53
Your Voice, 54

5. Effective Voice Production   55

Severity Level 1, 55
Severity Level 2, 55
Severity Level 3, 55
Common Causes of Voice Disorders, 56

6. Voice Assessment and Improvement   65

PERSONAL VOICE ASSESSMENT, 66
A. Respiration Assessment, 66
B. Phonation Assessment, 67
C. Resonation Assessment, 68
D. Pitch Assessment, 69
E. Loudness Assessment, 70
F. Rate Assessment, 71
Results, 72
Voice Improvement, 72
Respiration Improvement, 73
Phonation Improvement, 75
Resonation Improvement, 78
Pitch Improvement, 81
Loudness Improvement, 84
Rate Improvement, 86
Voice Quality Improvement, 86

PART FOUR   ARTICULATION   89

7. The Nature of Articulation   91

Background Information, 91
Speech Sounds Are Phonemes, 91

The Nature of Phonemes, 92
The Phonemes of English, 92
International Phonetic Alphabet, 94
How English Phonemes Are Produced, 96
Phoneme Classification, 98
Summary, 104

8. The Sounds of English   107

Introduction, 107
Chapter Format, 108
Consonants, 108
Vowels, 137
Diphthongs, 153

9. Assessing Your Articulation   157

Background Information, 157
Assessment, 162
A Plan for Improvement, 163
Test Format, 164

10. Articulation and Pronunciation Improvement   165

Using this Chapter, 165
Improving Listening Skills, 166
When to Ask for Help, 166
Design of this Chapter, 166
Consonants, 167
Vowels, 219
Diphthongs, 241
PASSAGES FOR PRACTICE, 247
Stops, 247
Fricatives, 249
Affricates, 252
Nasals, 253
Glides, 254
Front Vowels, 256
Central Vowels, 258
Back Vowels, 259
Diphthongs, 260
Pronunciation Lists, 262
Substitution, 262

CONTENTS

Omission, 263
Addition, 263
Incorrect Stress Placement, 264
Syllable Reduction/Deletion, 265

PART FIVE APPENDICES: READING FOR VOICE IMPROVEMENT 267

Appendix 1. Phrases and Sentences Graduated in Length   269

Appendix 2. Paragraph Readings   275

Appendix 3. Poetry Readings   281

References   288

Appendix 4. Student Pronunciation/Articulation Test (SPAT)   289

Glossary   297

Index   305

Preface

We marvel at the strength and agility of gymnasts and figure skaters. We applaud the precision and coordination of basketball, soccer, and baseball players. The physical skills required for these sports, however, cannot compare with the strength, agility, control, coordination, and precision required for another human activity—speech.

Speaking requires precise, coordinated interactions of many body systems, including our neurological, respiratory, phonatory, resonatory, and articulation systems. Since speech is a learned behavior first developed in early childhood, the skills it requires are largely taken for granted. Most of us, in fact, have never considered what a significant skill we have developed. Only those who have some breakdown in one or more of the systems required for speech production are unable to communicate adequately through speech. We all therefore may be considered speech athletes.

Some athletes are more skilled than others; speech is no exception. With a complete understanding of the systems required for effective speech production, an accurate evaluation of your present speech skills, and a systematic practice plan for improving weaknesses, you, too, may become a superior athlete in the arena of human communication.

This book is intended to guide you in achieving two major goals: (1) to expand your knowledge and appreciation of your ability to use speech as your primary communication strategy; and (2) to evaluate and improve your skills as an oral communicator by improving your voice production and articulatory strategies. As with great athletes, superior communicators most often become successes in their fields. Effective voice and articulation is the overt part of this communication system.

Chapter 1 of this text introduces you to individuals like yourselves who would have benefitted from the knowledge and skills you will achieve in this course. Chapter 2 is an introduction to language and speech, the major components of oral communication, while chapter 3 discusses the five processes required for oral communication (cerebration, respiration, phonation, resonation, and articulation). Chapters 4, 5, and 6 detail the nature of effective voice production and systematic assessment and improvement of your own voice. Chapters 7 and 8 discuss the nature of articulation and the correct way to produce sounds. Chapters 9 and 10 focus on assessment and improvement of your articulatory skills. As you read this text, note the highlighted terms; these are defined in the glossary in the back of the text. Also, though extensive exercises and practice materials are included in the text, you may wish to supplement these readings from other courses you are taking, such as English literature.

The authors wish to acknowledge the many people who aided them in the development of this text. This text could not have been completed without the support of our editor, Vicki Knight, whose encouragement and skills at keeping us on task are greatly appreciated. We would also like to thank Sandra Napier, Kathy Dean, Sharon Belmonte, Cynthia DeAngelis, and Andrea Riley for their various editorial and manuscript-preparation contributions. We wish to thank the reviewers for the advice and direction they provided in the development of this manuscript: Paul R. Hoffman, Louisiana State University; Margaret Thompson, University of Georgia; Jeanne M. Lutz, The Pennsylvania State University; Maryon Matsuda, California State University; John Palmer, University of Washington; Wayne Secord, The Ohio State University; and Dwight Freshley, University of Georgia.

Part One

Introduction

Chapter 1

The Importance of Effective Communication

After graduation from college five years ago with a marketing degree, Michelle, age 28, worked as a middle-level manager in a pharmaceutical company. In this position, she was responsible for the day-to-day operations of one division of the marketing department. She supervised the various jobs assigned by the different marketing directors. Though her performance reviews in this position had always been good to excellent, Michelle felt that she was not being seriously considered for positions that would be advancements with additional responsibilities. She was beginning to feel more like an office clerk.

When one of Michelle's colleagues, with fewer years of experience, was promoted to a position higher than her own, she decided to act. She made an appointment with the marketing director and confronted her with her concern. Imagine her surprise when she was told that, in the opinion of her supervisors, she didn't project a strong enough "image" to be given the responsibilities of a higher-level position. Indeed, the marketing director was somewhat surprised that Michelle had taken the initiative to discuss her concerns.

Michelle was crushed. What image was she projecting? Why would the marketing director think that she would lack initiative? She knew from her reviews and from feedback from her immediate supervisors that her performance in her present position was more than adequate. As she saw things, she had two choices for action. One, she could seek employment elsewhere, where her skills might be more appreciated; or two, she could try to determine why she had developed this image problem in her present position.

After working through her emotions of hurt and then anger, Michelle decided on the second alternative. If her image was a problem in her present employment, whatever this image was might follow her anywhere she would go. She must determine what changes needed to be made.

CHAPTER 1

Today, Michelle is 34 years old and is a marketing director for a medical supply company, a position she has held for eighteen months. She changed companies only after being promoted two times within the pharmaceutical company. What did Michelle discover about herself that she was able to effect such a positive change?

Michelle's situation has demonstrated that, in the business world, the image we project, whether accurate or not, may ultimately determine personal success or failure. Our personal appearance, hairstyle, choice of clothes all project an image. In examining herself, Michelle decided to become more conservative in her appearance, trading slacks for suits and wearing a shorter hairstyle. She was pleased with these personal changes and received some positive feedback from coworkers. Michelle began to feel more professional. She had made positive strides in modifying her image.

Michelle then began closely observing the upper-level managers and how they interacted with others. She began to discover that the manner in which they spoke to people seemed often to command a level of respect. They seemed to be able to project a more powerful image by using strong, effective communication tools. Michelle knew that she had always been described as a soft-spoken person. Perhaps this description of her communication strategies yielded an image of a weak individual who lacked initiative.

The ultimate improvement in Michelle's communication effectiveness came with help from a commercially available self-improvement course. During this course, she discovered that she was consistently using a weak, breathy voice quality with somewhat imprecise articulation, especially with people she saw as authority figures. Her ineffective communication skills added to her overall weak image. After she discovered that her communication was more effective around close friends and family, it didn't take Michelle long to improve her voice production and articulatory strategies in her work situation.

Michelle was intelligent enough and open enough to recognize the need for change. Her personal appearance changes were important. But, had poor communication strategies continued, chances for professional advancement would have remained limited.

Unlike Michelle, Mark could never accept the need for improving his communication skills, even though poor skills had even a greater effect on his career. Mark was a 31-year-old lawyer. He had been with the same law firm for six years and was consistently given the cases that needed only very limited client contact. Mark was very complete and accurate in the work he produced, but he had always wanted to be assigned to trial cases. For several years, Mark was told that his value to the firm rested with his ability to do the tedious type of work that required hours of research and writing legalese. As the years passed, Mark became more dissatisfied with his work, but too entrenched in his position to consider leaving. He continued to request trial cases. Trial cases were not forthcoming, so Mark finally decided to confront the senior partner of the law firm to demand an explanation for his exclusion from such cases.

The senior partner, having dealt several times with Mark's requests, finally decided to be frank with him. Mark was told bluntly that he did not possess the communication skills necessary to represent a client effectively in a courtroom situation. The senior partner went on to say that Mark's speech was like the work he produced—slow and monotonous, without the "fire" necessary to be effective in front of a jury. Instead of accepting the criticism in a positive manner, Mark took the comment as a personal insult. Not long after, he sought employment with a different firm.

Effective communication is important also in what have traditionally been considered nonprofessional work environments. John is a 46-year-old line supervisor at a local automobile assembly plant. He had worked in the factory for twenty-six years and had been a supervisor for the past eight years. John's duties involved instructing workers on the line regarding their duties for the day, troubleshooting mechanical problems with maintenance workers, and spot-checking the products that came off the line.

John began having communication problems when he noticed an intermittent type of hoarseness developing almost every workday by midafternoon. This hoarseness became more persistent during the week and then cleared somewhat on the weekend. This pattern continued for several weeks until John finally was examined by the plant physician. The plant physician thought John probably was suffering from an infectious type of laryngitis, so John was placed on antibiotics for ten days. Meanwhile, the hoarseness persisted, making it very difficult for John to talk loudly enough over the noise of the assembly line to be heard adequately by his workers.

John remained hoarse following the course of antibiotics. The plant physician therefore referred him to a throat specialist, who diagnosed the presence of swollen (edemic) and red (erythemetic) vocal folds. This vocal fold condition was causing the hoarseness and was thought to be the result of long-term abuse of the vocal folds. This abuse took the forms of habitual loud talking and shouting over the noisy background of the factory, resulting in banging and rubbing of the vocal fold tissue, as well as tissue irritation from 29 years of relatively heavy cigarette smoking. The vocal fold tissues simply couldn't withstand the abuse anymore and had begun to break down. No medical or surgical treatment would take care of this problem. If John were to continue in his present supervisory position, it would be necessary that he modify these abusive behaviors to reduce the impact of the behaviors on his vocal folds.

John chose to attempt to modify the vocal abuse. First, he decided to stop smoking, a task he subsequently described as the "hardest thing I've ever done in my life." Second, he examined his use of voice in the plant and on the line. He discovered that approximately sixty percent of his communications were purely social and could be reduced significantly. The other forty percent of his talking was directly related to his supervisory work. Though this could not be reduced, he was often able to call the worker into his office, a quieter environment, to give instructions rather than compete vocally with the line noise. By reducing and/or eliminating these vocally abusive behaviors, John's vocal fold tissue improved, thus reducing and finally eliminating the hoarseness. John, again, was able to talk effectively even over the noise on the line when it was absolutely necessary. He also learned an important lesson about not taking any one part of the communication system for granted.

Michelle, Mark, and John are all very different individuals, with very different types of environments and goals. They are all similar, however, because the communication skills of each had a significant impact on their lives. The effectiveness or ineffectiveness of their oral communication skills dictated in some part the success they found in life.

The importance of your oral communication skills to your success in daily living cannot be overstated. The manner in which you are perceived and judged by others is often reflected in your ability to communicate orally. Because the two major components of oral communication are voice and articulation, this text is designed to review your present abilities in these areas and to guide you toward improvement. Your use of effective voice and articulation will be a plus in whatever life situation you find yourself.

In developing communication skills, few of us have ever stopped to wonder, to be amazed at, or to try to understand this fascinating, complex system. This text will introduce you to the components of the communication system and, it is hoped, a better understanding and appreciation of this unique human skill.

The communication skills that you have developed to this point in your life have been molded by many different influences. These influences might include family, environment, geographic location, and basic personality, to name a few. A positive aspect of oral communication is that it may continue to be molded and continue to be improved. The processes of voice and articulation are amenable to change. They may continue to be made more effective throughout your life.

For some of you, this course will be the first time you have ever examined the effectiveness of your use of voice and articulation. For all of you, the course is designed for self-improvement—that is, improvement of voice quality and articulatory precision, both of which lead to improved intelligibility and more effective communication abilities.

Everyone can improve oral communication skills. To do this, however, some time and effort must be given to understanding the component parts of communication. Chapter 2 will introduce you to the basics of language and speech. You will learn that language can live without speech, but that speech is not present without language.

Chapter 3 is an overview of all the physiological processes of speech. These processes will include cerebration, or brain and nervous system functions associated with speech production; respiration, including the anatomy and physiology of breathing for speech and voice; phonation, with a description of the nature of sound, the types of sounds, and the voice-producing mechanism; resonation, which gives sound production its distinctive quality; and finally articulation, including information regarding phonemes, distinctive features, phonetics, sounds, syllables, and words.

Chapters 4, 5, and 6 will then guide you through the nature of voice production, including the anatomy and physiology of the vocal mechanism, a description of ineffective vocal habits and more serious voice disorders, a means of assessing the effectiveness of voice quality, and a step-by-step guide for improving the properties associated with the production of effective voice.

Finally, Chapters 7 and 8 will guide you through the nature of articulation and the sounds of English, including detailed descriptions of how sounds are produced. Chapters 9 and 10 will then provide you with a systematic method of first evaluating and then improving the effectiveness of your articulation.

Open your ears and open your eyes. Be brave enough to listen, to see, and to try. Effective voice and articulation is available to everyone. So let's begin.

STUDY QUESTIONS

1. How important is your ability to communicate in your present everyday classroom environment? Could you successfully complete all of your course work without using oral communication?

2. What professions can you think of that have a strong dependence on the use of effective voice and articulation?

Part Two
Bases of Oral Communication

Chapter 2

Your Communication, Language, and Speech

*I*n the movie *Cool Hand Luke*, the warden says to Paul Newman, playing a recalcitrant prisoner, "What we have here is a breakdown in communication." At that point, Paul Newman, as Luke, was not interested particularly in exploring just what the warden meant by "communication." However, *you* may bring some questions to this chapter, especially after seeing the chapter title. You may feel that your only objective in this course is to improve your speech; i.e., voice and articulation. However, speech is the way we express language, and language is one mode we use to communicate. We feel that your overall goal should be to improve your communication effectiveness. If you have ever had the experience of being videotaped, you may have been made painfully aware of awkward body posture, nervous habits, and incomplete sentences, with false starts and hesitations. Our aim is not to provide suggestions for improving these aspects of communication behavior, but we want you to be aware of their contribution.

In this chapter, we will examine the nature and process of communication. Then we will discuss language, a vehicle for communication. Finally, we consider speech and how it is produced and processed.

COMMUNICATION

Communication has often been considered the "glue" of culture. It serves to maintain the connections among all of us who share humanity and culture. You are on either the sending or receiving end of some communication during many of your waking hours. You are aware of obvious instances of communication: listening to a professor's lecture, chatting with friends, watching the evening news. Just as important are more subtle examples of communication—exchanging smiles with a passing stranger, shaking a fist at the motorist who just cut in front of you, or shaking your head in dismay at the latest exploit of your friend.

Communication is the process of exchanging information and ideas. Intuitively, we know that the process is more complex. Speakers must put ideas into some sentence form; then the words expressing those ideas must be inserted into the sentences. Listeners must break sentences into their parts and sort through relevant and irrelevant information. As a speaker, you want to have some effect on your listener or group of listeners. You may want to request a favor, persuade an audience to action, or deny a charge. As a member of an audience, you listen to receive such information. Communication, when viewed in this way, is actually a tool that you use, more or less effectively, to accomplish goals and intents. We do not communicate with each other for no reason. Even idle chatter has a purpose—to pass some time!

To understand what occurs in communication situations, researchers have created models that express the dynamics of this setting. The mechanics of the models may differ, but the elements are consistent. There are six basic variables in the communication process—source, message, channel, receiver, feedback, and noise. We will consider each of them and then put them in their places in a model of communication.

The **source** is the sender or the originator of some communication. An individual or a group can be a source. The source decides what to communicate, how to phrase it, and how to send it. For example, a source, a labor organization, decides to respond to proposed legislation regarding unions by formulating a stand and issuing a position paper. You, as a source, call a friend on the phone to arrange a study session. Among major influences on what and how the source communicates are experiences, beliefs, and values of that source. Management personnel of a company might issue a very different position paper than the labor union representing workers of that company, each reflecting particular attitudes and objectives.

The **message** is a collection of ideas and feelings that the source is trying to communicate. In formulating thoughts into symbols (in our case, words), the source is doing something called **encoding.** We all encode our messages quite easily and unconsciously. We will discuss this encoding process later.

The **channel** is how the source elects to send the message. Spoken messages are sent through sound or auditory channels. A glance or gesture is sent through visual channels. The message encoded by a reassuring embrace is sent through the channel of touch. In general, sound and sight are our major channels of communication.

The **receiver** is the intended target for the message. Just as the source encodes the message in preparation for communication, the receiver must decode the message. **Decoding** is the process of extracting meaning from the message. Like the source, the receiver has a set of beliefs, values, and experiences that influence how the message is interpreted.

As our model is now constructed, the sending of messages is strictly one-way. How does the source know when the message was not received or was misunderstood? **Feedback,** a verbal or nonverbal response by the receiver, provides the source with information to adjust his message. You have experienced a certain quizzical look from a communication partner who doesn't quite understand what you were trying to say. "Pardon?" or "What?" or "Huh?" are verbal ways we provide feedback to the source.

When a communication attempt is incomplete or unsuccessful, there are several possible causes for breakdown. One important factor in communication failure is **noise.** In our model, noise is any distraction that interferes with communication. You might be most aware of distractions when you are concentrating intently on studying. You can be annoyed by the bass beat emanating from the stereo speakers of your upstairs neighbor. The jackhammer of a street maintenance worker is disruptive to a conversation you conduct on a nearby sidewalk. These are examples of external noise. Noise can be internal also. A growling stomach or distracting thought can reduce your concentration as a speaker or listener. Remember how difficult concentrating on schoolwork can be the day before summer vacation? You create internal noise with your thoughts of summer plans and pleasures. You can increase your effectiveness by monitoring these situations and modifying your speaking or listening accordingly.

When we combine these elements, a model of communication results. In Figure 2-1, we see how these might come together. It is important to understand that the process is interactive, not simply unidirectional. The source is a listener also, in a sense, trying to interpret the feedback of the receiver. In turn, the source modifies his message. Let's take a communication example and follow it through the model. You get onto an elevator in the lobby with two other people for a ride to the 44th floor. You make eye contact with another passenger, smile and say, "Long ride, isn't it?" That passenger responds to your statement with a curt smile and turns away and you terminate your conversation. What happened? You, as the source, sent your message (verbal and nonverbal) through the channels of air and light (auditory and visual) to the other passenger, the receiver.

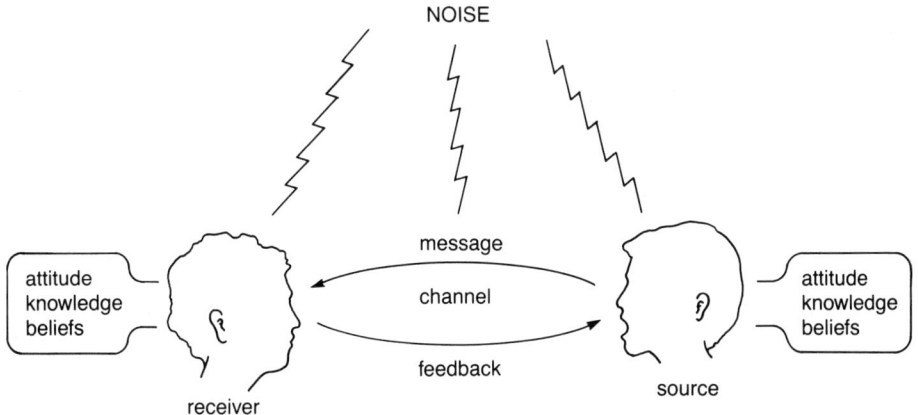

FIGURE 2-1 Model of communication

He decoded your message and gave you feedback: he smiled briefly and turned away. His obvious rejection of communication made you decide to end your attempt.

What was your last communication effort? Can you analyze it in terms of our model?

Human communication is unique in its diversity and flexibility. Communication between two or more people, or interpersonal communication, may be divided into two areas of study. Researchers who examine **verbal communication** are interested in studying language and paralanguage. Language, a system of symbols for communicating thoughts and feelings, is discussed in the next section. **Paralanguage** is the set of vocal qualities—stress, intonation, pause, and rate of speech—that communicate additional meaning to speech. We discuss these qualities in Chapter 4. When we consider the second aspect of interpersonal communication, **nonverbal communication,** we describe eye contact, facial expression, gesture, and the use of space.

Nonverbal behavior can function in communication in several ways. It can complement speech—as when praise is offered with a smile. When someone says "I'm happy for you" and leans forward to touch you, that touch enhances communication. Nonverbal communication also regulates conversations. Eye contact and gesture are usually the regulators. People look at you when they want to begin a conversation and look away when they are ready to end it.

Studies of eye contact have shown that there is more looking recorded when a person is listening. However, staring is perceived as being threatening. Speakers do relatively less looking. Eye contact is controlled also by culture. Asians, Indians, and northern Europeans have less eye contact than Arabs, Latin Americans, and southern Europeans. You may be familiar with the phrase "Look at me when I talk to you," spoken by an irate adult to a child or adolescent. Breaking eye contact with an elder is considered disrespectful in segments of American culture. However, a Puerto Rican child would be punished for making eye contact when she was being chastised.

Facial expressions may be innate; that is, they may be genetically determined. Electric recordings of muscle activity in persons instructed to think only sad or happy thoughts with an immobile face have shown increases in activity in those muscles involved in making the facial expressions of those emotions. Expressions of joy, hatred, disgust, sadness, and excitement seem to be constant across many different cultures. Facial expressions are indicators of emotion. When the words someone speaks and the facial expressions someone makes are considered together, we tend to interpret the communication on the basis of the facial cues. When a friend says to you "I really enjoyed that dinner you made"—with a look of distaste on her face—you don't interpret that comment as a compliment.

Gestures are an important aspect of our communication. Unlike facial expressions, gestures do vary across cultures. At birth, infants move in rhythm with speech that they hear. As we grow older, we continue this behavior in a more refined way. Our movements are timed with the speech of our conversational partners. A listener will nod his head at pauses in the speaker's conversation.

Proxemics is the study of the use of space by partners in a conversation. Hall (1966) has developed a classification of social distances. Based on observations of middle class Americans of northern European extraction, personal distance ranges from 1.5 to 4 feet, with an average of 2.5 feet. Social distance ranges from 4 to 12 feet, with 7 feet an average distance between partners in a business interaction. Vision and hearing are the most important sensory channels for these two situations. You can test average distances by gradually moving toward your conversational partner until he begins to back up. Other variables, such as age and sex, will affect your definition of distance, as will culture. Hall (1966), in his research, determined that Germans required the most personal distance, followed by Americans, Latin Americans, and the French. Arabs required the least personal distance. Measurements can be quite precise. Most people are well aware of the threatening feeling experienced when someone begins to infringe on personal "territory."

> Personal space is quite real in our daily lives. Try experimenting with moving toward and away from various communication partners. What is their reaction?

What is the importance of studying the communication process for the student of articulation and voice? In understanding the process, you should realize that as a source you can make your message more clear by overcoming the noise in the system and by monitoring your speech according to your feedback and that of the receiver. You can minimize the effect of noise in the process of communication by changing an inappropriate voice (altering loudness, eliminating hoarseness, improving intonation) and by improving imprecise articulation (learning correct pronunciation, producing clear consonants). By monitoring the reactions of your receiver (questioning looks, disinterested facial expressions), you can modify your speech to clarify and capture the attention of your audience. You can be aware that what you don't say, but show, is just as important as the content of your speech.

We now turn to language, an instrument of communication.

LANGUAGE

Before we discuss language and its components, we must define two important concepts. **Language competence** is a speaker's knowledge of a language. **Language**

performance is what a speaker says—how she uses her language knowledge. These concepts influence and reflect communication expertise.

Language competence allows you to understand every sentence that you read in this book, even though you have never seen them before. Your language knowledge enables you to judge whether *safloy* and *gobfl* are possible English words. As you read the following list of sentences, mark those you feel are not good English sentences.

1   Mary married a drunken sailor.
2   It was a drunken sailor that Mary married.
3   It was Mary that married a drunken sailor.
4   That was it Mary married a drunken sailor.
5   It was drunken that Mary married a sailor.
6   It was nice that Mary married a sailor.
7   It was sailor that Mary married a drunk.
8   It was strange that Mary married a drunk.
9   It was a drunk that Mary married strange.
10 It was drunk that Mary married a strange.
11 It was a drunk that strange Mary married.
12 That Mary married a drunken sailor was strange.
13 That Mary married a strange sailor was drunk.
14 That Mary married a drunk was sailor.
15 That Mary married a drunk was inevitable.
16 Mary's marrying a drunken sailor came as a surprise to us.
17 Mary's drunken sailor came to surprise us.
18 Sailor Mary's drunken to surprise us came.
19 What shall Mary do with a drunken sailor?
20 What with a drunken sailor Mary shall do?
21 Shall Mary do drunk with what a sailor?
22 Shall Mary have fun with such a sailor?
23 With what a sailor shall Mary do drunk?

(Lindfors, 1987)

If you noted that 4, 5, 7, 9, 10, 13, 14, 18, 20, 21, and 23 were not possible English sentences, then you have the language competence you need as a speaker of English. Language performance is a description of the sounds that you utter as you speak. Take some time today to listen to how someone else uses language. Hear *everything* they say; that is, listen to their filler words, false starts, and abrupt changes of topic. People rarely talk in complete, cohesive sentences, except in formal speeches, such as a presidential address. In the past, you have been aware of instances where you have been careful of your word choices and grammar. "Everyday" speech is much less restricted. Here is an excerpt of someone's language performance, transcribed from an informal interview.

My older sister works for a bank and she just got a promotion last week so we're all excited about that um they just appointed her uh bank official or some . . . something which is really good cause she's only been there for like a year and a half so that's real good and um then my younger brother goes to Auburn University and his major's psychology and he will be a senior next year and I live in Sidney, Ohio I don't know if you've heard of that and that's not that exciting but it was okay to grow up there's not that much to do.

Reading this segment is difficult because it is not separated into discrete sentences. However, if you heard this passage spoken, your language competence would enable you to decode the sentences without difficulty. If you are skeptical about whether we truly speak this way, take some time to tape a brief conversation between you and a friend. Make a transcript of the tape and you will discover how your speech may appear to be disorganized and nonfluent.

> Tape yourself while you describe the plot of a movie you enjoy. Listen to your monologue. Do you speak in distinct sentences?

What are we using to express ourselves? A **language** is a system of arbitrary symbols used for communication. These symbols are agreed upon by a speech community composed, in our case, of those of us who speak English. Notice that the phrase "arbitrary symbols" was used instead of "words." We also did not say "verbal" communication. The system of arbitrary symbols used by American deaf persons is a language known as American Sign Language, or ASL. Just as English or any other spoken language, ASL has its own set of rules governing structure of the symbols and how they are strung together to produce sentences. We will discuss the use of English and several of its varieties in this book.

We focus now on the notion of "system." Discussing systems of various sorts naturally brings us to talk about rules. Linguists endeavor to describe the rules that hold for the various languages of the world. They must discover the rules that form the basis for the subsystems of sounds (phonology), word meaning (semantics), grammar (syntax), and communication (pragmatics).

Phonology is the system of rules for combining sounds into words. The phonology of any language tells us which sounds are important and in what order those sounds may be combined to form words. In English, the sounds /t/ and /s/ may not be together at the beginning of a word as in *tsap*. However, they may appear together at the end of a word—*cats*. (Of course, we have the word *tsar*, borrowed from Russian, but this is not a word native to English.) The trilled /r/ of Spanish is not in our phonology nor are the clicks from Hausa, an African language. The sounds of English that are meaningful are called **phonemes.** Phonemes are significant because they make a contrast. For example, *pig*, *big*, *rig*, *dig*, and *wig* are different by only one sound. The sounds that distinguish the five words—/p/, /b/, /r/, /d/, and /w/—are considered to be phonemes. We will discuss 42 of the phonemes of English, but many more sound variations have been described. Say *top* with your hand held in front of your mouth. Do you feel the puff of air as you release the /t/? Say *pat*. You should feel air only as the /p/ is released; your tongue stays up for the /t/. If you release both sounds with a puff, it sounds artificial. You have just demonstrated two of the possible varieties of /t/. One of these is made with a puff of air—/t/ (aspirated)—and one is not—/t˘/ (unaspirated). We call these variations of a phoneme **allophones.** In Hindi, /t/ and /t˘/ are considered to be two separate phonemes. Hypothetically, /tik/ and /t˘ik/ are two different words for the speaker of Hindi, but we would have difficulty noticing the difference as speakers of English.

Contrast your production of these words: *kite—take; puck—cup; tub—but.* Can you distinguish the two allophones of each phoneme—/k/, /t/, /b/, /p/? Say *leave* and *veal.* What is different about the two allophones of /l/?

Semantics is the system that contains rules regarding the meaning of words. Our semantic system contains a sort of dictionary, or "lexicon." The lexicon is a "vocabulary list" of all the concepts in our world grouped into categories. For example, under the category "apple," we might find the features red, green, shiny, tart, sweet, and round. These features describe the concept. The concept "apple" itself could be described further under the category "fruit." Children who are learning the meaning system might display their emerging semantic knowledge by using the word "apple" to refer to all fruit. They might use the word "doggie" to mean any four-legged animal. They haven't incorporated all the features of the adult semantic system—barks, wags its tail, hates cats—into their understanding of what "doggie" means. When you hear "The mice stampeded across the field," what is wrong about that sentence? Right, mice cannot stampede. Similarly, "The elephants scurried across the field" disturbs your sense of what is appropriate. You have used your knowledge of semantics to identify these sentences as poor English sentences (or, at the very best, humorous sentences). Other dubious sentences include

> We picked apples from the vine.
> The bird slithered through the air.
> The snake walked from its nest.
> Snow flowed from the sky.

Create other sentences that do not make sense. Do young children (ages 4 to 7) understand what makes your sentences "bad" English sentences?

Syntax is simply the set of rules that determine how words are combined to form sentences. Your English teacher in high school called these grammatical rules. Syntax helps you determine that "The mouse was caught by the cat" means the same as "The cat caught the mouse." Syntactic rules tell us in what order nouns, verbs, articles, and other parts of speech should appear in a sentence. A young child who is learning language might say "cookie there" or "allgone kitty." At this stage of syntactic development, word order is not yet fixed. Soon, however, that child will be exclaiming, "There's my cookie," or "No more kitty," demonstrating a burgeoning understanding of syntactic rules.

Have you ever had the experience of being interrupted by a friend in the midst of a sentence? You were annoyed because that person violated one of the rules of pragmatics. Your friend violated the rule that states that conversational partners take turns in speaking. **Pragmatic** rules govern the appropriate use of language in social situations. You are using pragmatic rules when you start a conversation, change a topic, end a conversation, greet someone, use more formal speech with a stranger, or joke with a neighbor. We do not think about pragmatics, but when we talk we are quite aware when some pragmatic rule is violated, as when a friend comes up to you and starts talking without saying, "Hi, how are you?"

We have described the components of language—phonology, semantics, syntax, and pragmatics. How do these components come together in the production and comprehension of language? The linguist Noam Chomsky, in 1965, developed a theory that might account for how this process works. Chomsky's model has two levels for representing a sentence. **Deep structure** is the most abstract representation of a sentence. At this point, only the skeleton of a sentence exists. Gradually, all of the phonological and semantic elements of a sentence are added and **transformational rules** are applied which change the sentence. Transformational rules reorder and change the sentence components so that the final form of a sentence—its **surface structure**—emerges. The surface structure of a sentence is how you intend to say that sentence. From deep structure, representing sentence meaning, to surface structure can be quite a complicated process, as shown by Figure 2-2. The basic sentence frame "Mother eat something" can evolve into "Mother ate German chocolate cake," "Mother didn't eat anything," or "Why isn't she eating?" An ambiguous sentence, "He

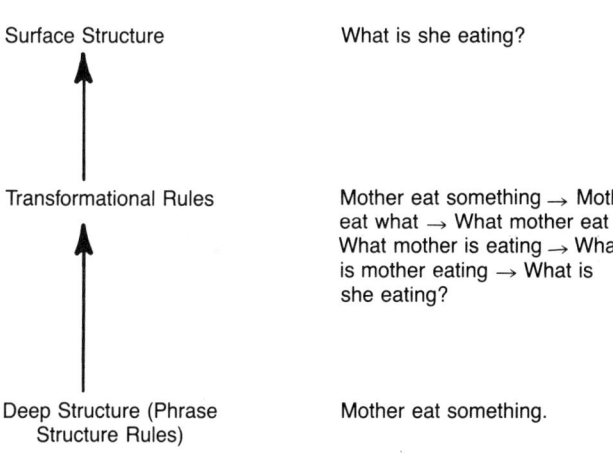

FIGURE 2-2 Language-processing model

Note: From *Language Development: An Introduction* by R. E. Owens, Jr., 1984, Columbus: Charles E. Merrill Publishing Co. Copyright 1984 by Bell & Howell Company. Reprinted by permission.

likes entertaining guests," would be represented in deep structure in two ways, depending on your interpretation: "He likes something" and "He likes to do something." Gradually, through the use of transformational rules, these become "He likes guests who are entertaining" and "He likes to entertain guests." The dual meanings of the sentences "Flying planes can be dangerous" and "Visiting relatives can be a nuisance" can be explained by the concepts of deep and surface structure. Chomsky's explanation accounts for the production and processing of an infinite number of sentences. Many of these sentences have never been encoded or decoded before.

As you can see, our simple definitions of language competence and performance have become more complex. Before you utter a word, a sequence of events has occurred to bring your thought to expression. Figure 2-3 is an abstract representation of the steps in language processing and language production. Next, we will discuss one particular aspect of that model—the realization of surface structure to speech.

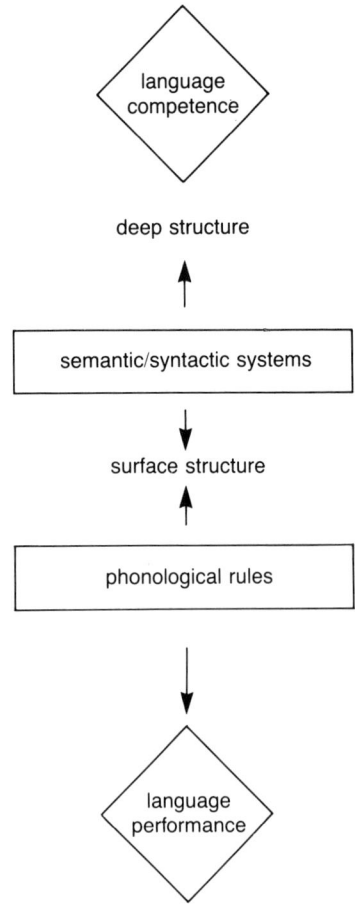

FIGURE 2-3 Steps in language production and language processing

21
SPEECH

As cultures and societies change over the years, so do the languages that represent those groups. We may be able to read the writings of historical persons in the founding of our country, but their speech was different from our own. Earlier in historical literature, the English of Shakespeare was pronounced differently, as we can see by words that he rhymed in his plays:

break	speak
boot	foot
cough	laugh
where	sphere
crab	bob
fear	there

Changes in spoken language occur more rapidly than in the written code. Alterations can happen in any of the parts of language that we discussed in the previous section: pragmatics, syntax, semantics, or phonology. We recognize the sound differences most readily.

Many factors influence the development of differences within a language. They include geographical region, socioeconomics (social class, education, employment), gender, and first language. As a speaker of the English language, you would be able to read any newspaper published in the United States: the *San Diego Union*, the *Boston Globe*, the *Atlanta Constitution*, or the *Chicago Tribune*. However, you recognize that the readers from those areas may speak differently from yourself, perhaps with another "accent." A linguist would consider these different types of English to be **dialects.** A dialect is a variety of a language. Dialects can exist for all languages of the world.

You are aware of dialects in the United States. These varieties of English have been described in a collective project called "The Linguistic Atlas of the United States." The atlas was designed to bring together evidence of language changes throughout the U.S. Areas where similar patterns of language change occurred were labeled as dialect areas. Hans Kurath, the original director of this project, designated four major dialect areas: Northern, North Midland, South Midland, and Southern (Fig. 2-4). Within these areas were several subdivisions. For example, the Northern area contains a distinctive Eastern New England dialect and a New York City dialect. We will deal with specific pronunciation differences in Chapter 8, but we can talk about some word, or semantic, differences here. For example, Northern dialects typically use *pail*; Midland and Southern dialects use *bucket*. Southern dialect uses *carry* to mean *escort* or *take*, as in "She'll carry me to the store."

Dialects that are spoken by people in positions of political and economic power are considered to be **standard dialects.** You are familiar with the standard English dialect spoken by anchorpersons on the evening network news. These standard dialects (e.g., Standard English, Southern Standard English) all share

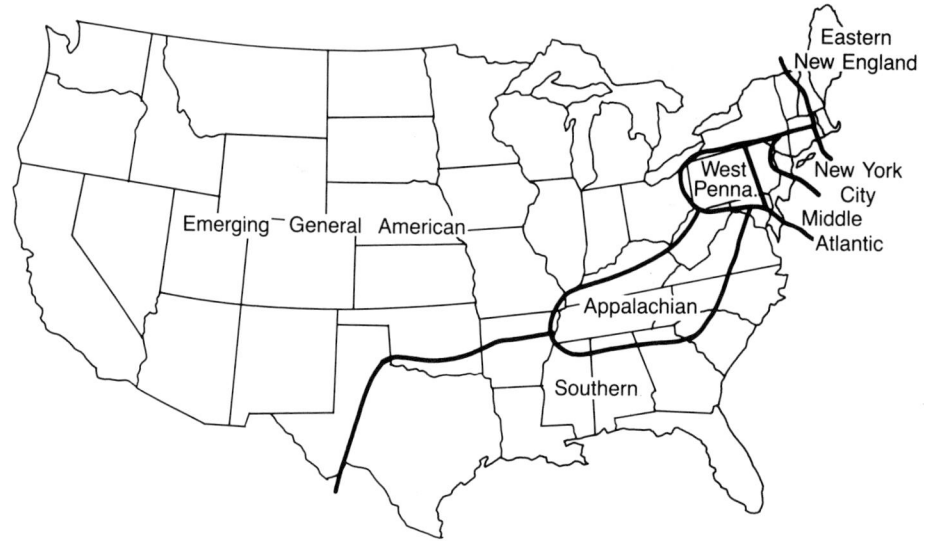

FIGURE 2-4 Major American English speech varieties

Note: From *A Structural History of English* (p. 371) by J. Nist, 1966, New York: St. Martin's Press. Reprinted by permission.

the same grammatical rules, but may differ in phonology, semantics, and pragmatics. **Nonstandard dialects,** however, are characterized by different grammatical rules. Examples of nonstandard English dialects include Black English, Appalachian English, and Southern White Nonstandard English. "He ain't got any" (He doesn't have any) and "I might shoulda ate that" (I should have eaten that) are examples of syntactic differences in these dialects.

People often have a set of beliefs about dialects other than their own. As linguists study dialects, no dialect is superior to another; each follows a set of rules and has evolved through a complicated history. As adults, some people choose to speak their native dialect exclusively or may choose to speak Standard English in certain situations. We will present Standard English pronunciation in our discussion of articulation. Dialectal variations will be presented in Chapter 8.

What are standard and nonstandard dialects in your area?
Do you have words that are found only in your community?
What slang words do you use?

Speech production is the way we express language. This complex process of coordinated anatomy and physiology permits us to produce speech efficiently. If you remember the effects on your speech of running a distance, having a bad cold, missing front teeth, or wearing dental braces, then you are aware of the components of speech production. Speech production is controlled ultimately by specific areas in the brain. We still do not understand how the process of formulating speech occurs. We do know that for most persons, both right- and left-handed, the most significant events take place in the left hemisphere of the brain. Specialized areas of the left hemisphere are responsible for encoding concepts into the electrical signals that will travel down the pathway from the brain, then through the brain stem and spinal cord, and arrive finally at their destination. We consider the lungs, trachea (windpipe), larynx (voice box), pharynx (throat), nasal cavity, and oral cavity (mouth) to be the parts of anatomy most involved with speech production. A breath of air initiates the complex process that will result in a string of sounds recognized by others as speech. If you consciously consider the muscular movements (beginning with chest and abdomen) necessary to say *production*, it quickly becomes apparent that the system is an intricate and finely tuned one. We will describe speech production in more detail in the next chapter.

Speech processing is the system of decoding the sound or acoustic signal that reaches your ears. Two major components of this process are hearing and perception.

Hearing is the first step. When we describe the hearing mechanism, we refer to the path that sound travels from the outer ears (those appendages on the outside of your head) to the auditory area of the brain. As we discuss it here, the hearing process does not require interpretation of the sound signal, although some basic analysis does take place immediately.

The ear itself is divided into three segments (Fig. 2-5). The **outer ear** focuses sound to the eardrum (tympanic membrane). In the **middle ear,** the three bones—malleus (hammer), incus (anvil), and stapes (stirrup)—transform the acoustic signal into mechanical vibrations that stimulate the fluid of the **inner ear.** The fluid in turn stimulates movement of receptor cells. The receptor cells are connected to the auditory nerve. At least four connections in the brain are necessary along the auditory pathway before the specialized auditory segment of the brain "hears" the sound. Two ears allow you to localize a sound. The range of human hearing is immense; the ear responds to very low to very high pitches or frequencies. However, the ear is receptive especially to a range of frequencies that coincides with the sounds of speech.

You sense a sound with the system described above, but you perceive, or discriminate, the sound with your brain, specifically the auditory cortex. **Speech perception** enables us to discriminate "meaningless" sounds such as slamming doors or singing birds from speech sounds. To do this, we have built "categories" of speech sounds. Infants have the capacity to perceive speech differences shortly after birth. They can discriminate voice differences between their parents and strangers, preferring to turn their heads toward parents when hearing competing voices. At one month, infants can detect the difference in onset of voice between *pa* and *ba* of 0.02 second. They have not developed categories of sound, but

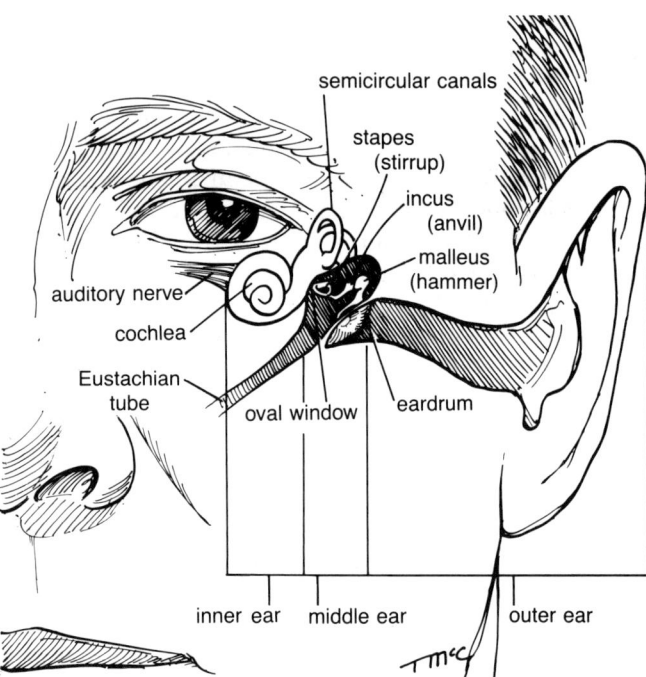

FIGURE 2-5   Anatomy of the ear

demonstrate the emergence of such a system. As competent speakers, we have created a category of silent or voiceless sounds like /p/, /t/, /k/, and /s/, which are separated in our speech perception system from the voiced sounds /b/, /d/, /g/, and /z/. ("Hiss" an /s/ sound and place your hand on your neck in the area of the larynx. Repeat with a /z/ sound. Feel the vibration? The sound /s/ is "voiceless," /z/ is "voiced.") Vowels and consonants are in separate categories. Once we have heard a sentence and transmitted the acoustic signal to the auditory cortex, we are ready to discriminate the speech sounds, put them into categories, and begin the process of making sense of the sentence.

We have outlined briefly the steps involved in producing and processing speech. These steps are, for speech production, origination of an idea in the brain, transmission of signals to the muscles involved in speech, and production of sounds. For speech processing, the steps are "collection" of sound by the ear, transmission of the electrical signal to the brain by the nerves, and perception and interpretation of the sound by the brain.

The two systems are considered separately, but in reality they are intimately linked as a **servosystem.** A servosystem is a system in which some movement is accomplished and a feedback loop monitors the performance of that movement. In speech communication, the central nervous system (CNS) plans a movement, neural impulses travel to the muscles responsible for the movement, and the sound is executed. For the sound /p/ in *potato*, the CNS plans the sequence of respiratory, laryngeal, and oral movements necessary to produce /p/, and nerve impulses travel to muscles responsible for respiratory, laryngeal, and lip movements. The lips are compressed, air pressure increases behind them, and the /p/ is released with a puff of air as the vocal folds begin to vibrate and the tongue is poised for the vowel to follow. Our feedback system tells us whether the /p/ was produced properly. Persons who lose their hearing in adulthood often begin to have slurred speech because they have lost an important channel for feedback. They must be taught to rely on the other feedback mechanism of sensation. Research has demonstrated that as a motor movement is performed, sensory cells send nerve signals back to the CNS. These impulses are compared in some way with the original motor plan and, if necessary, appropriate adjustments are made.

You now understand the nature and process of communication. You are a source and receiver of messages, primarily through the channel of verbal communication, but you know that components of nonverbal communication, eye contact, body movement, and facial expression contribute significantly. Language, as your transport of communication, is the sum of your knowledge of sound, meaning, grammar, and language use. You put that knowledge into action when you speak your native dialect. Speech production and processing are incredibly complicated sequences. You coordinate these aspects of speech communication through feedback loops to produce intelligible sentences.

In Chapter 3, we examine the various physiologic processes required for speech production and discuss their coordination. You will begin to comprehend the basis for voice and articulation. In understanding the anatomic and physiologic underpinnings for speech, you will appreciate the manner in which we classify and analyze voice and articulation.

STUDY QUESTIONS

1. What are the six variables in a model of communication?
2. What are some of the ways in which we communicate nonverbally? What are the two functions of nonverbal communication?
3. What is the distinction between language competence and language performance?
4. What are the four components of language?
5. What is a dialect? Identify your dialect area geographically. Does your dialect have any cultural or ethnic influences?
6. How are speech production and speech processing related in a servosystem?
7. How are communication, language, and speech related?

Chapter 3

Basic Speech Processes

The production of speech requires the coordinated functioning of several physiological processes. These processes are cerebration, respiration, phonation, resonation, and articulation (see Fig. 3-1). Your understanding of each of these basic processes and their interactions with one another will permit you to better analyze and manipulate the various process functions for improving both your voice and your articulation.

Imagine that you are walking across campus when, at some distance, you see an old friend. You wish to gain his attention, so you shout his name, "Bob!"

Now, stop and think. How did you initiate and accomplish that one-word utterance. Prior to taking this course, your answer might have been that you simply thought about what you wanted to say and you said it. We submit to you, however, that the process of saying just one word requires a sophisticated, coordinated system of activities involving the five major physiological processes just mentioned. That humans are able to coordinate these systems for even one word is a major anatomical and physiological accomplishment. The coordination of the processes for conversational speech is remarkable. Let us examine each process in some detail.

CEREBRATION

All of our bodily functions, including the production of speech, are under the control of the nervous system. Viewed as a command control center, this complex system, made up of billions of nerve cells called neurons, may be divided into the central nervous system and the peripheral nervous system.

The **central nervous system** is composed of the brain and the spinal cord, which are completely surrounded by a protective tissue covering called meninges. The cerebrum, the major portion of the brain, is composed of literally billions of

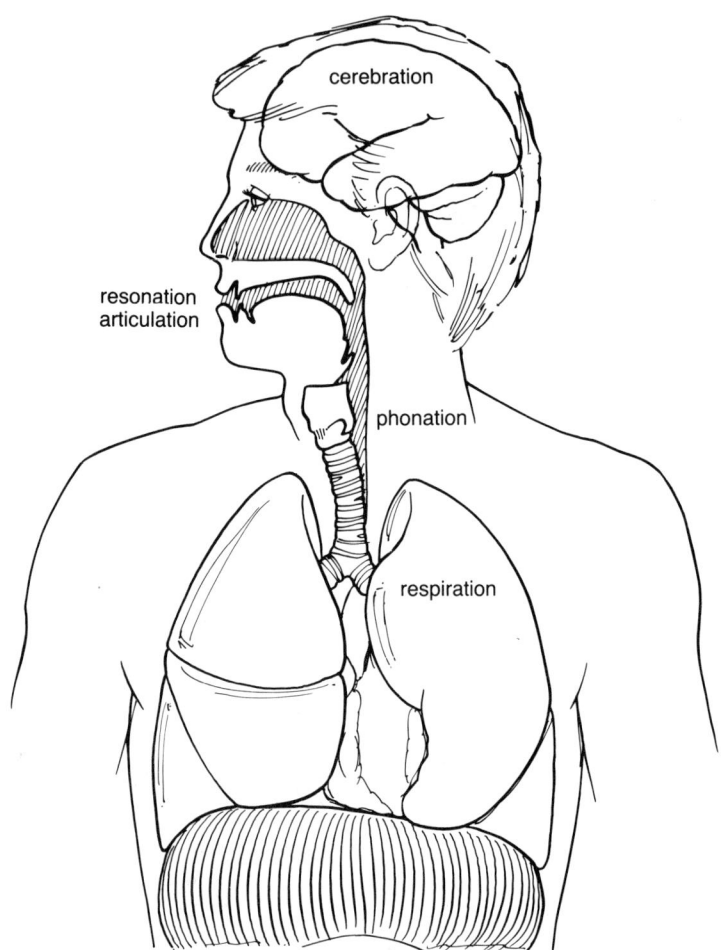

FIGURE 3-1 Basic speech processes

specialized neurons and is divided by fissures into four major lobes (Fig. 3-2). Each lobe is an organization of specialized nerve cells specific to either motor or sensory functions or highly specialized sense integrators for taste, smell, sight, and so on.

The four lobes are the frontal, temporal, parietal, and occipital lobes. A portion of the frontal lobe contains the area associated with the common motor pathways to the skeletal muscles, including the speech musculature. A small portion of this lobe, the left inferior frontal gyrus, is called Broca's area and is said to be the specific control of the motor activity for oral speech production.

The parietal lobe is the primary sensory control area of the brain; the occipital lobe is responsible for vision. The left temporal lobe serves an important function in the processing of auditory language.

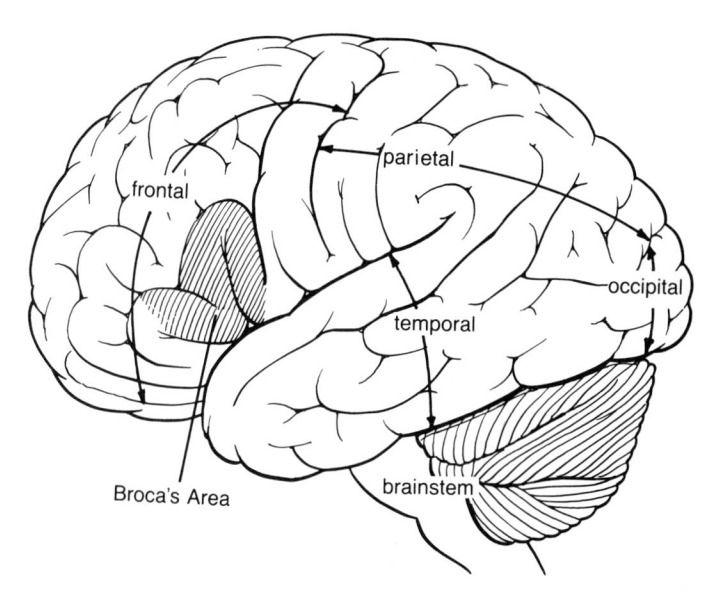

FIGURE 3-2 Four major lobes of the brain

Messages passed and received by the central nervous system pass through the sensory and motor nerves, which comprise the **peripheral nervous system.** The brainstem, an organizational structure and the lower part of the brain, gives rise to the major **cranial nerves,** which make up the long sensory and motor nerves that travel to and serve the many structures associated with speech (Fig. 3-3). The twelve paired cranial nerves, identified by both Roman numeral and name, may be sensory or motor or both sensory and motor in function. The cranial nerves related to speech and voice production include

- V Trigeminal—provides sensory innervation to the face, mouth, and lower jaw; motor innervation to muscles of mastication and the soft palate

- VII Facial—provides motor and sensory innervation to the face, lips, head, and upper neck

- VIII Acoustic—sensory nerve of hearing

- IX Glossopharyngeal—provides motor and sensory innervation to the tongue and pharynx

- X Vagus—provides motor and sensory innervation to the larynx, pharynx, and soft palate

- XI Accessory—provides motor innervation to neck muscles

- XII Hypoglossal—provides motor innervation to the tongue

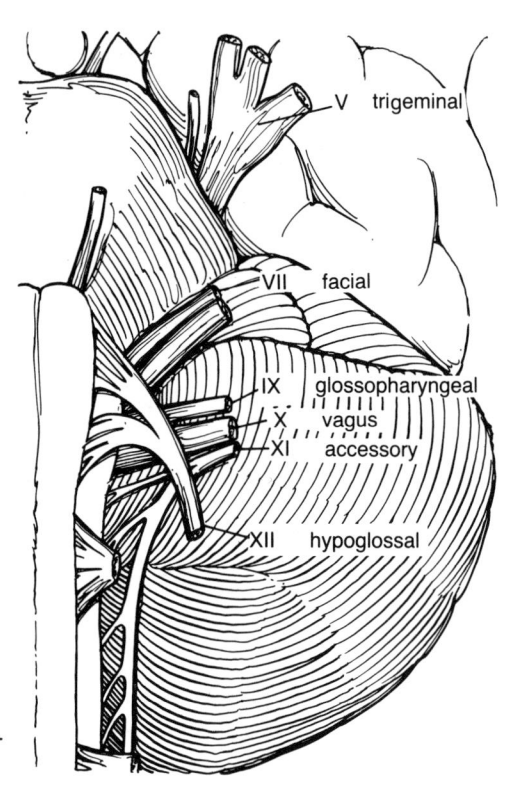

FIGURE 3-3 Cranial nerves serving the speech structures

As you initiated the word *Bob*, the process of **cerebration** began organizing and sending both motor and sensory messages from the central nervous system through the appropriate nerve channels. The correct anatomical and physiological relationships were established in the appropriate structures in order for the production to begin. Without the nervous command control center, speech is not possible. Breakdown can occur within the cerebration process (i.e., stroke or head trauma), causing various communication problems. Let us assume, however, that no breakdown has occurred to interrupt your speech production. The next step is to provide a support system that may drive the voice and speech mechanisms. For this support, we depend on the process of respiration.

RESPIRATION

Technically speaking, the respiratory function involves the exchange of oxygen and carbon dioxide into and out of the bloodstream through tiny capillaries in the lungs. This gas exchange supports our lives by providing the oxygen necessary for our bodies' energy conversion needs. This is the primary respiratory function—it supports our lives.

The secondary respiratory function is for the support of speech. Breathing for life and breathing for speech involve only minor physiological modifications of the same anatomical structure. Both breathing purposes involve **inhalation** (breathing in) and **exhalation** (breathing out) of air. Breathing for life is mostly automatic and passive; breathing to support speech requires that the air be exhaled under pressure. The anatomical structures responsible for the respiratory support of speech are shown in Figure 3-4 and described in the following sections.

Thoracic Cavity
Located between the base of the neck and the diaphragm, the **thoracic cavity,** or chest cavity, contains a bony structure, a muscular portion, and the respiratory passages.

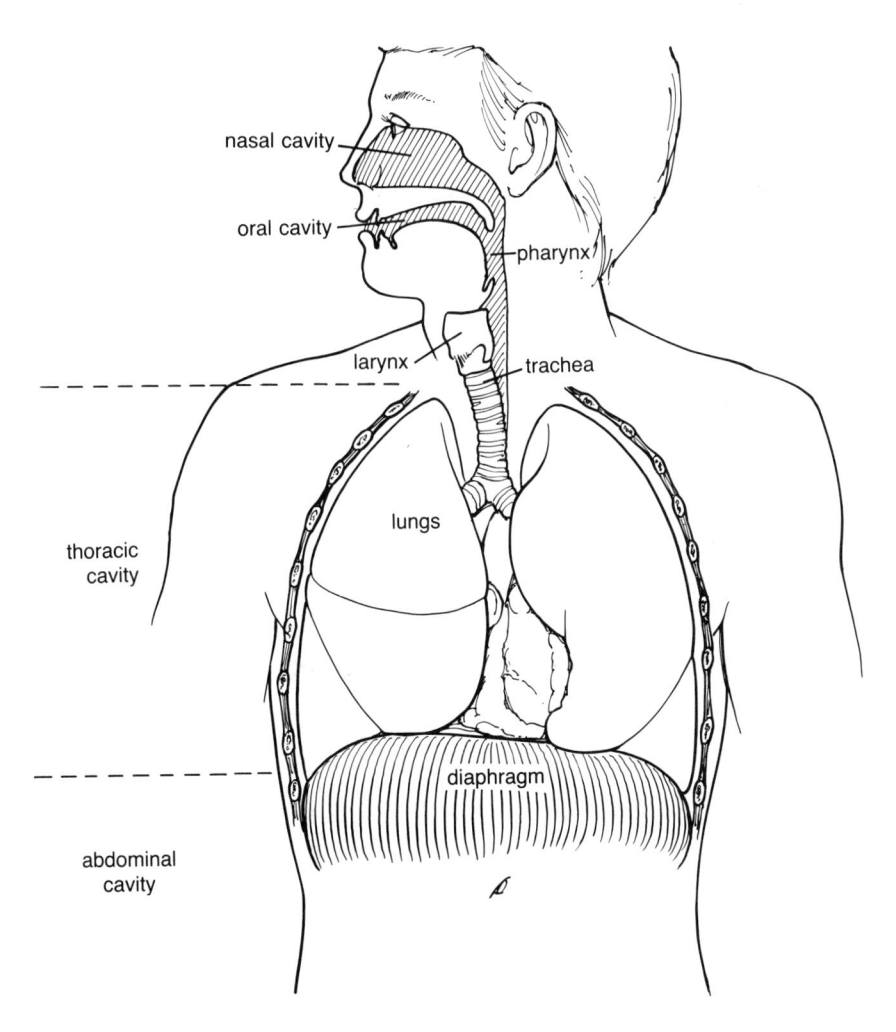

FIGURE 3-4 Respiratory support structures

The bony structure makes up the framework of the cavity and is composed of the 12 thoracic spinal vertebrae, 12 pairs of ribs, and the sternum.

The muscular portion of the thoracic cavity includes the external and internal intercostal muscles and the subcostal muscles. Eleven pairs of external intercostals raise the ribs up and out to increase the diameter of the cavity for inhalation. There are also 11 pairs of internal intercostal muscles, which are responsible for pulling the ribs down, thus decreasing the diameter of the cavity for exhalation. The number, size, and shape of the subcostals vary. The subcostals also pull the lower ribs down and apart, decreasing the cavity size.

The respiratory passages located within the thoracic cavity include the trachea, the bronchial tubes, and the lungs. The **trachea,** about 11 cm long in the adult, is the main conduction chamber for air. It lies near the middle of the thoracic cavity below the **larynx** (voice box) and divides or bifurcates into the right and left primary bronchi. As the bronchi enter the lungs, they further subdivide into bronchioles. The **lungs** themselves are two spongy, pink, elastic sacs that are divided into several lobes. These lobes contain specialized air cells called alveoli, which are brought into close proximity to the blood in a rich capillary network in the lungs. It is at this level that the exchange of blood gases occurs.

Diaphragm

The **diaphragm** is an arch-shaped muscular sheath that is located at the bottom of the thoracic cavity, separating it from the abdominal cavity. This large muscle group is usually recognized as the major muscular support for respiration. Contraction of the diaphragm muscles in a downward direction will expand the size of the thoracic cavity during inhalation.

Abdomen

The **abdomen** is the lower portion of the body's trunk and contains major organs such as the liver, gall bladder, pancreas, spleen, stomach, intestines, and bladder. The wall of the abdomen (abdominal wall) is composed of another sheath of muscles, which run horizontally and vertically as well as diagonally. Downward contraction of the diaphragm during inhalation may cause an outward expansion of the abdominal wall.

Breathing for Speech

The respiratory support system for speech, as seen in Figure 3-4, may, in its simplest terms, be viewed as a closed box. The thoracic cavity is the box, with the back and sides being the spine and rib cage, respectively. The front of the box is the sternum and the bottom is the elastic diaphragm. The shoulders are represented by the top of the box. Only one small opening is provided in the top of the box; this represents the trachea, which connects the elastic lungs to the outside air.

Standing at rest, the air pressure inside and outside the box may be equal (Fig. 3-5). For speech to occur, however, the air pressure must be increased inside

BASIC SPEECH PROCESSES

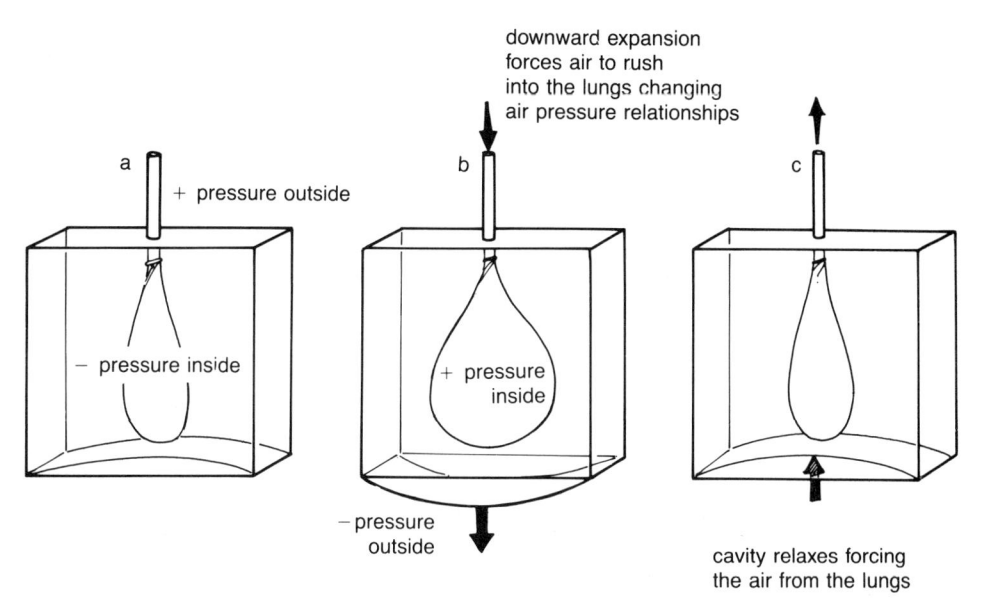

FIGURE 3-5 Breathing for speech

the box to permit air to rush into the lungs. To accomplish the increase in air pressure, the box must somehow expand its size. During the box expansion, greater outside air pressure and less inside air pressure will cause air to be drawn into the trachea and lungs. Because the majority of healthy adults use thoracic breathing, the following sequence will occur:

1. The bottom of the box (diaphragm) will flatten downward, increasing the size of the box (thoracic cavity) and creating a negative air pressure in the lungs.

2. The positive outside pressure causes air to be inhaled through the mouth and the nose. The air travels through the trachea and into the lungs as equalization between the inside and outside air pressure is again sought.

3. As air rushes into the lungs (inhalation), the box (thoracic cavity) expands even more via the floating ribs until the air pressure inside becomes greater (positive) than the air pressure outside the cavity (negative).

4. The bottom of the box (diaphragm) then relaxes and returns to an arch-shaped position, decreasing the size of the box. The sides (ribs) of the box lower. These motions act to force air from the lungs (exhalation).

The ability to control the respiratory process for speech is inherent in all healthy humans. Sometimes a person will develop inappropriate or ineffective breathing habits that create ineffective speech or voice patterns. Ineffective breathing for speech will be further studied in Chapter 5.

The cerebration and respiratory processes have worked together to build the proper breathing support for speech and voice production. At the same time, the vibratory system for speech has begun its activities. Let us now examine the process of phonation.

PHONATION

Phonation is the term that describes the production of sound by the vocal folds. This sound is voice. Because effective voice production is a major component of this text, the anatomy and physiology of voice production will be discussed in detail in Chapter 4. At this time, let us discuss phonation in terms of voice sounds.

For sound to be created, an object must be made to vibrate. In musical terms, the vibration may be created by striking a drum, strumming a guitar string, blowing air on a reed, or vibrating the lips through a mouthpiece. Sounds may also be created by hitting a steel beam with a hammer, exploding a firecracker, slamming a door, and so on. Stop and listen to all the sounds around you at this moment. Every sound you hear is a vibratory pattern that is being carried through the air.

These vibratory patterns may be described by very specific terms including frequency/pitch, intensity/loudness, and spectrum/quality.

Frequency refers to the number of times a vibration occurs per second. The higher the number of vibrations, or vibratory cycles per second, the higher the pitch level we perceive. **Pitch,** then, is the psychological correlate of frequency. A 60-cycle-per-second (cps) tone, measured in a unit called a **hertz** (Hz), would be perceived as a low pitch; an 8,000-Hz tone would be perceived as a high pitch. The human voice may produce a rather wide frequency range but it is rarely lower than 60 Hz in men or higher than 1200 Hz in the female singing voice.

In the same manner as frequency/pitch, **loudness** is the psychological correlate of **intensity.** The greater the intensity, the louder we perceive the sound to be. Intensity is measured in units called **decibels** (dB). The normal conversational intensity level of the human voice is between 50 and 70 dB. A decibel level of 100–120 dB would be considered a very loud shout.

The **quality** of sound will be determined by its **spectrum,** or spectral components. For example, when the vocal folds produce voice, the sound produced is not a single tone or a pure tone; rather, the sound produced is a complex tone made up of many frequencies. The number of times the vocal folds vibrate per second is called the voice's **fundamental frequency.** The average fundamental frequency in the male voice is 90–150 Hz; the average for females is 170–220 Hz. Many people may possess the same fundamental frequency, but their voices will sound different owing to the spectral components of their phonation. Variations in the length, mass, tension, and elasticity of the vocal folds will influence the spectrum, or quality of the vibration. For example, if your fundamental frequency were 120 Hz, your voice would also be producing various overtones that would be multiples of the fundamental—240 Hz, 480 Hz, and so on. These overtones will have their own multiples, with the entire voice signal forming a spectrum of sound, or a voice quality distinctive to each individual.

Within your own vocal fold structure, you have the capability of modifying the frequency, intensity and quality through the manipulation of the vocal fold musculature. For example, by increasing the length and tension of the vocal folds, you can increase your pitch. Also, by squeezing the vocal folds tightly together and increasing air pressure below the folds, you can increase your loudness level. We will discuss vocal variations in much greater detail in following chapters.

The **vocal folds** are located in the structure called the larynx (Adam's apple), which is located at the top of the trachea. The major function of the larynx is to serve as a protection valve for the trachea and lungs, protecting the structures from the accidental inhalation of things that you swallow. Everything that you breathe will pass between the vocal folds on the way to the lungs. The air pressure built up in the lungs during inhalation may be blocked or impeded from being exhaled by approximating or adducting the vocal folds. Indeed, you will soon learn that voice is produced when the air from the lungs overcomes the resistance of the closed folds, setting them into vibration. When this phonation occurs, it provides for a medium upon which speech may be carried. Let us now examine how the sound of voice is made even more distinctive for each individual as it is treated by the process of resonation.

RESONATION

As sound travels through the air, it will come in contact with objects that will be sympathetic to its vibratory pattern. When an object is sympathetic to a particular sound, the sound may cause that object to vibrate also, thus enhancing the sound. The sound may also come in contact with other objects that, instead of enhancing, may dampen the sound through absorption of all or part of the sound waves. The enhancing and dampening effect on sound will change the spectral components of the sound, thus yielding a new and distinctive sound quality. This effect is called **resonation.**

Sound produced by the vocal folds will also be subject to dampening and enhancing as it travels through the upper airway. The process of resonation will provide each individual with a distinctive voice quality. Individual voice qualities occur because the structures that serve as vocal sound resonators (pharynx, oral cavity, nasal cavity) vary in length, width, and shape. These variations yield different resonating qualities.

Resonation within one individual may also be manipulated through modification of the sizes, shapes, and openings of the resonators. For example, you may produce a rather pinched resonant quality by elevating the entire larynx in the neck and retracting your tongue. These actions will decrease the size and modify the shape of both the pharynx and oral cavity, thus changing the quality of your voice. Or, a person may create a "nasal" quality by not permitting the normal opening of the soft palate for nasal sounds. This person will sound as if he or she has a cold. Let us further examine the resonators (Fig. 3-4).

Pharynx

The **pharynx** is a part of the upper airway above the larynx and is often referred to as the throat. The size and shape of the soft muscular pharynx may be modified by the vertical positioning of the larynx in the neck (high or low) and by how the tongue is permitted to rest in the mouth (forward or back). The base of the tongue is attached in the pharynx. When the tongue is permitted to be in a retracted position, it will tend to damp sound production, thus decreasing the effectiveness of voice. A more forward tongue position, which permits a frontal placement of voice, is more desirable.

Nasal Cavity

Various sizes and shapes of the nose provide a great opportunity to modify the resonant quality of voice. Technically, only three sounds—/m/, /n/, and /ng/ (as in *bang*)—are nasal sounds. Only these sounds are to be permitted to travel through the nose during speech production. The opening and closing control mechanism for the **nasal cavity** is the soft palate. During speech production, the soft palate will elevate and make contact with the posterior pharynx. This contact will seal off and separate the nasal cavity from the pharynx and oral cavity. Problems associated with nasal resonance will be discussed in detail in a later chapter.

Oral Cavity

The size and shape of the **oral cavity** (mouth) are only two factors associated with oral resonance. Other factors affecting oral resonation include jaw movement and excursion; tongue size, shape, and positioning; and the height, length, and width of the hard palate. The teeth, jaw mass, and cheekbones will also affect sound resonation.

To this point we have discussed the individual voice resonators. You should understand, however, that the resonators do not work as individual units; rather, they are coupled together in various configurations to produce your distinctive voice quality. Manipulation of these couplings may be a necessary step in your quest for a more effective voice.

Your brain is now firing off thousands of orders for the production of "Bob!" You are providing the respiratory support and the voicing component, and you've begun to couple the appropriate resonators. It is now time to complete this speech act through the precise and accurate formation of the appropriate speech sounds via the articulators. Let us, therefore, examine the complex process of articulation.

ARTICULATION

The process of **articulation** involves the manipulation of oral and nasal structures in such a manner as to produce clear, precise speech sounds. The sculptors of these sounds are the anatomical structures responsible for their production. Figure 3-6 illustrates the locations of these structures and their relationships to each other. Notice that we have subdivided the tongue into several different parts. The tongue is the single most important structure for speech in the oral cavity. When scientists investigated the area of the brain responsible for sending and receiving messages about movement and sensation to the tongue, they discovered that there were a proportionately greater number of neurons assigned to the tongue than were assigned to several other larger parts of the body. Their findings confirmed what we already knew: the tongue must make many rapid, intricate movements in coordination with other structures to produce speech sounds.

Other anatomical parts in the oral cavity involved in articulation are the lips, teeth, mandible (lower jaw), hard palate (roof of the mouth), and velum (soft palate). Some languages, such as Arabic, also use the pharynx as an articulator. If you mouth the words of this sentence as you read it, you will begin to acknowledge that articulation is certainly a complex task.

Articulation is the process of creating speech sounds, as you know. What constitutes a speech sound in English? Is a click a speech sound in English? What about a whistle? You *are* using oral cavity structures to modify a stream of air in some way when you click your tongue or whistle. Do clicks and whistles create new words in our language when attached to some sequence of other sounds? Do they make a difference, as does the /r/ or /b/ sound in *rat* or *bat*? No, clicks

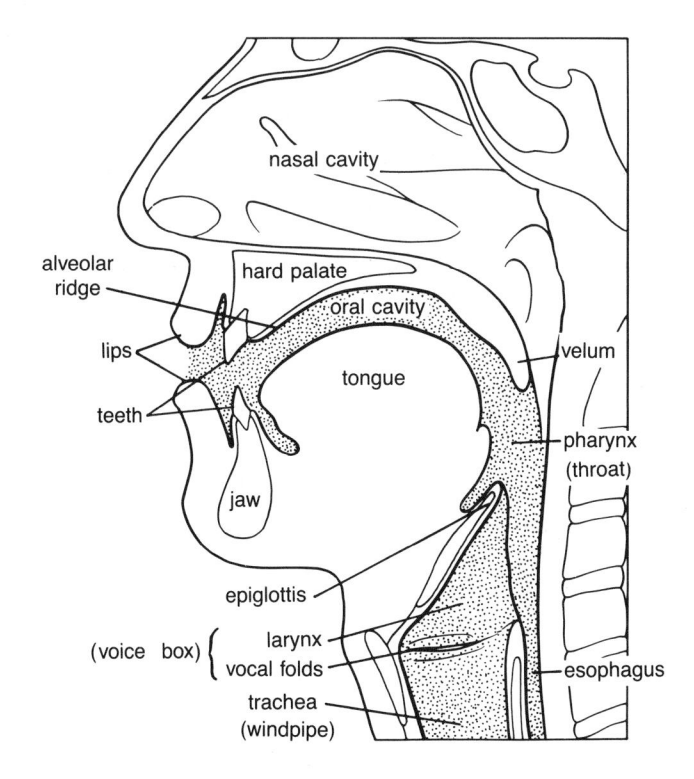

FIGURE 3-6 Structures involved with articulation

and whistles do not. We call sounds like /r/ and /b/ phonemes. Phonemes are not only sounds that make a difference, but they also may be described by their special qualities of production. In Chapter 7, you will learn the classification system that describes English phonemes, as well as any phoneme in any language, by the way they are articulated.

Phonemes, as consonants and vowels, combine together to produce syllables. Syllables connect to form words. Words merge into a stream of sentences and you are involved in the process of language. Your discussions with others have at their source individual phonemes reliably and precisely produced by a coordinated voice and articulation system.

"Bob!" Congratulations, you said the word. You completed one of the most complicated processes of human accomplishment. But did Bob respond? Were your voice and articulation adequate to complete the communication act effectively? Let us further study the effectiveness of your oral speech production.

STUDY QUESTIONS

1. What are the five basic speech processes?
2. How do the central and peripheral nervous systems interact to permit speech and voice production?
3. What is the major difference in breathing for life and breathing for speech?
4. What major anatomical change must take place in order for air to be inhaled or exhaled?
5. Do we hear voice as it is produced by the vocal folds or is the voice changed in some way? If it is changed, can you explain how it is changed?
6. What are the major articulators? What do you think would happen to the speech production of a person who lost feeling in his or her tongue? Has this ever happened to you during a dental appointment?

Part Three
Voice

Chapter 4

The Nature of Voice

One of the fascinating things about the human voice is that the mechanism responsible for its production—the larynx, or voice box—did not develop primarily for the purpose of voice production. In fact, voice is a secondary or an overlaid function of the larynx; its major biological function is protection of the lungs and trachea. Because the trachea (windpipe) connects to the pharynx (throat), anything that we swallow could drain into the trachea were it not for the muscular valve we call the larynx. When we swallow, three strong muscular contractions take place in the larynx, effectively closing off the trachea and diverting what we swallow into the esophagus (foodpipe). One of these contractions is the approximation of the vocal folds which protects us from aspirating or inhaling what is swallowed. We have all experienced mild aspiration when something "went down the wrong pipe." When we want to produce voice, which is called phonating, the true vocal folds are brought together (adducted) and are set into vibration by air that we expel from our lungs. Let us examine the anatomy and physiology of the structures responsible for voice production.

ANATOMY OF THE LARYNX

The laryngeal mechanism is a complex system of cartilages, muscles, and connective tissues. Your understanding of the basic structure and function of the larynx will help you to better understand why you sound the way you sound. This knowledge will also enable you to identify the changes you may choose to make in voice production in order to produce voice as effectively as possible.

The larynx is a cylindrical tube with folds or floors of muscle tissue that extend from the inside walls toward the middle of the tube. This tube sits directly on top of the windpipe, or trachea, which directs the air to and from our lungs.

Directly above the tube is the pharynx, the base of the tongue, and the oral and nasal cavities (Fig. 4-1).

The easiest way to visualize the larynx is to imagine that you are looking at a cylindrical tube in which the bottom and the top have been removed. When we look inside the tube we see that it is divided by two partitions into three separate chambers (Fig. 4-2). Each partition and each chamber represent different parts of the laryngeal mechanism. The top rim of the tube represents the part of the larynx called the **aryepiglottic folds.** The aryepiglottic folds are made of a circular muscular band of sphincteric tissue that contracts when we swallow. This contraction helps to divert swallowed food and liquid away from the larynx and into the food pipe, or **esophagus.**

The top partition of the tube represents the false vocal folds, or the **ventricular folds.** These muscular folds contract tightly and impound air in the lungs to help support lifting heavy objects, coughing, defecating, and vomiting. The ventricular folds also serve as a second line of defense against things that we swallow, deterring them from entering the trachea and lungs. The space between

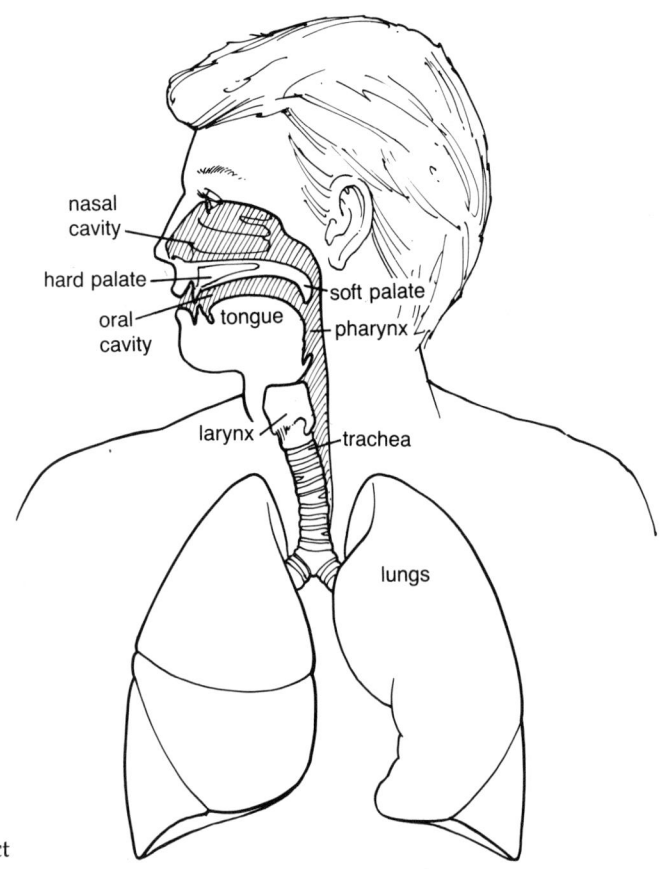

FIGURE 4-1 The vocal tract

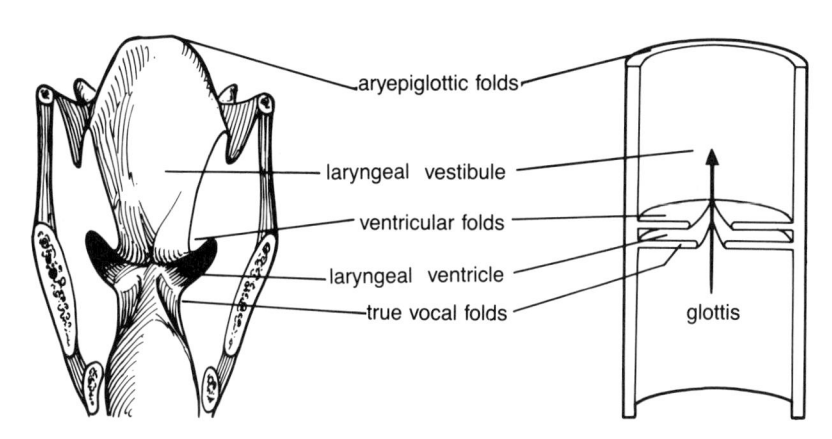

FIGURE 4-2 The laryngeal tube

the aryepiglottic folds and the ventricular folds is called the **laryngeal vestibule.** Vestibule is a term that is often used to describe the entrance of a building. The laryngeal vestibule is the entrance of the larynx. If food or liquid reaches this level of the larynx, we react by coughing violently and clearing our throats to expel the foreign substance from the airway.

The lowest partition in the tube represents the true vocal folds. The true vocal folds serve as the third line of defense for the trachea and lungs. The true vocal folds also provide the vibration necessary for the production of voice. The space between the true vocal folds and the ventricular folds is called the **laryngeal ventricle;** the gap between the two vocal folds themselves is called the **glottis.**

The Laryngeal Framework

cricoid cartilage	cuneiform cartilage
thyroid cartilage	epiglottis
arytenoid cartilages	first tracheal ring
corniculate cartilages	hyoid bone

The structures represented by the cylindrical tube can define the very basic outline of the larynx; like all structures, however, the larynx requires a framework and a foundation to support the framework. The laryngeal framework consists of nine cartilages, with the base cartilage, called the **cricoid cartilage,** resting on the **first tracheal ring,** which serves as the support foundation (Figs. 4-3 and 4-4). The cricoid cartilage looks much like a signet ring with the front (anterior) part looking similar to the ring band; the back (posterior) part looks like the section that would contain the engraving. Attached to both sides of the cricoid cartilage (lateral) by movable joints is the main body of the laryngeal frame, known as the **thyroid** cartilage. The thyroid cartilage rises above the cricoid and may be easily felt in the neck. It is commonly called the "Adam's apple."

The laryngeal framework also has a support attachment from above. This superior supporter is called the **hyoid bone,** which is attached to the upper arm

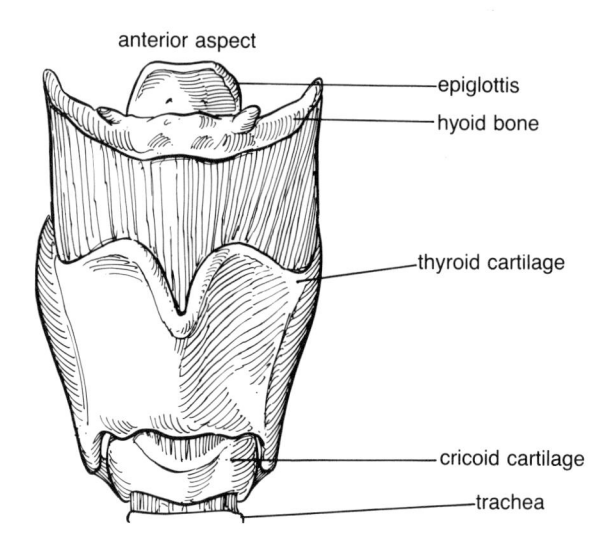

FIGURE 4-3 Laryngeal framework, anterior

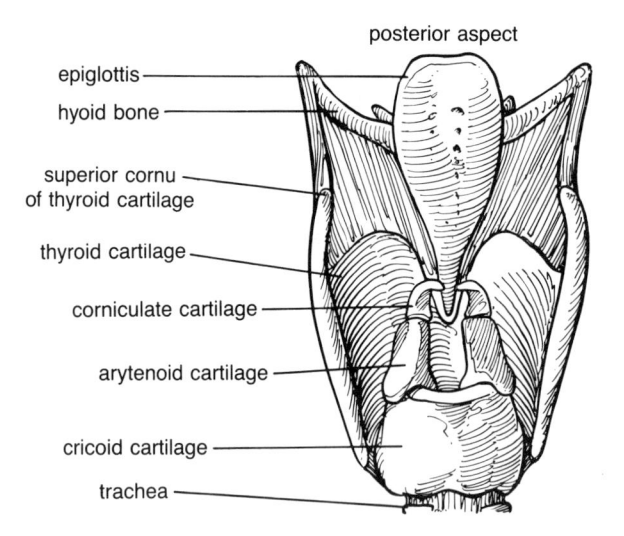

FIGURE 4-4 Laryngeal framework, posterior

(superior cornu) of the thyroid cartilage. The hyoid bone is simply suspended in the neck by a series of strap muscles. The larynx, therefore, is essentially hung from above by the hyoid bone and grounded below on a tracheal ring foundation.

Sitting on the top of the back side (posterior) of the cricoid cartilage are two very important movable cartilages called the **arytenoid cartilages.** The arytenoids are shaped somewhat like pyramids and will be very important in our discussion of how the vocal folds approximate (adduct) to make voice. Two other pairs of very small cartilages contribute to the framework of the larynx. These are the **corniculate** and **cuneiform cartilages.** The corniculate cartilages sit on top of the arytenoid cartilages, forming the point of the pyramid. The cuneiform cartilages are embedded in supporting laryngeal tissues just lateral to and above the corniculates. The large leaf-shaped cartilage that completes the laryngeal framework is the **epiglottis.** The epiglottis attaches to the inside angle of the thyroid cartilage.

The Laryngeal Muscles

The framework of our structure is completed. It is now time to build the functional components. The major functional components of the larynx are muscles; specifically, muscles that

1. are the vocal folds,
2. separate the vocal folds (abductors),
3. approximate the vocal folds (adductors), and
4. stretch the vocal folds.

These muscles, called intrinsic laryngeal muscles, are connected at both ends within the laryngeal framework.

The Vocal Folds

vocalis muscles
thyroarytenoid muscles

The vocal folds themselves are made of two pairs of muscles, the **vocalis muscles** and the **thyroarytenoid muscles** (Fig. 4-5). These muscles share common fibers and form the flat vocal folds. The vocal folds attach to the framework or the laryngeal cartilages in two places. The front, or anterior, ends of the vocal folds attach to the inside angle of the thyroid cartilage near the attachment of the epiglottis. The back, or posterior, ends of the folds attach to the arytenoid cartilages, which sit on top of the cricoid cartilage. The **adduction,** or approximation, of the vocal folds is one step in the production of voice.

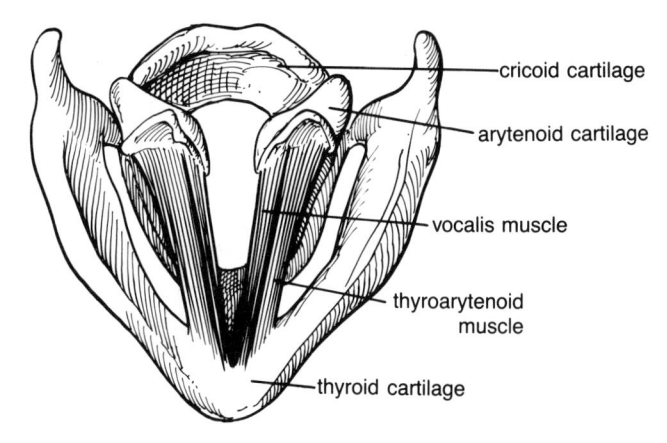

FIGURE 4-5 Vocal fold muscles

Vocal Fold Separators (Abductors)
posterior cricoarytenoid muscles

When we are not talking and are simply breathing quietly, the vocal folds are separated, or in an **abducted** position. When the folds are in this position, the space created between the vocal folds is called the glottis. One pair of muscles is responsible for abducting the vocal folds. These are the **posterior cricoarytenoid muscles** (Fig. 4-6). Because the name of a muscle often reflects its attachments, we can see that this muscle connects to the back, or posterior, part of the cricoid cartilage on one end and to the arytenoid cartilage on the other end. When the posterior cricoarytenoid muscles contract, they cause the arytenoid cartilages to swivel toward the sides (laterally) of the larynx. Because the vocal folds are attached to the arytenoid cartilages, they will also be moved laterally, causing them to separate (abduct). The posterior cricoarytenoid muscles are the only muscles that separate (abduct) the vocal folds.

Vocal Fold Approximators (Adductors)
lateral cricoarytenoid muscles
transverse arytenoid muscles
oblique arytenoid muscles

When we swallow, lift something, defecate, cough, clear our throats, or produce voice, our vocal folds must approximate or adduct. Vocal fold adduction is accomplished through the interaction of several intrinsic laryngeal muscles. These muscles are the **lateral cricoarytenoid muscles,** the **transverse arytenoid muscles,** and the **oblique arytenoid muscles** (Fig. 4-5). The lateral cricoarytenoid muscles

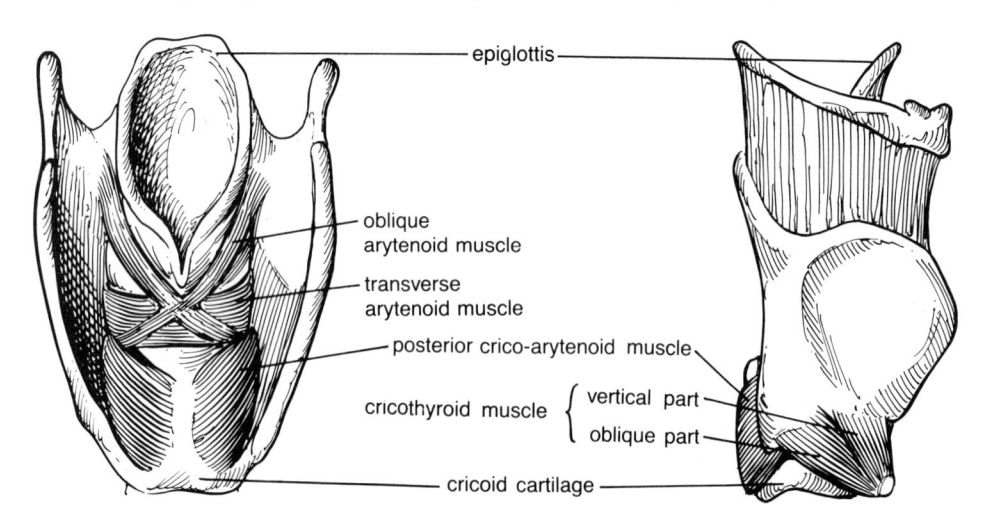

FIGURE 4-6 Abductor and adductor muscles

are responsible for swiveling the arytenoid cartilages toward the middle (medially) of the larynx. The vocal folds, which are also attached to the arytenoid cartilages, will also move medially and eventually approximate (adduct). To help guarantee proper adduction, the transverse and oblique arytenoid muscles, which cross between the arytenoid cartilages, also contract, pulling the cartilages closer together.

Vocal Fold Stretchers

      cricothyroid muscles (pars rectus, pars oblique)

In order to make our speech sounds variable, we tend to use many different pitches when we speak. Pitch changes in an individual are dependent upon the lengthening of the vocal folds. As you know, one end of the vocal folds is attached to the thyroid cartilage and the other end is attached to the arytenoid cartilages, which sit on the cricoid cartilage. If the thyroid cartilage is permitted to tilt forward while the cricoid cartilage remains stationary, the vocal folds will be obliged to stretch, or elongate, yielding a higher pitch. The muscles that contract to cause this tilting action are the **cricothyroid muscles** (Fig. 4-7). The erect portion of the cricothyroid tends to tilt the thyroid cartilage downward; the oblique portion slides the thyroid forward. These actions cause the stretching of the vocal folds.

Nerve Supply

All muscles must be supplied by nerves in order to function. Indeed, damage to a nerve will cause a paralysis of the muscle it serves. The major nervous supply of the larynx comes from two branches of cranial nerve X, known as the vagus nerve. The vagus nerve courses down from the brain and gives off branches called the **superior laryngeal nerve** and the **recurrent laryngeal nerve.** The

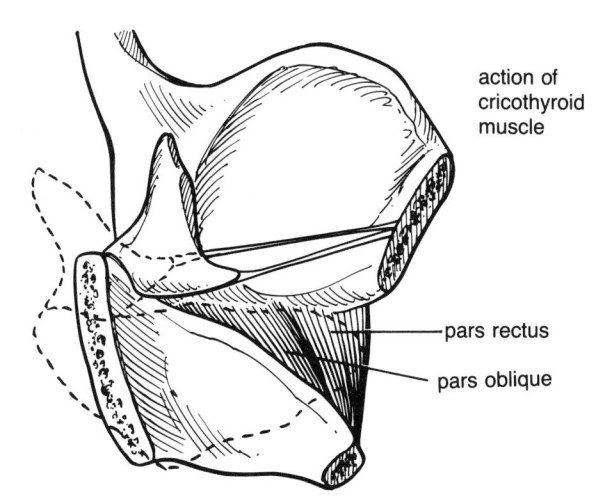

FIGURE 4-7 Action of cricothyroid muscle

superior laryngeal nerve courses directly to the cricothyroid muscles (the stretcher muscles), which are the only laryngeal muscles that it services. The recurrent laryngeal nerve takes a long winding course before it ends up servicing all the other intrinsic laryngeal muscles. In fact, the left recurrent laryngeal nerve loops all the way around the aorta of the heart, and the right recurrent laryngeal nerve courses around the subclavian artery. Both nerves run under the thyroid gland before entering the larynx. You can see how heart or thyroid disease could damage the recurrent nerves, leading to vocal difficulties.

BASIC PHYSIOLOGY OF THE LARYNX

We have discussed the muscles that make up the vocal folds and how other muscles cause the folds to separate (abduct) and approximate (adduct). Once the vocal folds are approximated through these various muscular contractions, they are in position to vibrate to give us sound for our speech. Vibration of the vocal folds for speech is called phonation.

Exactly how the vocal folds phonate has been debated for many years. The most accepted theory of phonation is called the myoelastic-aerodynamic theory (Vandenberg, 1958). This theory states that, following the approximation of the vocal folds, air pressure from the lungs is built up against the resistance of the approximated folds. Eventually, that air pressure becomes great enough to overcome the resistance of the folds, forcing them to momentarily separate, thus releasing one small puff of air. This release creates a sudden drop in air pressure directly between the vocal folds, causing a suction action to begin. This suction, called the **Bernoulli effect,** along with the natural static positioning of the adducted vocal folds, causes the folds to draw back together. The closer the folds draw, the greater the suction becomes until the folds totally approximate again, thus completing one vibratory cycle.

During normal conversational speech, human vocal folds will vibrate from about 100 cycles per second to about 500 cycles per second. The faster the vibration, the higher the pitch that we hear. The rate of vibration for producing various pitches is determined by the length and mass of the vocal folds as well as the tension of the folds during phonation. For example, imagine that you have a rubber band. If the rubber band is thick, it will have a deeper sound when set into vibration than will one that is thinner. A longer rubber band and a shorter one of equal thickness will also vary in pitch because both the length and the mass of the longer one are greater. Which one do you think will produce the higher pitch (Fig. 4-8)? Now, if we put additional tension on the rubber band by stretching it to various lengths while setting it into vibration, we will also vary the pitch. Indeed, the stretching and contraction of your own vocal folds permit you to manipulate your pitch for conversational inflection as well as for singing purposes.

Male and female voices typically vary in pitch because of mass and length variations. Following the changes that occur during puberty, male vocal folds are

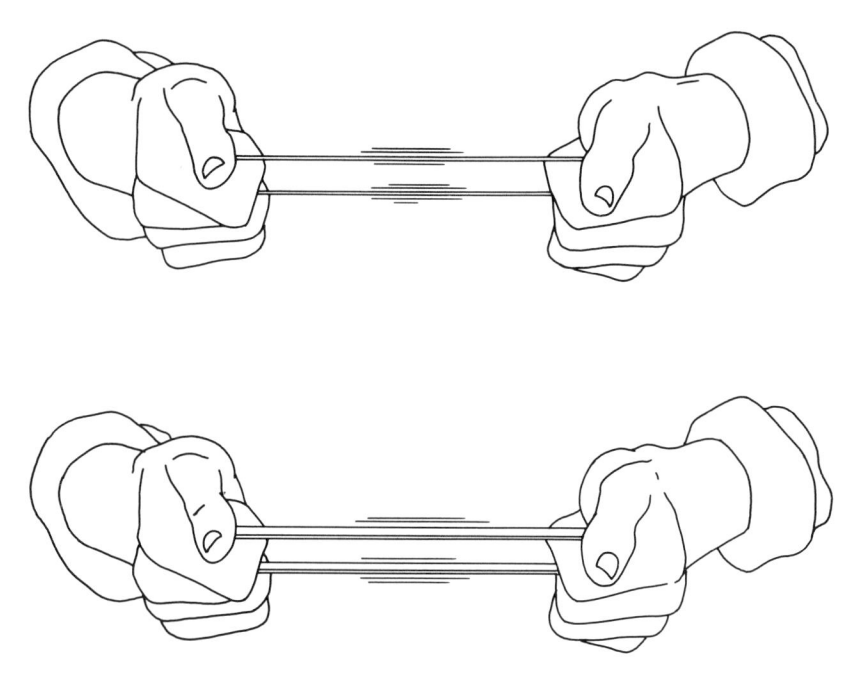

FIGURE 4-8 Two rubber bands

thicker and longer than female vocal folds. The adult male vocal fold averages 15 to 20 mm in length compared to the female average of 9 to 13 mm. Variations in pitch that you are able to make in your own voice are dependent upon how far the cricothyroid muscles are able to stretch your folds as well as the amount of tension you place on the vocal folds. Try gliding from a low note to a high note on the sound /o/. Do you notice more laryngeal area tension the higher you glide? Does it take more effort to sing higher notes? When the vocal folds are stretched they become stiffer. More air pressure is then required to separate the stiff vocal folds in order to produce the higher-pitched phonation.

Loudness or intensity variations of voice are dependent on the amount of air pressure built up beneath the vocal folds and on the amplitude of the vocal fold vibration. Amplitude refers to how far the vocal folds are forced open during phonation. In order to shout, you will notice that you first take a deep breath. This deep breath enables you to easily build up a greater amount of air pressure beneath the adducted vocal folds. Then when you shout, the vocal folds are blown farther apart than normal so that the distance the fold travels laterally is greater. This lateral excursion is the amplitude of vibration. The resultant voice is therefore louder or more intense.

You now have some understanding as to how you are able to vary your pitch and loudness levels. With this knowledge, can you speculate as to how you whisper? If you guessed that the vocal folds do not approximate during the whisper then you were partially correct. The folds do not make a total approximation but do move into a parallel position, permitting air to pass between the folds, thus producing a turbulent airy sound. Warning: Long-term whispering can be abusive to the vocal folds in that the friction created by the air turbulence can damage the tissues of the folds.

VOICE PRODUCTION

As adult human communicators, we are usually able to interpret the identity of sound through our storage system of previous listening experiences. When you stop to think about it, the multitude of sounds that we are able to recognize and interpret for meaning is truly amazing. Indeed, the process of sound recognition begins as soon as we are born, if not before. We begin by recognizing the sound of our own parents' voices and the voices of other family members. Environmental noises such as food preparation, the running of bath water, the telephone ringing, television sound, and so on are soon introduced and filed away in our sound recognition systems.

Stop reading now and take a moment to listen to all of the sounds around you. How many sounds do you hear? Are there any sounds that you don't recognize?

As we grow older, it is expected that our ability to recognize sound will very quickly develop further into the ability to place extended meaning to the sound. For example, the infant who heard the sounds of food preparation began to anticipate that the hunger feeling would soon be satisfied. This was a basic conditioned response to what was heard. Eventually, as the child became more aware of the environment, these sounds of food preparation developed into the understanding that someone was preparing food and therefore it would soon be time to eat.

Sound recognition and the assignment of meaning to what is heard is inherent in the normal development of language and speech production. Though speech can certainly be produced with very little sound, as when we just whisper or move our mouths, it is very difficult to understand speech produced only in this manner. Few people can "read lips" efficiently. Successful lip reading is based upon prior experience with and understanding of speech and language production. We may well imagine the difficulty a deaf child would have developing speech and language when the sounds of speech are not available. The visual components of speech produced by the parents are present, but without the auditory or sound stimulation the child is not able to receive enough language stimulation to develop normal speech.

> Ask a friend to read to you at a normal rate of speed while only mouthing the words. Can you see the value of the voice component of speech?

Definition of Voice

As you have just demonstrated through the above exercise, the sounds of speech play a very important role in human communication. **Voice** is the major element of speech that provides the speaker with the vibration signal upon which speech is carried. Voice provides the **melody** of speech. Beyond the spoken meaning of words, it provides additional expression, intent, and mood to our spoken thoughts. It permits the speech signal to be carried loudly enough that, in normal circumstances, it may be easily heard and understood.

We normally think of melody in terms of music or in relation to the singing voice, but the speaking voice acquires its own form of melody. We can readily recognize melody in the form of spoken poetry, with its inherent rhythms and rhyming sounds. Melody is also present in our everyday conversational speech. We may describe this melody in terms of the rhythm, rate, and inflection of speech production. In fact, effective use of voice is dependent upon the proper use of these three voice components. Let us examine each one in more detail.

Rhythm refers to the periodic flow of speech without the presence of unusual or inappropriate hesitations, blocks, or repetitions. Probably one of the most severe problems of rhythm—one that we all have heard at some time—is that caused by stuttering. Severe stuttering will make it very difficult for a person to communicate in everyday situations. Most of us have even experienced unusual hesitations in our own speech. Remember the first time you were required to speak in front of a large group? Your nervousness probably caused a slight breakdown in the normal rhythm of your speech production. This breakdown probably reduced the effectiveness of what you were saying.

> The next time you give or listen to a class presentation, notice if the rhythm of speech is as effective as possible.

Rate refers to the speed at which we deliver our speech. The effective rate is neither too slow nor too fast; nor is it monotonous or the same in all speaking situations. When we are excited or angry we tend to talk much faster than when we are in more relaxed or intimate situations. Appropriate rate will also vary according to location and dialect. For example, the rate of speech produced in the northeastern United States tends to be much faster than in the southern states. Appropriate use of rate is important for effective speech production. Speech that is too slow or fast or monotonous in rate draws attention to how the speaker is talking rather than what is being said, thus reducing the effectiveness of the communication.

Inflection refers to the many pitch and loudness variations that we include in our running conversational speech. For example, we will stress certain important words by slightly increasing our loudness level and raising our pitch. This is especially evident at the end of questions. Try to say "How are you" using the same pitch and loudness level for each word. As you can see, the sentence loses meaning without the appropriate inflection. Without inflectional changes, speech production would be described as monotone. It would be very boring to listen to this type of vocal presentation; thus the effectiveness of speech would be diminished.

Say the sentence "I love you" as many ways as you can by using a different inflectional pattern each time. How does this change the meaning, intent, mood, or feeling?

Indeed, the rhythm, rate, and inflection of our voice productions determine to a very large extent the power and effectiveness of our overall communication abilities.

"Normal" Voice

It is very difficult, if not impossible, to define "normal" voice. There exists in human communication a very wide range of acceptable voice productions. The ones who therefore determine normalcy are those who must interact with the speaker. In other words, we are all judges of normalcy. We all have an opinion as to whether a person "sounds good" or uses voice effectively. Because of the wide range of acceptable voices, it may be easier to define or describe the abnormal voice.

The abnormal or unusual voice will call attention to the speaker if the overall **voice quality,** pitch, or loudness differ from those of other persons of similar age, sex, cultural background, or geographic location. For example, it is quite acceptable in some eastern societies of the world for the male to use an unusually high-pitched voice. The same voice used by a male in western society would call attention to the speaker. So, what is common and accepted in one culture or society may not be considered "normal" in another.

Even within a single culture, there are great variations in acceptable voice productions. To demonstrate this fact to yourself, simply listen to the many different voices being produced by your friends, teachers, and classmates. You will hear voices that are high and low, loud and soft, and voices that are more pleasant to listen to than others. All may be within acceptable limits. One of the most common variations within a single culture is the manner in which the voice is resonated. In fact, people from different geographic locations may be identified by the way they resonate voice. More or less nasal resonance is characteristic of different parts of the country.

> Listen to your classmates. Can you guess which part of the country they were raised in on the basis of their nasal resonance?

This brings us to the question, What makes one voice more or less effective than another voice? It is important to realize that good voice, like good wine or food, is a matter of personal opinion. Some people may prefer to listen to the deep, resonant voices of professional newscasters; others may prefer a less formal, lighter voice production. What is your opinion? What qualities do you think contribute to an effective voice? We suggest that the most effective voice production results when we combine, in the most optimum manner, the most appropriate pitch, loudness, resonation, rhythm, and rate that our physical structures enable us to produce. Effective voice, then, is the interaction of these components in such a manner that voice is produced efficiently and effortlessly. Some people may automatically produce voice in this manner, but most of us may benefit from analyzing our own vocal components and working to improve their interactions.

VOICE AND PERSONALITY

The need to use effective voice is determined by the owner of the voice. Indeed, we would suspect that an individual planning a career in which the voice would be used professionally—a radio broadcaster, a preacher, a trial lawyer, and so on—would strive for the most effective voice possible. Because there exist many standards of adequate voice production, you are the one, in the long run, who will determine the level of effectiveness for your own voice. Will you be the beneficiary of a positive image projected by your voice or a victim of ineffective voice production?

We ask this serious question because the way you sound—your voice quality—projects a very definite image of yourself to those around you. Voice quality is often one means by which others perceive your personality. You may be perceived as friendly, aloof, strong-willed, intractable, powerful, and so on. How do you perceive those around you on the basis of their voice qualities?

Social stereotypes, like personality, may also be established on the basis of quality of voice. People with very nasal qualities may be viewed as "snobbish" or "uppity." Males with high-pitched voices may be stereotyped as effeminate. Indeed, in a study by Blood et al. (1979), it was demonstrated that the personalities of people with less than effective voice qualities were described in more negative terms than were those with normal voice. These stereotypes may or may not be true representations of the actual people who are projecting the image. Nevertheless, the image is present.

> The successful election of politicians is often based upon the image projected to the electorate. What part do you think voice plays in the development of a positive public image?

YOUR VOICE

So, what do you sound like? Have you ever really taken the time to listen to yourself? We "hear" ourselves all the time, but most of us have never really listened to and analyzed our voices. You will take time to listen to yourself in this class. When you listen, you will find that your voice is very individual and distinctive. No one else sounds like you. Your voice characteristics began developing with your first cry at birth, have constantly changed as a result of your changing physical and anatomical structures, and have been influenced and molded by the "normal" standards of voice in your cultural setting.

Because voice is so dynamic, or changeable from moment to moment, we are blessed with the ability to produce many voices. The most obvious example of this is the professional impressionist, who can produce adequate vocal imitations of many different famous people. You are blessed with the ability to produce many voices. This text is designed to encourage and direct you in a systematic experiment of voice manipulation in order to discover and cultivate the voice that is most effective for you. For your voice to be judged effective, the overall quality, pitch range, loudness variations, and vocal melodies must fall within acceptable bounds for each of these common variables. Chapter 5, "Effective Voice Production," will lead you through descriptions of ineffective vocal habits and more serious voice disorders. By understanding the nature of voice production you have taken the first giant step toward voice improvement.

STUDY QUESTIONS

1. In the most simplistic terms, how would you describe the physical nature of the larynx?
2. The framework of the larynx consists of what type of tissue?
3. Muscles comprise the functional components of the larynx. These muscles are divided into four major functional groupings. What are the four groupings? How many total laryngeal muscles are there? What is an intrinsic laryngeal muscle?
4. How do phonation and respiration combine to produce voice?
5. How are pitch and loudness modified?
6. What parts do rhythm, rate, and inflection play in effective voice production?

Chapter 5
Effective Voice Production

*H*ow effective is your voice as a part of your overall communication system? This chapter is designed to help you answer this question. It will help you to identify the component parts of voice, which through systematic modification and practice, may be significantly improved. You have learned that ineffective or **abnormal voice** may exist when the quality, pitch, or loudness vary from an accepted norm. There are, however, various severity levels of vocal difficulties, with each level requiring a different or combined improvement approach. Let us examine these levels.

SEVERITY LEVEL 1

Level 1 voices are those identified as aesthetically unpleasant or ineffective in the presence of a normal laryngeal mechanism and vocal tract. Identification of the voice components that cause the voice to be judged ineffective, followed by a self-improvement program, are possible and desirable at this level.

SEVERITY LEVEL 2

Level 2 voices are those identified to be ineffective to the point that they require professional therapeutic management by a speech pathologist. These disorders may be the result of abnormal laryngeal mechanisms or vocal tracts caused by inappropriate vocal habits. These inappropriate vocal habits may lead to the development of laryngeal growths or pathologies.

SEVERITY LEVEL 3

This final level includes those voices that require medical or surgical management by a physician. These voices may be affected by minor disorders, such as infectious laryngitis, that may be easily treated by a family physician. More serious disorders or pathologies may occur which require examination and treatment by a specialist called an otolaryngologist (*oto* means ear and *laryng* means larynx). This specialist is therefore sometimes called an ear, nose, and throat doctor. The otolaryngologist will examine the larynx and vocal folds and treat the pathology through either medication or surgical management. Following the appropriate medical management, the physician will often make referrals to the speech pathologist for evaluation of the functional causes of the disorder and follow-up voice therapy.

The vast majority of students in your class will be operating at the Level 1 severity. You are interested in improving the effectiveness of voice production while utilizing a perfectly normal and healthy laryngeal mechanism. If, however, you or your instructor suspect that the quality, pitch, or loudness of your voice is quite unusual or if you are experiencing intermittent or persistent hoarseness, then examination by an otolaryngologist would be in order while you are participating in this class.

COMMON CAUSES OF VOICE DISORDERS

Many factors may contribute to the development of ineffective voice production. These factors may be as simple as using an ineffective pitch level or as serious as a neurological disorder. Your understanding of these causes will help you to avoid them or will explain to you the need to modify them if they are already present. We will divide these common causes into three major groups: vocal misuse, medical causes, and personality-related causes.

Vocal Misuse
Whenever we use our voices incorrectly we are potentially causing vocal changes or promoting characteristics that may cause the voice to be ineffectively produced. **Voice misuse** may take place through inappropriate use of the several vocal components that combine to make voice possible or simply through vocally abusive behaviors.

The components that make voice possible include respiration, phonation, resonation, pitch, loudness, and rate. Any one component or combination of components that are functionally used in an inappropriate manner may yield an ineffective voice production. Indeed, this course will concentrate on the manipulation of these voice components to find the optimum balance for effective voice production.

Respiration **Respiration,** or **breath support,** refers to the proper exchange of air for support of vocal fold vibration. As you learned in Chapter 4, vocal fold vibration is dependent upon overcoming the resistance of the approximated vocal folds by the buildup of air pressure below the folds. Although the majority of people breathe adequately to support voicing, some problems in breathing techniques may be evident. These problems may include the use of inadequate breath support, or shallow breathing, or the use of residual air during speech production.

Breath support Three methods of creating air exchange between the atmosphere and the lungs are evident. These methods are called clavicular breathing, thoracic breathing, and diaphragmatic breathing. In Chapter 3, we described the breathing mechanism by use of the example of a closed box (Fig. 3-5). Imagine now that your chest or thoracic cavity is this closed box, with the only entrance being a tube. Attached to the end of the tube inside the box is a balloon. The tube represents your trachea; the balloon represents your lungs. If you want to draw air into the balloon (lungs), you may accomplish this simply by expanding the top, sides, or bottom of the box. The top of the box represents your shoulders. Because the upward mobility of your shoulders is limited, expansion of the box or thoracic cavity will be limited. Therefore your clavicular breathing is not particularly supportive of voice production. However, expansion of the sides of the box, or the chest wall, is much greater and normally allows enough air to be inhaled to support voice during normal conversational speech. This form of thoracic breathing is used by the majority of adults.

The most efficient method of air intake for the support of voice is through the downward contraction of the bottom of the box, or the diaphragm. The diaphragm is a dome-shape muscle that forms the bottom of the thoracic cavity. When it contracts downward, the muscles of the abdomen are forced outward and the entire cavity or box expands to its maximum extent. This maximum expansion permits a maximum inhalation of air for the support of voice production. As young infants and toddlers we all breathed diaphragmatically. As we grew older we switched to the more common thoracic breathing pattern. Actors and singers and those who tend to use their voices professionally often attempt to redevelop the diaphragmatic breathing pattern because of the increased demands on their voices. Inadequate use of breath support will often lead to an ineffective or disordered voice production.

Breathing effectively for voice requires the appropriate buildup of air pressure below the vocal folds. Differences in pitch production, loudness variations, and inflection patterns initiated at the level of the vocal folds will require subtle, rapid air pressure changes. A simultaneous relationship must also be developed between the breathing pattern for speech and the length of the spoken phrases. Conversational speech is the stringing together of multiple phrases. All major inhalations should occur between phrases so as not to interrupt the meaning of the phrase. All phrases, however, do not require a separate inhalation. Effective breathing will occur at a point where lung ventilation is needed *and* following completion of a phrase unit. When too many breaths are taken, the conversation becomes disjointed and difficult to follow. When too few breaths are taken, the speaker may "run out of breath." When this occurs, the speaker is using residual air for speech.

CHAPTER 5
58

Residual air **Residual air** is a term that describes the volume of air still in the lungs that may be forcefully expelled following a normal exhalation. People who continue to talk following the normal expiration of air are said to be "talking on residual air." Because residual air does not provide adequate breath support for voice, this type of voicing will increase laryngeal muscle tension, straining the vocal mechanism and leading to ineffective voice production.

Begin counting. Do not take a breath until you have totally exhausted the air in your lungs. Do you feel the vocal strain?

Another important, though somewhat obscure, factor in the relationship between breath support and voice is how efficiently the vocal folds are utilizing the breath stream in producing the voice. As you will learn in another section of this text, some consonant sounds may be voiced while others do not require voice. For example, the consonants /s/ and /z/ are produced by the same articulatory positions, with /s/ being voiceless and /z/ being voiced. If the vocal folds are strong and their muscular control is well balanced, then the breath support required to support each consonant will be nearly equal. The overall health and general condition of the folds may therefore be tested by sustaining the two consonants for as long as possible following maximum inhalations, timing each effort, and comparing the times (Boone, 1979). The times should be nearly equal.

Breathe in as deeply as possible; then sustain the /s/ consonant as long as possible until you have totally exhausted the air in your lungs. Repeat the same instructions for the /z/ sound. Time both consonants. Are the times nearly the same?

The maximum inhalation and subsequent exhalation continued until all possible air is forced from the lungs is called the **vital capacity.** We will use this technique later as one means of assessing your vocal efficiency.

Phonation Phonation is a term that refers to the actual way in which the vocal folds vibrate. Inappropriate phonatory behaviors may include the use of hard glottal attacks, breathy phonation, glottal fry phonation, and hoarseness.

Hard glottal attacks (HGAs) are the most common inappropriate phonatory behavior. As you know, the glottis is the space between the vocal folds. When the vocal folds are forced together too tightly while saying vowels, the glottis or space is "attacked," causing the vocal folds to vibrate too hard. The hard glottal attack can therefore place a strain on the vocal folds, leading to an ineffective voice production. To produce a hard glottal attack on purpose you could

1 inhale,
2 squeeze the vocal folds tightly together as if you are lifting a heavy object, thus building up air pressure below the folds, and then
3 sharply release the air while producing any vowel sound.

This harsh form of glottal attack may be evident in conversational speech.

> Say the vowels /a/, /e/, /i/, /o/, and /o͞o/, using a hard glottal attack.

The opposite extreme of the HGA is the use of the breathy voice, or **breathy phonation**. A breathy voice is produced when the vocal folds are not approximated tightly enough to prevent an unusual escape of air. Breathy voice production is ineffective and potentially harmful to the vocal folds owing to air turbulence and friction created between the folds. The breathy voice will often project an image of weakness or shyness—an image not often desirable in today's society.

> Some actresses use a breathy voice quality to project a sultry image. Can you imitate an actress with a breathy voice?

Less common is the production of glottal fry phonation. A **glottal fry** is the low-pitched growl-like sound that sounds like the sputter of an outboard boat motor. Sometimes, people who try to make their voices sound more authoritative will functionally produce an inappropriate glottal fry phonation. The sound of the glottal fry is distracting and may draw attention away from the content of the speech production.

Hoarseness refers to an aperiodic vibration of the vocal folds and may be described by terms such as harsh, raspy, gravelly, and so on. Hoarseness may result from temporary swelling of the vocal folds due to some form of **voice abuse** such as shouting or may be the result of more serious growths of the vocal folds. Hoarseness that persists for more than 5–7 days should be examined by a physician.

Resonation Resonation refers to the appropriate coupling of the pharyngeal, oral, and nasal cavities for the most effective enhancement of vibrations from the vocal folds. Resonation yields the individual vocal qualities that make your voice production unique to you. Inappropriate coupling of the resonating cavities or improper posturing of the tongue or larynx will cause ineffective voice production. Inappropriate resonation may be described by the terms hypernasality, cul de sac nasality, assimilative nasality, or denasality.

Hypernasality is present when excessive nasal emission occurs during phonation. This quality results when the soft palate fails to close the nasal cavity during the production of all sounds except /m/, /n/, and /ng/. All sounds therefore may travel into the nasal cavity and be expelled through the nose. Failure of the soft palate to close may be a functional behavior in the presence of normal anatomical structure or may be the result of palatal or pharyngeal damage or inadequacy. **Cul de sac nasality** refers to the nasal resonation of all sounds without the presence of a great deal of nasal emission.

Assimilative nasality occurs when the sounds adjacent to the three nasal consonants /m/, /n/, and /ng/ are nasalized along with these sounds. It is presumed that the soft palate may open too soon and then remain open too long before and after the nasal consonant.

Densality, or **hyponasality,** occurs when normal nasal resonance is not present on the sounds /m/, /n/, and /ng/. We have all sounded denasal when he have had a bad cold and appropriate sounds have not been permitted to pass through the nasal cavity.

Block your nasal cavity with your soft palate and talk to a friend as if you have a cold. Do you see how this changes your voice production?

Proper resonator coupling is important to the effective production of voice. The coupling of the resonators will also be influenced by how the tongue is positioned in the mouth and pharynx (forward, back, up, down) and the positioning of the larynx in the neck (up, down).

Pitch   Pitch is the property of voice that describes how high or how low a voice is being produced. We all have a habitual pitch range that we use rather consistently in conversational speech. Habitual use of an inappropriate pitch level will cause the voice to be ineffective and may place unusual strain on the laryngeal mechanism. The use of an inappropriate pitch may draw attention to the speaker and is considered one of the primary components of ineffective voice use.

In Chapter 3, we discussed the terms fundamental frequency and overtones. Several other terms may be used to describe the pitch use of an individual. These terms are pitch range, habitual pitch, optimum pitch, pitch inflection, and pitch breaks.

Pitch range   **Pitch range** refers to the total range from low to high that an individual is able to achieve. Depending on sex, age, physical structure, and the ability to manipulate the laryngeal mechanism, pitch range will vary tremendously among individuals. A wide pitch range is not required for effective voicing if the range that is present is utilized efficiently. On the contrary, some individuals possess very wide pitch ranges but, conversationally, use only a narrow portion of that range.

It is difficult to say what a normal pitch range should be because of the tremendous variability in voices. Most people, however, should be able to demonstrate a range of approximately sixteen notes on a musical scale. To test your pitch range you begin by finding the lowest note you can produce with your singing voice. Call this note *one* and sing up the musical scale as high as you possibly can, singing *one, two, three, four, five,* and so forth. You may need the help of a piano or a pitch pipe to match the appropriate notes. If necessary, ask for the help of a friend or your instructor. Sometimes a narrow pitch range may reflect an ineffective voice or even a more serious voice disorder. If you have a limited pitch range, you and your instructor may determine that a laryngeal examination is desirable.

Habitual pitch **Habitual pitch** refers to the narrow portion of total pitch range in which you tend to focus your voice. The habitual pitch is not one pitch level; rather, it is a range of pitches that you use in conversational speech. Your habitual pitch use may be effective, too high, or too low. The effectiveness of your pitch is ultimately determined by the listener, but you may subjectively judge whether your habitual pitch range is the same as your optimum pitch.

Optimum pitch **Optimum pitch** is a term that has been debated for many years. Although an individual does not have one optimum pitch level, he or she will possess a pitch range that is most effective for voicing. The goal in voice development is to match the optimum pitch range to the habitual pitch use. Fairbanks (1960) suggested finding the optimum pitch by first determining the entire pitch range (including falsetto) and then counting one-fourth of the way up the range. The pitches around this level would constitute the optimum pitch. Most college females will focus their pitch levels around middle C on a musical scale; males will focus one octave lower (C_3).

Pitch inflection **Pitch inflection** refers to the variability in pitch levels used during conversational speech. This variability will add much to the mood, intent, and meaning of your speech. A simple inflection such as "well ➚ " will add significant meaning to a single word. The "well ➚ " could mean "What do you want?" "What do you mean?" "I'm waiting," depending upon the conversational context. Pitch inflection will occur between and within phrases. Inflection patterns will be determined by the intent or meaning of the phrase. For example, the phrase "I'm going today" may be inflected various ways.

I'm going today.   Focus on speaker
I'm going today ➚ .   Focus on time

Between phrases, the inflection pattern may require a shift in pitch. For example, the statement "I'd like to do it for you ↑ but I just can't" describes the frustration of the speaker in not being able to help a friend. A flat pitch inflection, or **monotone,** is difficult to listen to and quickly becomes boring. Effective speakers will use pitch inflection as a powerful communication tool.

Pitch breaks **Pitch break** is a term that refers to sudden uncontrolled and inappropriate change in pitch during speech production. A pitch break is normally the result of inefficient or inadequate breath support or a weakness in the laryngeal muscles that permits a loss of pitch control. Frequent pitch breaks, such as might occur in the voice of an adolescent male, are not appropriate in the voice of a college-age student and would need to be resolved to make the voice more effective.

Loudness Loudness is the perceptual term that relates to vocal intensity. In Chapter 4, we discussed appropriate use of loudness as demonstrated in voices that are habitually too soft or too loud. Speakers who habitually use inappropriate loudness levels during conversational speech may project harsh or overbearing images or images of shyness or weakness. Beyond the image problems that may arise, inappropriate use of intensity levels may be seen also within phrases and words. Like pitch inflection, variability of intensity levels will add to the overall meaning, intent, and mood of speech. The ability to inflect words or phrases is aided by the additional stress that a change in loudness can provide.

For example, the phrase "It's not time to go" may be aided by varying the intensity levels as follows:

It's *not* time to *go*.

The speaker of this phrase is emphatic and is not simply making a declarative statement.

Notice in daily conversational speech how loudness levels offer significant contributions to the mood, intent, and meaning of what is said. Anger, disgust, joy, surprise, and so on can be exhibited simply through changes in loudness levels.

Rate Rate of speech may create problems in voice production when the rate is either too fast or too slow. Rate may be measured by dividing the number of words said by the elapsed time. A convenient scale is words per minute. The ideal rate of speech is between 160 and 170 words per minute. When speech is produced too rapidly, the speaker cannot use appropriate breath support and often speaks on residual air. When the rate of speech is too slow, the laryngeal mechanism may not be supported well by the air stream and the phonation may be breathy. Rate that is either too fast or too slow will yield an ineffective vocal production. At times the rate of speech may be monotonous. When this is the case, the speech pattern is said to lack rhythm. You will further examine your speech rate in Chapter 6.

Vocally abusive behaviors Whenever the vocal folds are forced to adduct too vigorously, this may be considered a vocally abusive behavior or **vocal abuse.** When such behavior is more or less habitual, it may cause changes to occur in the tissues of the vocal folds, thereby yielding an ineffective voice quality. These tissue changes may be swelling, redness, or the development of various growths. Some of the more common vocally abusive behaviors include chronic shouting, such as a cheerleader might do at sporting events; loud talking, perhaps over noise in a social situation or a factory; the screaming of small children or the production vocal noises to simulate trucks, animals, machine guns, and the like; and coughing and throat clearing caused by cigarette smoking, allergies, sinus conditions, or simply habit. Voice abuse is one of the primary causes of vocal difficulties and needs to be identified and modified or eliminated in order to make the voice as effective as possible.

> Have you ever shouted loudly enough at a sporting event that you become hoarse for a day or so? Chronic hoarseness is a Severity Level 2 or 3 type of problem.

Medically Related Causes

Many medical/surgical conditions and situations exist which would yield an ineffective voice production. These conditions may be the result of direct or indirect surgical intervention for cancer or other lung problems or may be the effects of chronic illness or disorders such as allergies, sinusitis, smoking, or alcohol abuse. In addition, a number of other primary medical problems produce vocal difficulties as a secondary symptom along with the major disorder. For example, people who are deaf will not be able to monitor their voices well; people with neurological disorders such as stroke may have many problems with voice and speech.

Personality-Related Causes

The way we feel, both physically and emotionally, is often directly reflected in the quality of our voices. The tensions and stresses of everyday life may contribute directly to the ineffective functioning of the sensitive vocal mechanism. One term used to describe the many occurrences in human life that can cause emotional and psychological stresses is **environmental stress.** Personal, work, school, social, or family situations may well create difficulties that increase whole body and/or laryngeal muscle tension to a level that causes a hyperfunctioning of the voice. This hyperfunction may lead to an ineffective voice production.

At times, environmental stress may become so severe that avoidance behaviors may develop to counteract stressful situations. These avoidances, called psychological conversion, permit people to avoid awareness of the stress or emotional conflict. Conversion behaviors associated with ineffective voice production are aphonia (whispering), muteness (inability to speak or produce voice), or unusual dysphonias. These voice problems are used to draw attention away from the stress-producing cause.

The final personality-related cause of an ineffective voice production is that of identity conflicts. Persons who experience difficulty in establishing their own personalities may develop ineffective voices as a result. These may include a high-pitched voice in the post-adolescent male or the weak, thin, juvenile-sounding voice of an adult female.

In Chapter 4, we discussed the basic nature of voice and how voice relates to your total communication success. In this chapter we have discussed the individual components of voice that make voice either effective or ineffective depending upon their usage. Let us now examine your voice and set you on the course of voice improvement.

STUDY QUESTIONS

1. Many causes may contribute to an ineffective voice production. What are the three *major* causes presented in this chapter? With which of these major causes are you most concerned?

2. What type of breathing pattern do you use to support your speech production? Is the type of breathing pattern you use considered to be the most effective for the support of speech?

3. Can you think of any communication situations in which hard glottal attack phonation may be required for effective communication?

4. Why is your voice quality changed significantly when you have a cold? Give two possible explanations.

5. What is the difference between a habitual pitch range and an optimal pitch range?

6. Inflection involves the manipulation of two basic voicing components. What are these components? How does the respiratory system contribute to inflection?

7. What are common vocally abusive behaviors? When was the last time you abused your voice? What were the circumstances and what were the abusive behaviors?

Chapter 6

Voice Assessment and Improvement

Thus far we have discussed the various components of voice which, when used appropriately, will lead to an effective voice production. How effective is your voice?

Given that it does not fall into Severity Levels 2 and 3, then we may assume it is either as effective as possible or the various voice components could use a little attention to make the overall voice production more effective. It is possible to examine your own voice production and to determine which voice components may be improved. This personal assessment may be accomplished in a very systematic manner by assessing the effectiveness of each major component of voice separately. When the total assessment is completed, those components with the lowest ratings may be systematically improved. It is suggested that you complete this assessment in a small group situation or individually with your instructor. However it is accomplished, you should be as accurate and honest as possible. The Personal Voice Assessment begins on the next page.

CHAPTER 6

PERSONAL VOICE ASSESSMENT

Tape record the following reading in your natural normal speech. Many voicing components will be analyzed utilizing this tape.

> If you walk along the main street on an August afternoon there is nothing whatsoever to do. The largest building, in the very center of the town, is boarded up completely and leans so far to the right that it seems bound to collapse at any minute. The house is very old. There is about it a curious, cracked look that is very puzzling until you suddenly realize that at one time, and long ago, the right side of the front porch had been painted, and part of the wall—but the painting was left unfinished and one portion of the house is darker and dingier than the other. The building looks completely deserted. Nevertheless, on the second floor there is one window which is not boarded; sometimes in the late afternoon when the heat is at its worst a hand will slowly open the shutter and a face will look down on the town. It is a face like the terrible dim faces known in dreams—sexless and white, with two gray crossed eyes which are turned inward so sharply that they seem to be exchanging with each other one long and secret gaze of grief. The face lingers at the window for an hour or so, then the shutters are closed once more, and as likely as not there will not be another soul to be seen along the main street.
>
> *Ballad of the Sad Cafe* (Carson McCullers)

A   RESPIRATION ASSESSMENT

Purpose: To assess lung capacity, vocal fold/breath support efficiency, and respiratory strategies for running speech

1. Sustain the /ah/ sound as long as possible. Breathe in as deeply as you possibly can and sustain the /ah/ as long as possible until you totally expel all of the air from your lungs. Time this production and rate it on the following scale.

    Scale 1

1	2	3	4	5
0–3 seconds	4–7	8–11	12–15	16+

    Goal: 16+ seconds

2. Sustain the sound /s/ (like a snake) for as long as possible. Breathe in as deeply as possible and sustain the /s/ as long as possible until you totally expel all the air from your lungs. Time this production. Repeat the same procedure for the sound /z/. Subtract the difference in time between the two sounds. Record the difference on the following scale.

VOICE ASSESSMENT AND IMPROVEMENT

Scale 2

1	2	3	4	5
15+ seconds	14–12	11–9	8–6	5–3 or less

Goal: 5–3 seconds difference or less

3 Listen to and silently read along with your tape-recorded paragraph. Draw a line marking each place where you took a breath. Compare the number and place of inhalations taken to those reported in your instructor's manual. Choose one of the following scales and record the number of inhalations.

Scale 3

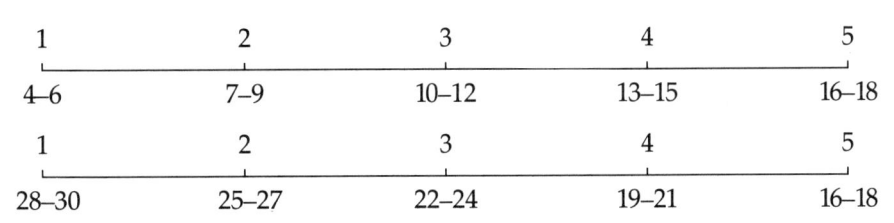

1	2	3	4	5
4–6	7–9	10–12	13–15	16–18

1	2	3	4	5
28–30	25–27	22–24	19–21	16–18

Goal: 16–18 inhalations

Complete the following calculation:
Scale 1 _____ + Scale 2 _____ + Scale 3 _____ = _____ ÷ 3 =
Respiration score _____

B PHONATION ASSESSMENT

Purpose: To assess the presence of hard glottal attacks, breathy phonation, glottal fry phonation, and hoarseness

Play the sample tape back to your instructor or small assessment group. Listen very closely to your voice production. Rate the actual phonation characteristics on the following scales.

Scale 1 Hard glottal attacks

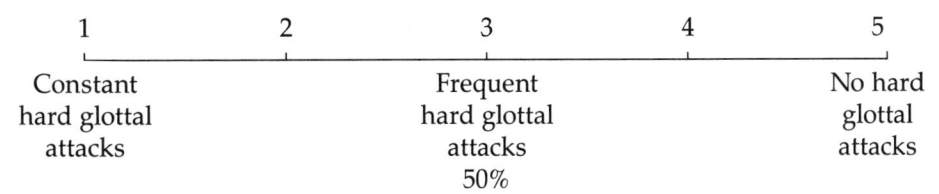

1	2	3	4	5
Constant hard glottal attacks		Frequent hard glottal attacks 50%		No hard glottal attacks

Goal: No hard glottal attacks

Scale 2 Breathiness

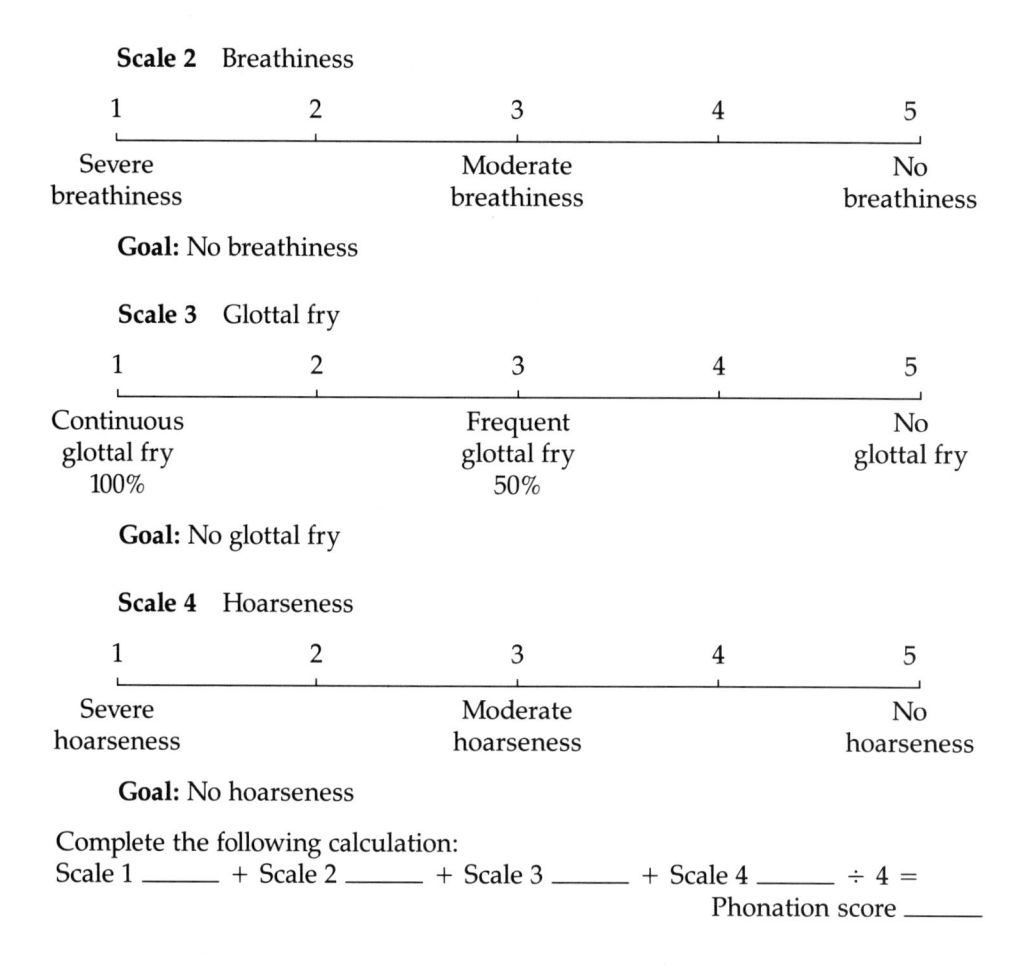

```
1          2          3          4          5
|——————————|——————————|——————————|——————————|
Severe                Moderate              No
breathiness           breathiness           breathiness
```

Goal: No breathiness

Scale 3 Glottal fry

```
1          2          3          4          5
|——————————|——————————|——————————|——————————|
Continuous            Frequent              No
glottal fry           glottal fry           glottal fry
  100%                  50%
```

Goal: No glottal fry

Scale 4 Hoarseness

```
1          2          3          4          5
|——————————|——————————|——————————|——————————|
Severe                Moderate              No
hoarseness            hoarseness            hoarseness
```

Goal: No hoarseness

Complete the following calculation:
Scale 1 _____ + Scale 2 _____ + Scale 3 _____ + Scale 4 _____ ÷ 4 =
Phonation score _____

C RESONATION ASSESSMENT

Purpose: To assess the presence of hypernasality or denasality

Listen again to the tape-recorded paragraph with your instructor or your nearest assessment group. Listen closely to your resonation characteristics. Then choose *one* of the two resonation scales below and rate your resonation component.

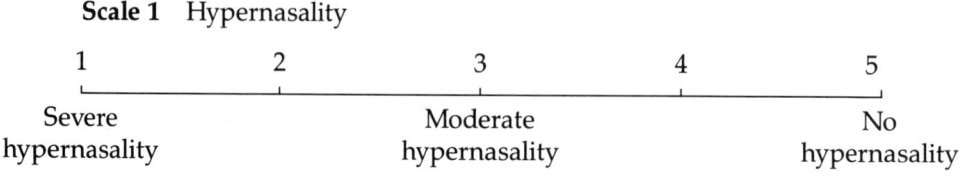

Scale 1 Hypernasality

```
1          2          3          4          5
|——————————|——————————|——————————|——————————|
Severe                Moderate              No
hypernasality         hypernasality         hypernasality
```

Goal: No hypernasality

Scale 2 Denasality

1	2	3	4	5
Severe denasality		Moderate denasality		No denasality

Goal: No denasality   Resonation score _____

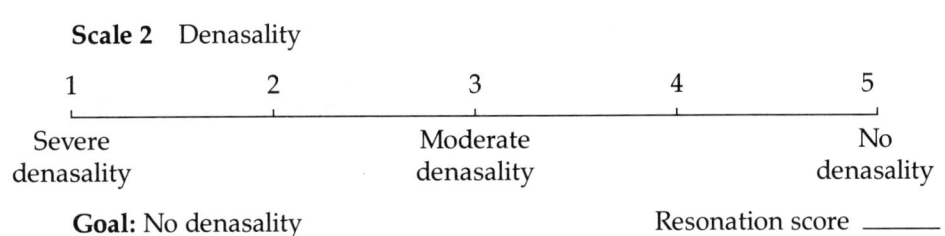

D PITCH ASSESSMENT

Purpose: To assess pitch range, habitual compared to optimum pitch, effectiveness of pitch inflection, and presence of pitch breaks

Scale 1 Pitch range

Sing the lowest note you can possibly sing on the word *one*. Beginning on that note, sing up as many whole notes as you possibly can singing *one-two-three-four-five*. . . . Record the number of notes you can sing on the following scale.

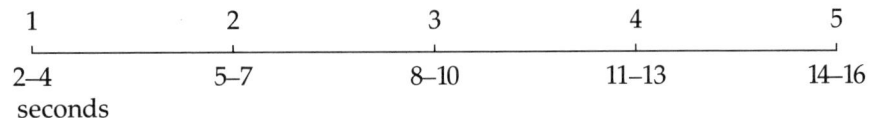

1	2	3	4	5
2–4 seconds	5–7	8–10	11–13	14–16

Goal: 14–16 notes

Scale 2 Habitual pitch

While listening to your tape-recorded reading passage with your instructor or your small assessment group, decide whether the overall pitch level is appropriate, too high, or too low when compared to your scale 1 pitch range. Rate your decision by choosing *one* of the following scales.

Pitch too low

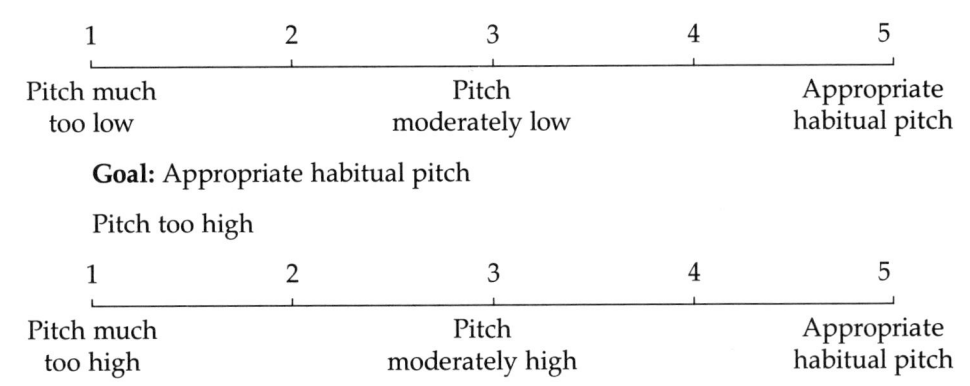

1	2	3	4	5
Pitch much too low		Pitch moderately low		Appropriate habitual pitch

Goal: Appropriate habitual pitch

Pitch too high

1	2	3	4	5
Pitch much too high		Pitch moderately high		Appropriate habitual pitch

Goal: Appropriate habitual pitch

Scale 3 Pitch inflection

Again, while listening to your tape-recorded reading, determine the effectiveness of your inflection strategies and rate the effectiveness on the following scale.

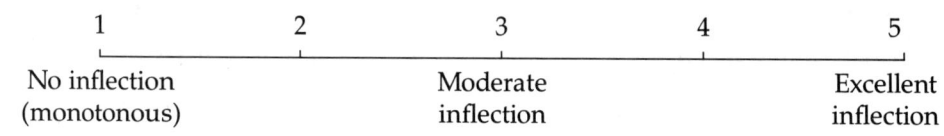

```
1          2          3          4          5
```
No inflection   Moderate   Excellent
(monotonous)   inflection   inflection

Goal: Excellent inflection

Scale 4 Pitch breaks

Review your tape-recorded voice sample for the presence of inappropriate pitch breaks. Rate the number of breaks on the following scale.

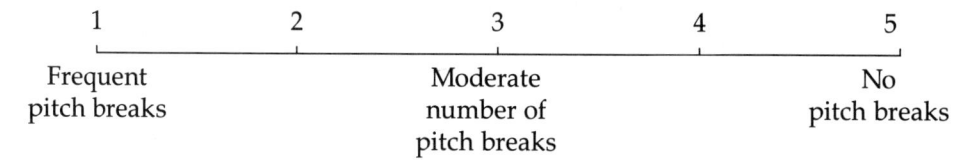

```
1          2          3          4          5
```
Frequent   Moderate   No
pitch breaks   number of   pitch breaks
                            pitch breaks

Goal: No pitch breaks

Complete the following calculation:
Scale 1 _____ + Scale 2 _____ + Scale 3 _____ + Scale 4 _____ =
_____ ÷ 4 = Pitch score _____

E LOUDNESS ASSESSMENT

Purpose: To assess the effectiveness of the overall loudness level (too loud, too soft) and the variability of loudness for purposes of inflection and stress

Scale 1 Loudness effectiveness

Using your tape-recorded reading, rate the effectiveness of your loudness level on *one* of the following scales.

Choose *one*.

Too soft

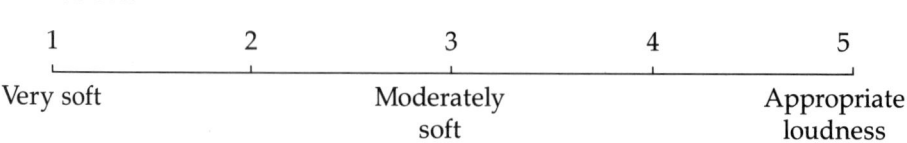

```
1          2          3          4          5
```
Very soft   Moderately   Appropriate
                            soft   loudness

Goal: Appropriate loudness

VOICE ASSESSMENT AND IMPROVEMENT

Too loud

1	2	3	4	5
Very loud		Moderately loud		Appropriate loudness

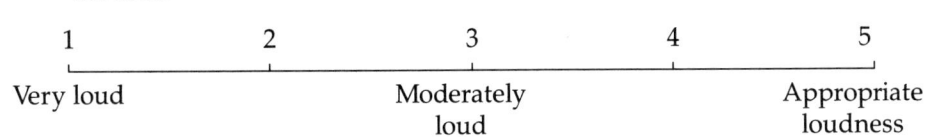

Goal: Appropriate loudness

Scale 2 Loudness variability

Using your tape-recorded reading, rate the effectiveness of your loudness variability for purposes of inflection and stress. Rate your effectiveness on the following scale.

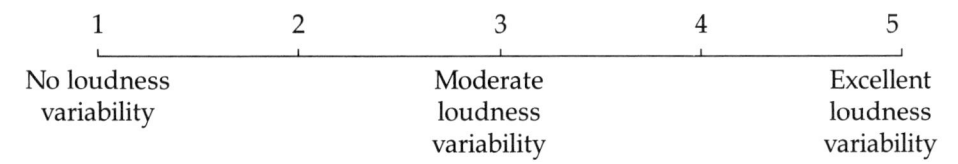

1	2	3	4	5
No loudness variability		Moderate loudness variability		Excellent loudness variability

Goal: Excellent loudness variability

Complete the following calculations:
Scale 1 _____ + Scale 2 _____ = _____ ÷ 2 = Loudness score _____

F RATE ASSESSMENT

Purpose: To assess the actual rate of your speech on a words-per-minute basis and to assess the variability, or rhythm, of your speech

Scale 1 Rate of speech

Count the number of words read in your tape-recorded sample. Then, using a stopwatch, time the length of your reading. Divide the number of words by the elapsed time to calculate words per minute. Then choose *one* of the following scales to rate the effectiveness of your rate of speech.

Too Fast

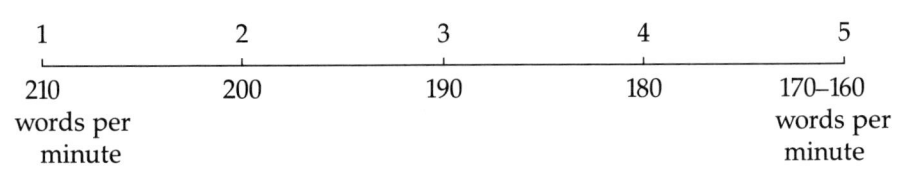

1	2	3	4	5
210 words per minute	200	190	180	170–160 words per minute

Goal: 170–160 words per minute

Too slow

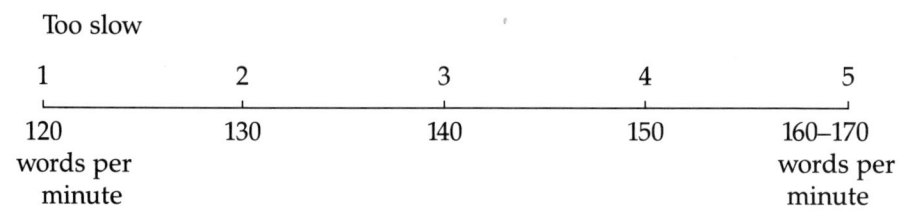

1	2	3	4	5
120 words per minute	130	140	150	160–170 words per minute

Goal: 160–170 words per minute

Scale 2 Rate variability (rhythm)

Listen to your tape-recorded sample with your small assessment group or your instructor. Assess the rhythm of your speech (or rate variability) and rate it for effectiveness on the following scale.

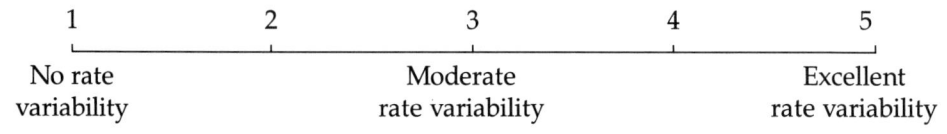

1	2	3	4	5
No rate variability		Moderate rate variability		Excellent rate variability

Goal: Excellent rate variability

Complete the following calculations:
Scale 1 _____ + Scale 2 _____ = _____ ÷ 2 = Rate score _____

RESULTS

You have now generated a single score for A, respiration; B, phonation; C, resonation; D, pitch; E, loudness; and F, rate. Add these scores and divide by six for your final voice effectiveness score.

A _____ + B _____ + C _____ + D _____ + E _____ + F _____ =
_____ ÷ 6 = _____

Goal: 5

If any one voice component was rated less than five, then this component will require personal improvement. The remainder of this chapter is designed to aid you in this task.

VOICE IMPROVEMENT

Now that you have completed your personal voice assessment, you have identified the various voice components that may benefit from an improvement program. Improving individual components will lead to a more effective overall voice production. The following is a series of exercise programs designed to improve the major voice components of respiration, phonation, resonation, pitch, loudness, and rate. Study your personal assessment results with your instructor and establish your voice improvement goals. When your goals have been established, find the exercise programs tailored to your needs and systematically practice each exercise as needed. When you think you have successfully modified each voice component, then ask your instructor to retest you utilizing the personal voice assessment. This will determine whether your improvement goals have been met.

RESPIRATION IMPROVEMENT

As described in Chapter 5, an efficient exchange of air is necessary for the production of normal voice. Problems in the respiratory support of voice may exist when

1. a person uses shallow breathing by not using enough of their lung capacity,
2. a person talks using residual air, or
3. a person's vocal cords do not vibrate as efficiently as possible.

Respiratory Exercises

Problem 1 Shallow breathing and poor lung capacity caused by poor or limited thoracic and/or abdominal expansion

Goal Expand and improve respiratory lung capacity.

Exercises Abdominal breathing

    A Stand upright. Place one hand on your chest and the other hand on your abdomen. Sharply inhale. The hand on your chest should remain relatively still while the hand on the abdomen should move out with the expansion of the abdominal muscles. Relax the abdominal muscles; lightly and slowly exhale. Repeat the inhalation and exhalation until you are able to easily maintain the proper movement of the abdomen—out during inhalation, in during exhalation.

    B Lie flat on your back on the floor. Place a hard-backed textbook on your upper abdomen. Inhale by expanding the abdominal muscles and contracting the diaphragm. Exhale through relaxation of the muscles. Watch the text rise during inhalation and fall during exhalation.

    C Add speech to exercises A and B. Begin by counting, saying one number per inhalation/exhalation. Then say two numbers, and then three, and so on. Say only as many numbers as you can comfortably say while the air is flowing easily. Do not push or strain.

CHAPTER 6

    D Continue using speech with abdominal breathing. Refer to the graduated sentences in Appendix 1. Inhale before each sentence and build your ability to produce each sentence through nine- and ten-syllable phrases on one controlled inhalation and exhalation.

    E While continuing to use abdominal breathing, practice reading the paragraphs in Appendix 2. Breathe only where a phrase marker indicates the appropriate place to breathe. Choose and mark your own phrasing in passages 4, 5, and so on.

Problem 2 Continuing to talk on residual air after the normal conversational lung capacity has been exhausted

Goal Learn to talk only on normal conversational exhalations. Eliminate the use of residual air for speech.

Exercises Residual air

    A Review problem 1 and make sure you are using your lung capacity to its optimum by utilizing a relaxed abdominal or diaphragmatic breathing technique. When satisfied that you are breathing in the appropriate manner, move on to B.

    B Refer to the phrases graduated by length in Appendix 1. Begin with the two-syllable phrases and inhale and exhale lightly while reading each phrase. Continue building this ability by adding longer phrases. As soon as you lose the relaxed inhalation/exhalation and begin to strain—stop. These phrases will represent the number of syllables that you can comfortably say on one exhalation without resorting to the use of residual air.

    C Refer to the reading paragraphs in Appendix 2. Choose one paragraph without phrase markers and read it aloud. Determine where you think the appropriate phrase markers should be and place them in the text. Practice reading this paragraph while breathing only in the places you marked. Make sure you place no strain on your breathing or respiratory system.

Problem 3 Inefficient use of the breath stream by the vocal folds as a result of lack of laryngeal muscle control

Goal Improve the periodic vibration of the vocal folds.

Exercises Inefficient vocal fold vibration

    A Inhale as deeply as possible and then sustain the vowel /e/ as long as possible on a comfortable tone. As you begin to run out of air, you may use residual air until the total lung capacity has been exhausted. Sustain the sound very softly. Listen for breathiness, wavering of tone, and phonation breaks. As much as possible, eliminate these three vocal behaviors.

B Inhale deeply and glide softly from your deepest note to your highest note using the vowel /o/. Make sure the glide is smooth and even, with no voice breaks.

C Inhale deeply and glide softly from your highest note to your deepest note using the sound /o/. Make sure the glide is smooth and even, with no voice breaks.

D Using a piano or a pitch pipe, sustain or hold out the sound /o/ as long as possible while matching your voice to the notes middle C, D, E, F, G (one octave lower for a male). Sustain the notes very softly. Listen for breathiness, wavering of tone, and phonation breaks. As much as possible, eliminate these three vocal behaviors.

E If you notice that your voice tires easily or if you become easily dysphonic, exercises A, B, C, and D should be done two times each, two times per day.

When you feel you have improved your respiratory support of voice, please reassess this vocal property, utilizing the personal voice assessment.

PHONATION IMPROVEMENT

Phonation is the term that describes the actual vibration of the vocal folds. Characteristics of phonation that may cause this property of voice to be ineffective may be

1 hard glottal attacks caused by too great a buildup of air pressure beneath the vocal folds or too much laryngeal area muscle tension,

2 breathy phonation caused by inefficient vocal fold closure or a lack of proper breath support,

3 glottal fry phonation normally associated with two other ineffective voice components, respiration and pitch, or

4 hoarseness caused by voice abuse, inappropriate use of voice components, laryngeal pathologies, medical diagnoses, or psychosocial/emotional causes.

Phonation Exercises

Problem 1 Hard glottal attacks caused by too great a buildup of subglottic air pressure and laryngeal muscle tension

Goal Eliminate the occurrence of hard glottal attacks.

Exercises Hard glottal attack

A Teach yourself to produce the vowel sounds by using a soft glottal attack or what may be called an easy sound onset. To accomplish this, practice saying each vowel preceded by the sound /h/. You will then say *ha, he, hi, ho,* and *hoo.* Drop the /h/ gradually until the vowel sound can be said lightly and easily without a glottal attack. Expand this new ability by reading aloud phrases and paragraphs located in Appendices 1 and 2.

B If more practice is needed when you have completed exercise A, begin a negative practice exercise. Produce each vowel sound with a soft glottal attack, followed by a hard glottal attack, and then soft again. Demonstrate to yourself that you have complete confidence in your ability to control this laryngeal behavior.

C Because increased laryngeal area tension may be a cause of hard glottal attack productions, exercises designed to reduce laryngeal tension may be necessary.

- Progressive relaxation: Alternately tense and relax all of the muscles in your body, beginning with your scalp and systematically moving down your body to your toes. When you have accomplished a level of relaxation through this exercise, practice reading phrases and paragraphs in Appendices 1 and 2 and monitor any decrease in glottal attacks.
- Chewing: Vegetative chewing may relax the jaw, tongue, neck, and laryngeal musculature. Pretend you are chewing food while at the same time you are lightly and easily saying the vowel sounds. Gradually eliminate the chewing but continue to say the vowels without the glottal attack. Expand the vowels into words, phrases, and paragraphs found in Appendices 1 and 2.
- Yawn/sigh: Another method of reducing laryngeal muscle tension is the yawn/sigh exercise. Pretend you are yawning. At the end of the yawn, you should then lightly sigh while saying a vowel sound. The yawn will loosen and relax the laryngeal muscles and the sigh will direct an easy onset of the vowel. Gradually decrease the yawn until the sigh/vowel can be produced without the glottal attack. Then extinguish the sigh and say the vowels; then words, phrases, and paragraphs in Appendices 1 and 2.

Problem 2 Breathiness caused by inefficient vocal fold closure and poor breath support

Goal Gain improved vocal fold closure and breath support, thus eliminating breathiness.

Exercises Breathiness

- **A** Mild breathiness may be improved simply by using more precise articulation, especially on the plosive sounds /p/, /t/, and /k/. Practice reading phrases and paragraphs found in Appendices 1 and 2 while using an exaggerated articulation pattern. The increased intraoral air pressure required for more precise articulation will decrease the mild laryngeal breathiness.

- **B** A moderate amount of breathiness may be modified by increasing your vocal intensity. Louder voice production requires that the vocal folds approximate more firmly, thus decreasing the amount of wasted air. Refer to Loudness Problem 1 and all associated exercises.

- **C** A greater amount of breathiness may require a more aggressive exercise program consisting of glottal attack exercises. Hard glottal attacks were previously described as an inappropriate phonatory behavior. However, a person with poor glottal closure may use this vocal behavior as an exercise to develop improved glottal closure. To purposely produce a hard glottal attack you must breathe in deeply; close your vocal folds and squeeze them together as if you are lifting a heavy object and then release the buildup of subglottic air pressure while saying the vowels /a/, /e/, /i/, /o/, and /o͞o/, one vowel at a time. These vowels should be said aloud, using the hard glottal attack, three times each, three times per day.

- **D** The most aggressive exercise to use with moderate to severe breathiness is the isometric push. The pushing exercise is accomplished by pushing the palms of your hands together while producing the vowel sounds using Hard Glottal Attack Exercise C. The combination of these two exercises will cause normal vocal folds to adduct vigorously and decrease breathiness. (We are not advocating that people should talk using a hard glottal attack. In the present context, this laryngeal behavior serves merely as a facilitator for glottic closure for a decrease in breathiness.)

- **E** An inefficient vocal fold vibration may also contribute to breathy phonation. Review Respiratory Problem 3 and all associated exercises.

Problem 3 Glottal fry phonation caused by ineffective respiratory support and inappropriate pitch production
  Goal Eliminate glottal fry phonation.
  Exercises Glottal fry

  A Review Respiratory Problems 1 and 3. Practice all associated exercises needed or until respiratory assessment scale 1 and 2 yield a respiratory score of 5.
  B Refer to Pitch Problem 1. Practice associated exercises to raise pitch; this will help to eliminate the glottal fry.

Problem 4 Hoarseness caused by voice abuse, inappropriate use of voice components, medical diagnoses, or psychosocial/emotional causes
  Goal Eliminate hoarseness and return voice to normal.
  Exercises Hoarseness

  A When hoarseness is the result of an acute laryngitis caused by voice abuse, place yourself on limited voice use (no whispering!) for three to four days. Hoarseness should resolve and the voice should return to normal.
  B Frequent intermittent hoarseness or chronic hoarseness requires medical examination and probable treatment by an otolaryngologist and a speech pathologist. Do not attempt to self-diagnose and treat should hoarseness persist.

When you have completed the appropriate exercise for improving or eliminating inappropriate phonatory behaviors, have your instructor reassess this component of voice using the personal voice assessment.

RESONATION IMPROVEMENT

Once the voice leaves the larynx it begins the journey through the vocal tract. The vocal tract is made of cavities that either dampen or enhance the voice vibration, giving each of us our own distinctive sounds. The resonance cavities include the pharynx, the oral cavity, and the nasal cavity. Effective vocal resonance is dependent upon the proper coupling of these cavities. The following characteristics of resonation may be ineffective.

1 Permitting too much air to pass through the nasal cavity. An extreme amount of air passage through the nasal cavity is called hypernasality. Too much nasal resonance but with less air passage through the nose is called cul de sac or dead-end nasality. When vowel sounds are inappropriately resonated through the nasal cavity following the normal nasal consonants (/m/, /n/, /ng/), assimilative nasality is said to occur.

2. Not permitting normal nasal resonance on the nasal consonants /m/, /n/, and /ng/. When this occurs, the person is said to produce voice with too little resonance or hyponasality (denasality). This voice quality may be evident when someone has a head cold.

3. Attempting to speak with a retracted tongue and jaw and an elevated larynx, which essentially pinches or traps the voice in the pharynx. The resultant quality is weak and lacks a full resonant sound.

Resonation Exercises

Problem 1 Hypernasality, cul de sac, and assimilative nasality caused by a lack of palatal-pharyngeal closure. (The assumption is made here that lack of closure is a functional disturbance and not organic in nature.)

Goal Attain normal palatal-pharyngeal closure and reduce nasal emission of air.

Exercises Hypernasality

A. Maximize the precision and correctness of your articulation. Work on the articulatory drills with exaggerated oral movements. Precise articulation will decrease the perception of hypernasality.

B. Utilize all the loudness exercises for increasing your loudness level. Inappropriate nasal resonance may be decreased with a slightly increased loudness level.

C. Do the obvious—produce voice as if you have a cold. In other words, practice a hyponasal resonance—the opposite extreme of the problem. A slight modification of the "cold" voice will then yield a normal nasal resonation. Utilize the phrases in Appendix 1 for this purpose.

D. Practice contrasting pairs while attempting to produce a definite and distinct difference for each word. Use the words

beat	meet	boot	moot
bit	mit	boat	moat
bait	mate	bought	mop
bet	met	bite	might
bat	mat	bout	mouth

E. Use negative practice by repeating all the /b/ words in exercise D with too much nasal resonance. Then produce each word with the normal amount of resonance.

F. Expand your ability to produce a decreased hypernasality by practicing the phrases, sentences, and paragraphs in Appendices 1 and 2.

Problem 2 Hyponasality caused by completely or partially blocked nasal passages. Assuming this blockage is not caused by a cold, allergies, or a growth such as nasal polyps, the problem is generally the result of fixing the soft palate too high against the pharyngeal wall.

Goal Attain normal palatal pharyngeal opening and increase nasalization of /m/, /n/, and /ng/.

Exercises Hyponasality

  A Chill a small mirror in the refrigerator. Place the mirror under your nose. With your lips pressed tightly together hum the sound *mmm*. If your lips are together, the airflow must go through your nose and the mirror will steam. Slowly modify the hummed *mmm* by (a) opening the mouth while humming and saying /ma/, (b) expanding to other vowel sounds (/ma/, /me/, /may/, /mo/, /mo͞o/), (c) eliminating the hum and then expanding into the words, phrases, sentences, and paragraphs in Appendices 1 and 2.

  B Utilize a hypernasal resonance. Practice the words in Resonance Problem 1D, using an exaggerated hypernasal resonation. Slowly decrease the degree of nasality until a normal coupling of the cavities is reached.

Problem 3 Decreased resonation due to speaking with a fixed jaw, a retracted tongue, or an elevated larynx. The size and shape of the oral and pharyngeal cavities can be modified by tongue, jaw, and laryngeal positioning. Positioning that decreases the size of these cavities will negatively affect voice by trapping and pinching its production. Thus, relaxation and mobility of the speech structures is essential for effective voice.

Goal Reduce tension of the jaw, tongue, and laryngeal strap muscles, thus increasing the size of the resonating cavities and freeing the laryngeal vibration.

Exercises Fixed jaw, retracted tongue, elevated larynx

  A Consciously loosen your jaw at the hinges next to your ears. With the loose jaw, open and close your mouth with wide jaw excursions. Continue to exaggerate this movement while repeating the vowel sounds /a/, /e/, /i/, /o/, and /o͞o/. Now add an /m/ before each sound while continuing to use wide jaw movements. Then, practice reading short phrases in Appendix 1 while exaggerating the jaw movement on every word. Expand this into sentences and short paragraphs (Appendices 1 and 2). Gradually decrease the exaggerated jaw movements into a more normal open jaw position. To guarantee that the jaw does not become fixed as you are practicing, place a finger between your front teeth as you practice. Do not let your teeth come any closer than the finger width for your practice purpose.

B The retracted tongue should be helped by loosening the fixed jaw position. An additional exercise for gaining more natural tongue placement is to exaggerate the movements necessary for producing the vowel /e/. Say the /e/ several times by protruding the tongue far forward through and between the teeth. Add the five vowel sounds to each /e/: /e/-/a/, /e/-/e/, /e/-/i/, /e/-/o/, and /e/-/o͞o/. Then gradually decrease the extension of the tongue until it is no longer protruding between the teeth but remains orally in a forward position.

C Improved forward placement of the tongue and increased jaw mobility should help to place the larynx in a less elevated position in the neck. Another way to lower the larynx in the neck is through gentle massage. Identify the edges of the thyroid cartilage of your larynx. Grasp the cartilage with your thumb on one edge and your finger on the other and gently massage downward in a circular manner. When you feel the larynx loosening, begin saying the vowel sounds lightly and easily while not permitting the larynx to stiffen and elevate. Also, make sure your jaw is loose and your tongue is forward. Expand this by saying the short phrases, sentences, and paragraphs in Appendices 1 and 2.

When you have completed the appropriate exercises for improving resonation, have your instructor reassess this voice property using the personal voice assessment.

PITCH IMPROVEMENT

In Chapter 4, we described how pitch variability added to the natural melody of speech through inflectional changes. Chapter 5 described the possible problems that may arise if an inappropriate pitch level is used. An ineffective use of the component of pitch may exist when

1 a person uses a pitch range that is either too high or too low for his or her laryngeal anatomy to successfully produce; we often see this problem in individuals who, while attempting to sound more authoritative, will artificially lower the voice.

2 a person uses a rather flat, or monotonous, pitch pattern, decreasing the effectiveness of the vocal variety.

CHAPTER 6

Pitch Exercises

Problem 1 Utilization of a habitual conversational pitch range that is either too high or too low

Goal Establish use of an optimum pitch range.

Exercises Determination of optimum pitch range

- **A** When working with pitch problems, it is often helpful, but not absolutely necessary, to have use of a pitch pipe or piano. Begin by singing the sound /o/ on a comfortable level. Now, in whole-note steps, sing down the scale until you reach the lowest note that you can produce comfortably. If a piano or pitch pipe is available, match this tone and document the note. Now from this low note sing up the scale as high as you can possibly go in whole notes. As you sing up, count the number of notes. If possible, match the highest note to a piano. This is your pitch range. A range of 14–16 notes would be considered adequate for conversational voice production. Your optimum pitch range would be located approximately one-fourth of the way up your entire range. Therefore, if your total range is 16 notes, your optimum voice use would fall around the fourth note.

- **B** To some people, the concept of notes and singing to find the optimum pitch range is very difficult. If you find this to be the case, try the following. In a natural conversational voice, say *um-hum*, as if you are answering *yes* to a question. The *hum* part of this production is usually produced in a very relaxed tone near your optimum pitch level. If possible, have your instructor or a friend match this tone to a pitch pipe or a piano so that a reference tone is available for further exercises.

- **C** Now that you have found a more appropriate pitch range, it is time to begin practicing speaking within that range. Using the reference note matched to the pitch pipe or piano, say each vowel sound several times at this level. Listen to how your voice sounds and how it feels to produce voice. Then, using phrases and sentences (Appendix 1), expand your speech gradually at the optimum level. Eventually your auditory feedback system will become accustomed to this level and you may then expand its use into longer readings (Appendix 2) and eventually into conversational speech. Monitor each exercise program level by listening to a tape recording of your practice for additional feedback and reinforcement.

D One way of confirming the use of the optimum pitch range is through negative practice. Practice saying exercise sentences using pitch levels that are too high and too low. You will soon see that it is more comfortable and takes less effort to utilize the optimum pitch range.

Problem 2 Utilization of monotonous pitch patterns in conversational speech

Goal Improve vocal variety through use of improved inflectional pitch patterns.

Exercises Improvement of inflection

A You have established your habitual pitch range. Variety of pitch usage with that range is one characteristic of effective voice usage. Were you to use only a limited part of your pitch range, your voice would be flat and monotonous. Pitch should, however, inflect in several directions including up, down, up and down, and down and up. In Chapter 4 we used the phrase "I love you" to demonstrate these various inflectional patterns. Practice saying this phrase in the following ways:

I love you.	(robot voice)
I love you?	(like a question)
I love you.	(simple statement)
I love you.	(declarative)
I love you.	(who do you love?)

It is easy to see how meaning can change simply by changing pitch patterns used with the exact same words.

B Utilize the phrases and sentences in Appendix 1 for practicing inflection patterns. Give each 2–5-syllable phrase as many meanings as possible simply by changing the pitch inflection patterns. Some of the phrases are already marked for inflection exercise; others are not. Follow the arrows for upward and downward pitch change. After you have practiced the marked phrases and are comfortable with the inflection patterns, practice and mark additional sentences on your own. Then move on to the paragraphs in Appendix 2, practicing improved use of pitch inflection to add excitement and meaning to the readings.

When you have completed the appropriate exercise materials for improving your use of pitch, have your instructor reassess this voice property using the personal voice assessment.

LOUDNESS IMPROVEMENT

Another determinant of effective voice production is the use of an appropriate loudness level in various situations as well as the ability to use loudness changes for inflectional purposes. Problems associated with the vocal property of loudness may include

1. speaking too softly as dictated by the situation,
2. speaking with a habitual loud level in most situations, and
3. permitting the loudness level to be monotonous, thus decreasing vocal variety and expression.

Loudness Exercises

Problem 1 Speaking in a loudness level that is habitually soft
Goal Improve the effectiveness of voice by increasing the loudness level.
Exercises Increase of loudness level

A Because your ability to increase your loudness level is dependent upon a good respiratory support of voice, review exercises A through E under Respiratory Problem 1. Make sure you have appropriate respiratory support for increasing loudness.

B Raise your level of awareness as to how softly you are talking by tape recording a conversation of you and a friend. Compare the loudness level of your friend to your own. Understand that people who talk too softly are constantly asked to repeat themselves, they may be ignored, or they may project a bashful or backward image.

C Using the graduated sentences in Appendix 1 and a tape recorder, practice direct manipulation of many loudness levels. Produce some phrases softly and some loudly. Tape record these and listen to the differences in your own voice.

D Use the loudness meter (vu meter) on your tape recorder to monitor your phrase productions at a reasonable, effective loudness level. Develop this improved level through phrases, sentences, paragraph readings (Appendices 1 and 2) and conversational speech.

> E Use a friend to monitor your loudness level in classroom and social situations. Permit your friend to be critical and use the feedback to improve yourself.

Problem 2 Speaking in a loudness level that is habitually too loud
Goal Improve the effectiveness of voice by decreasing the loudness level.
Exercises Decrease of loudness level

> A Raise your level of awareness as to how loudly you are talking by tape recording a conversation between you and a friend. Compare the loudness level of your friend to yourself. Pay attention to the reactions of those with whom you talk. Do people back away, look away, or cut you short? Understand that people who talk too loudly often project an image of being overbearing.
> B See Exercise C, Loudness Problem 1.
> C See Exercise D, Loudness Problem 1.
> D See Exercise E, Loudness Problem 1.

(Note: Sometimes when people have difficulty monitoring loudness levels the problem may be associated with hearing loss. If you have the opportunity to have your hearing levels screened, it would be a good idea to rule out this possibility.)

Problem 3 Use of a monotonous loudness level, thus decreasing vocal variety and expression
Goal Improve vocal variety and expression through use of improved inflectional loudness patterns.
Exercises Loudness variation

> A Practice loudness variation by counting from 1 to 10, beginning very softly and ending very loudly. Then perform the same task from loud to soft.
> B Sustain the vowel o beginning very softly and ending loudly. Try to maintain one pitch level. Then perform the task from loud to soft.
> C Practice manipulating loudness in the 2- to 5-syllable phrases in Appendix 1. Some phrases are marked for increased stress; others are not. After you have practiced the marked phrases and are comfortable with the intensity stress patterns, practice and mark additional sentences on your own. Move on to the paragraphs (Appendix 2) until you are comfortable with loudness changes in conversation.

When you have completed the appropriate exercise materials for improving your use of loudness, have your instructor reassess this voice property using the personal voice assessment.

RATE IMPROVEMENT

The rate at which we speak will contribute to the effectiveness of our overall vocal presentation. Rate is a timing characteristic that is influenced by the number of words we speak per minute, the duration of individual words, and the pauses we place between words.

Rate Exercises

Problems Speaking too fast or too slow; in other words, too many or too few words per minute

Goal Improve the effectiveness of speech by developing a more appropriate rate.

Exercises Rate adjustment

A Become aware of your rate problem by reviewing your rate assessment. Were you too fast or too slow? If you found that your rate was too fast, practice reading the phrases in Appendix 1. Try to read slowly, but instead of using longer pauses, exaggerate vowel durations within the words. For example: Iiiits tiiiime toooo goooo hooome; as opposed to: Its. . . . time. . . . to. . . . go. . . . home. Stretching vowels is a more efficient way of decreasing rate than making longer pauses.

B From deliberate vowel prolongations in phrases, you may move into reading poetry (Appendix 3). The inherent rhythms and inflectional patterns of poems are ideal for indirectly teaching timing and melody.

C When you feel you have made progress in modifying your rate through poetry reading, begin paragraph reading (Appendix 2). Use the tape recorder and time your words per minute.

D Use negative practice now by reading either too fast or too slowly. Compare this rate to your new rate of speed.

When you have completed the appropriate exercise materials for rate improvement, have your instructor reassess this voice property using the personal voice assessment.

VOICE QUALITY IMPROVEMENT

We have concentrated on improving your voice production by working on the weaknesses of certain components of your vocal production. It is the integration of all of these components in a balanced and efficient manner that leads to the production of effective voice quality. Even the "best" or most "effective" speakers can improve voice production by practicing the vocal interpretation of classical literature, poetry, and speeches. Some of these are included for your pleasure and practice opportunity in Appendices 2 and 3. By now, you should have improved any major weaknesses in your vocal presentation and you are ready to move on to the other considerations of effective speech. Remember, words alone do not tell the story. Words alone cannot give the meaning. Your vocal presentation is the melody, the rhythm, the intent, the mood, and the meaning of what you say. Voice it clearly and effectively and you will be a better communicator.

Part Four

Articulation

Chapter 7
The Nature of Articulation

*I*n this chapter, you are ready to proceed to the area of articulation—the process where the tone generated by the vocal folds is shaped by the tongue, lips, and teeth and directed to the oral or nasal cavity to produce a recognizable speech sound. In Chapter 3, you were introduced briefly to the components of articulation and its process; you are ready now to understand just how you coordinate your articulatory system to create intelligible speech.

BACKGROUND INFORMATION

The cry you made at birth was the genesis of speech. You learned to modify and refine that cry into speechlike sounds in the first year of life. At age seven or eight you had mastered the production of the sounds of English. You are now an experienced and competent speaker of English. What have you accomplished? In this chapter, we will discuss articulatory phonetics; phonology and its basic unit, the phoneme; symbols used to represent phonemes; anatomy and physiology of articulation; and how the two groups of sounds—consonants and vowels—are produced and classified.

> If you have access to preschool-aged children, listen to their speech articulation. Compare their speech to that of elementary-aged children.

SPEECH SOUNDS ARE PHONEMES

Articulatory phonetics is the study of how we use the speech mechanism to produce sounds. When you study articulation, you are concerned with the movements of the organs of speech. These organs of speech are the *articulators*, which consist of the lips, teeth, jaw, tongue, and hard and soft palates. Phonology, as you recall, is the study of the rules for the sound system of a language. We will discuss the concrete act of moving tongue, lips, and jaw to create sounds, but we also must represent the repertoire of speech sounds in an abstract manner. A phoneme is a representation of speech sounds. Although the production of single sounds varies from person to person and even within an individual, we articulate the sounds of English in the same general fashion. When we study articulatory phonetics, we consider the particular characteristics of each phoneme.

THE NATURE OF PHONEMES

A phoneme may be viewed in three different ways. First, it is a sound that makes a difference. *Pat, bat, rat, sat, cat, mat,* and *fat* are all different words. These words differ in only one element, the beginning sound. Each of those sounds is considered to be a phoneme.

If a phoneme is a sound that makes a difference, then there must be sounds that do not make a difference. A phoneme is also a family of sounds like itself. These other sounds do not change word meaning when we use them. We recognize the /t/ in *top* and *pot* as the same sound, or phoneme, but it is produced in a slightly different manner in the two words. What is the difference? The /t/ in *top* is produced with a burst of air; the /t/ in *pot* is made without such a puff of air.

Finally, a phoneme is a bundle of distinctive features. Just as the engine of a car has several internal components such as carburetor, air filter, and spark plugs, a phoneme has features that describe what the articulators are doing to produce the phoneme. We can also classify phonemes on the basis of these features. We will rely heavily on this definition later as we describe the phonemes of English in more detail.

THE PHONEMES OF ENGLISH

In the domain of English phonemes, there are specific sound-symbol relationships. When we represent phonemes, we enclose them between slash marks like this: /p/. We will consider 24 English consonants as follows:

CONSONANTS

Symbol	Representative Words
/p/	pine, flapper
/b/	back, rubber
/t/	top, flutter
/d/	deck, ladder

Symbol	Representative Words
/k/	cough, keel
/g/	goat, egg
/f/	feed, rough, physiology
/v/	view, leave
*/θ/	thought, bath
*/ð/	though, the
/s/	sink, cite, kiss
/z/	zebra, these, buzz
*/ʃ/	shop, rush, caution
*/ʒ/	vision, luge, casual
/h/	hope, who
*/tʃ/	check, batch
*/dʒ/	jury, ledger
/m/	meet, hammer
/n/	neck, banner
*/ŋ/	ring, bank
/w/	went, twice, one
*/j/	young, onion
/r/	rough, write, marry
/l/	letter, belly

Symbols that are starred are new to you for these sounds.

There are 18 English vowels: 14 simple vowels and 4 diphthongs, which are two-vowel sequences.

SIMPLE VOWELS

Symbol	Representative Words
/i/	meet, seal, field
*/ɪ/	mitt, will, hit
/e/	mate, aid, weight
*/ɛ/	met, many, let
*/æ/	mat, bad, act
/u/	cool, two, grew
*/ʊ/	cook, pull, would
/o/	coat, most, goes
*/ɔ/	caught, off, soft
/ɑ/	cot, father, top
*/ə/	above, upon, occur
*/ʌ/	above, cup, club
*/ɚ/	murder, dollar, older
*/ɜ˞/	murder, bird, work

Again, starred symbols are new to you as used here.

DIPHTHONGS

Symbol	Representative Words
/aɪ/	f**i**ght, h**ei**ght, tr**ie**d
/aʊ/	f**ow**l, **ou**t, p**ou**nd
/ɔi/	f**oi**l, t**oy**, c**oi**n
/ju/	f**eu**d, c**u**be, **u**se, **you**

Can you think of any other English spellings for these consonant and vowel sounds?

INTERNATIONAL PHONETIC ALPHABET

The symbols we use to represent each of the sounds of English are standard symbols from the **International Phonetic Alphabet (IPA).** The IPA was created in 1888 and further revised in 1949. The IPA and other phonetic alphabets were developed because spelling does not always represent how a sound is pronounced. In the list of phonemes and key words in the previous section, we included other possible English letters that can represent each phoneme. For example, /i/—as in *beet*—has these possible spellings: e, ee, ea, ie, ei, eo, i. When we use IPA symbols to represent a word, we have used *phonetic transcription*. /kæt/, /fit/, /sun/, and /fon/ are the phonetic transcriptions for the words *cat, feet, soon,* and *phone*. With practice, you will be able to read these symbols with more ease.

There are other phonetic alphabets that you may have encountered. You are most familiar with the phonetic alphabets found in various dictionaries as pronunciation keys. Table 7-1 compares IPA with other phonetic alphabet systems. In the last column, you will notice a "linguistic alphabet." Linguists, persons who study the languages of the world, require an alphabet system that will allow them to describe every language they study. In this way, any language researcher could "read" the symbols and pronounce the words of an obscure language. Extinct languages of some Native Americans have been preserved in this way.

Thus, phonetic alphabets overcome the difficulties of English spelling and assist linguists in describing languages. We are ready to discuss phonemes and their classification in more detail. First, we must address the anatomy and physiology of their production.

Try writing simple words in each of the phonetic alphabets and in IPA notation. Is any one easier to use than the others?

TABLE 7-1 Comparison of IPA with other phonetic alphabets

IPA	Random House Dictionary*	Oxford American Dictionary†	Webster's Collegiate Dictionary‡	Linguistic Alphabet
p	p	p	p	p
b	b	b	b	b
t	t	t	t	t
d	d	d	d	d
k	k	k	k	k
g	g	g	g	g
f	f	f	f	f
v	v	v	v	v
θ	th	th	th	θ
ð	<u>th</u>	*th*	<u>th</u>	ð
s	s	s	s	s
z	z	z	z	z
ʃ	sh	sh	sh	š
ʒ	zh	zh	zh	ž
tʃ	ch	ch	ch	č
dʒ	j	j	j	ǰ
h	h	h	h	h
m	m	m	m	m
n	n	n	n	n
ŋ	nˆg	ng	ŋ	ŋ
w	w	w	w	w
j	y	y	y	y
r	r	r	r	r
l	l	l	l	l
i	ē	ee	ē	iy
ɪ	i	i	i	i
e	ā	ay	ā	ey
ɛ	e	e	e	e
æ	a	a	a	æ
ə	ə	ĕ, ŭ	ə	ə
ʌ	u	u	ə	ə
ɚ	—	—	ər	ər
ɝ	ûr	ur	ər	ər
u	o͞o	oo	ü	uw
ʊ	o͝o	uu	ủ	u
o	ō	oh	ō	o
ɔ	ô	aw	ȯ	ɔ
ɑ	o	o	ä	a
aɪ	ī	I	ī	ay
aʊ	ou	ow	aủ	aw
ɔi	oi	oi	ȯi	ɔy
ju	yo͞o	yoo	yü	yuw

The Random House Dictionary of the English Language, College Ed., L. Urdang, ed. New York: Random House, 1968.
†*Oxford American Dictionary*, E. Ehrlich, S. B. Flexner, G. Carruth, and J. M. Hawkins, ed. New York: Oxford University Press, 1980.
‡*Webster's Collegiate Dictionary*, 9th ed. Springfield, MA: Merriam-Webster, 1987.

CHAPTER 7

HOW ENGLISH PHONEMES ARE PRODUCED

You now have a theoretical basis for understanding the nature and classification of speech sounds. It is useful to understand how the mechanism works to produce the phonemes of language. Although you cannot be conscious of the position your mouth assumes for every sound, you will be able to use your knowledge about articulation to correct your own speech if necessary or improve your intelligibility.

There are several anatomic organs, or structures, of articulation. You can see their relationship to each other in Figure 7-1. Movable articulators are the lips, tongue, jaw, and velum, or soft palate. The immovable articulators are the teeth and hard palate. Notice how each of these structures is placed in relation to the nasal, oral, and pharyngeal cavities.

The lips are the most visible articulators. In fact, young children usually first learn to make sounds using the lips. The lips come together as in the first phonemes in *might*, *beat*, and *pod*; they round as in *who*, *why*, *over*, and *hook*; the lower lip comes in contact with the upper teeth in *fight* and *vine*.

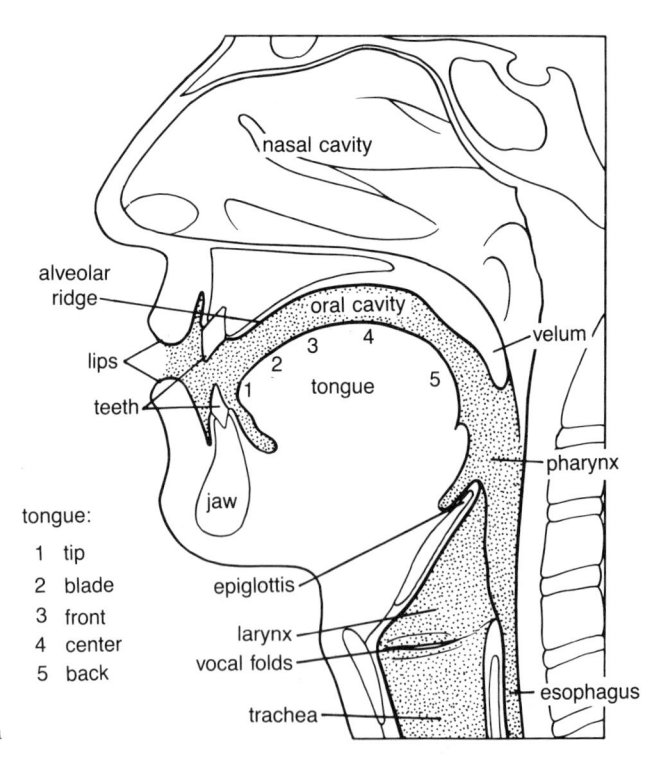

FIGURE 7.1 Structures of articulation

THE NATURE OF ARTICULATION

The tongue is probably the most important articulator. It is involved in producing all consonant and vowel sounds except /p/, /b/, /m/, /f/, and /v/. When someone has "slurred" speech, it can be attributed often to inefficient or incorrect tongue movement. If you have had a numbing novocaine injection for dental work, you are familiar with the strange effect it has on your tongue and your speech. If you attempt simultaneously to immobilize your tongue and speak, you instantly experience incoherent speech. The tongue is divided into different regions, each participating in various sounds. Feel the tip of your tongue make contact with other articulators as you produce the first sound of these words: *thought, this, toad, dine, lye, never.* The tongue blade forms the first sounds in the words *soup, zipper, short, chop,* and *gym* and the middle consonant in *leisure.* The back of the tongue forms the consonants in the words *kick* and *gig.* The tongue also assumes various positions for all vowels. The tongue raises high in the mouth for the vowels in *feel* and *fool.* The tongue bunches to the front of the mouth for *meet* and *mat.* For *coat* and *cot,* the tongue gathers to the back of the mouth. When you say the words *meet, mate,* and *mat,* you can appreciate the adjustments the tongue must make. As you can see, we depend heavily on the mobility and versatility of the tongue for most of the sounds of our speech.

The **velum,** or soft palate, remains in a raised position for all English phonemes except /m/ (**m**ight), /n/ (**n**ever), and /ŋ/ (si**ng**). To find the soft palate, run your tongue backward along the roof of your mouth (hard palate) until you arrive at the border of the bone and fleshy area. It is possible to watch the velum rise by aiming a penlight to the back of someone's mouth and asking them to say "ah." You will notice the upward movement of the velum immediately. More dramatically, have your experimental partner repeat "ah-ah-ah" in succession and you will see the rapid response of the velum. Inadequate velar movement results in excess air being expelled through the nose during speech and in a hypernasal quality to speech.

The lower jaw is the last movable articulator. While your jaw does not provide the articulatory finesse of your tongue, it does support the tongue in articulatory maneuvers such as producing the first phonemes in o**u**ght and **e**vil. The jaw is open for the first phoneme and relatively closed for the second.

The teeth, as one set of immovable articulators, are the contact point for other articulators. We have already mentioned their interaction with lips and tongue. Although you may be intelligible without teeth, edentulous (toothless) adults are more likely to prefer wearing dentures to enhance their speech as well as their appearance.

The other immovable articulator, the hard palate, may be divided into two sections. The **alveolar ridge** is the area just behind the teeth and just before the palate proper begins to rise up into the oral cavity. The alveolar ridge provides a contact area for the tongue for /t/, /d/, /s/, /z/, /tʃ/, /dʒ/, /n/, and /l/. The hard palate is used to produce /ʃ/, /ʒ/, /tʃ/, /dʒ/, /j/, and /r/.

Position each of the articulators (lips, teeth, tongue) and explore the sounds that are possible to make. Can you produce a bilabial fricative sound. A labiodental stop? A palatal stop?

PHONEME CLASSIFICATION

As you remember, when we discussed the three definitions of a phoneme, we said that a phoneme is (1) a sound that makes a difference, (2) a family of sounds, and (3) a bundle of distinctive features. Now we will use this last definition to assist us in the description and classification of English phonemes.

English phonemes fall into two main categories: consonants and vowels. **Consonants** are identified as those phonemes that result from some narrowing or closing of the vocal tract. **Vowels** are produced when the vocal tract is in a more open position. There are simple vowels and diphthongs. Diphthongs are produced by gliding two vowels together so quickly that they are impossible to distinguish. The vowels in *light* and *boy* are diphthongs.

Phonemes may be classified in different ways. In the next two sections, we will discuss consonants and vowels. Typically, we group phonemes by their articulation features—participating articulators, position of tongue and lips, tension of tongue, and so on. You will gain so much expertise in phoneme classification that when someone says, "I'm thinking of a voiced alveolar fricative," you will respond instantly with "/z/, of course!" The key to this admirable skill is to practice the various sounds as they are introduced, altering one feature at a time to produce another sound.

Consonants

You are giving a class presentation and when you are critiqued by your instructor, you notice that the content of your talk was good, but that your presentation style was given lower marks. In discussion with your instructor, you discover that your speech was not distinct enough to be understood by the class. What happened? You knew that your voice was loud enough. You had practiced that beforehand. If you had taped your talk, you might have noticed that your speech was somewhat distorted, not clear. What was the culprit? In most instances, incorrect articulation of consonants is to blame when someone does not understand your speech.

As you know, consonants are characterized by some degree of constriction at certain locations in the vocal tract. In addition, the stoppage of air can be complete, as in /p/ or /t/, or it can be partial, as in /s/ or /f/. Try saying those sounds and notice how they differ from each other in terms of the amount of airflow. Finally, consonants can be made with or without voice. When you say *pop*, you notice that voicing occurs only for the vowel. When you say *Bob*, you feel laryngeal vibration through the whole word.

These ways of classifying consonants have particular names. **Place** refers to the location of constriction in the vocal tract. Anatomical names are used to delineate them. Bilabial consonants /b/ and /p/ are formed with both lips. When you say /t/ or /d/, you are producing an alveolar consonant (referring to the ridge behind your upper teeth). Consonants /k/ and /g/ are velar (related to velum) consonants; /h/ is a glottal consonant. Glottal refers to the vocal folds; in this instance, they are open as air flows through them. You can also describe consonant sound by **manner,** or amount of constriction in the vocal tract. /d/ and /g/ are considered to be stop consonants, because the flow of air is "stopped." Occasionally, you will hear the term "plosive" in place of "stop." We have chosen "stop" to emphasize that airflow is momentarily halted. Other authors choose to emphasize the explosive nature of these sounds. The constriction of the vocal tract is complete for stop consonants. /s/ and /f/ are produced differently; while closure is almost complete, a rush of turbulent air moves constantly between the articulators. Such sounds are considered to be **fricatives.** Affricates are "compromise" consonants. In /tʃ/, as in *champion,* the air is stopped, but then released in turbulence. **Glides, laterals,** and **nasals** are similar to fricatives in that the air moves continuously through the vocal tract. The glides /r/ and /w/ are vowel-like, but with more constriction. When you say the lateral /l/, air moves out on either side of your tongue, while the tongue contacts the alveolar ridge. Nasal consonants /m/, /n/, and /ŋ/ (as in *sing*) are produced with the velum lowered so that air and sound come out the nasal passage. There is also constriction in the oral tract to prevent any air escaping through the mouth.

Finally, **voicing** distinguishes similar consonants. /b/ is the voiced bilabial stop counterpart of the voiceless bilabial stop /p/. Pairs like /p/–/b/, /t/–/d/, and /s/–/z/ are called cognates. Each pair of consonants differs in only one feature—voicing.

We are now ready to use the articulation features place, manner, and voicing to gather consonants together in a cohesive pattern. We often abbreviate these articulation features for consonants as PMV (for place, manner, voicing). Table 7-2 is a standard chart of consonant symbols.

Coarticulation

As you study these consonants, you may be seized by doubts that you actually talk in the precise manner in which these consonants are described. Do you move from consonant to vowel to consonant in a measured fashion, perfectly articulating each consonant? Do you make each consonant in the same way in every word in which it appears? Try saying *pool* and *pile.* The influence of the vowel results in lip rounding for the first word. This does not occur in the second. Compare your production of *key* and *cool.* You notice that the place of articulation of /k/ moves slightly forward for *key* and slightly back for *cool.* This blending of articulation features resulting from neighboring sounds is called **coarticulation.** Coarticulation exists in the real world of the stream of speech we produce.

TABLE 7-2 Traditional classification of English consonants

Place of Constriction	Plosives U	Plosives V	Fricatives U	Fricatives V	Affricates U	Affricates V	Semivowels V	Nasals V
Bilabial	p (pig)	b (big)					w (watt)	m (hum)
Labiodental			f (face)	v (vase)				
Linguadental			θ (thigh, thin)	ð (thy, this)				
Alveolar	t (tot)	d (dot)	s (seal)	z (zeal)			l, r† (lot) (rot)	n (Hun)
Palatal			ʃ (shoe, mission)	ʒ (visual, measure)	tʃ (choke, nature)	dʒ (joke, gentle)	j (yacht)	
Velar	k (coat)	g (goat)						ŋ (hung)
Glottal			h (happy)					

Manner of Production

*U = unvoiced; V = voiced.

†In production of /l/, air goes around the sides of the tongue. In contrast, air goes through a small aperture between the tongue and palate for production of /r/.

Source: From *Language Development: An Introduction* by R. E. Owens, Jr., 1984, Columbus: Charles E. Merrill Publishing Co. Copyright 1984 by Bell & Howell Co. Reprinted by permission.

Vowels

It's time for time travel. Take yourself back to your first-grade classroom. Mrs. Beasley is conducting one of her early language arts lessons. She begins, "There are only five vowels you'll need to remember. They are a, e, i, o, and u. Sometimes y is a vowel." From that fateful day forward, whenever you heard "vowel," those five or perhaps six little letters came to mind. Later that year, Mrs. Beasley might have told you that those vowels could be long or short. Long vowels were indicated by ē as in *beet*, short vowels by ĕ as in *bet*. You are now ready to make some major adjustments in this conceptualization of the vowels of English.

In truth, there are 18 vowels in English, 17 vowels for some Midwesterners and Californians. The vowels you learned in the first grade were the **letters** used to represent, alone or in various combinations, the vowel phonemes of English for spelling. The "short" and "long" vowels that haunted you during your elementary years are actually different vowels. Just as you expected, you will be learning different symbols for each of these 17 or 18 vowel sounds. Vowel "length" or duration is related to whether the vowel is in an open or closed syllable. For example, say *why* (open syllable). Now contrast that with *white* (closed syllable). You notice that the vowel is "shorter"—that is, articulated for less duration—in the second word.

Vowels have certain characteristics that make them quite different from consonants. All vowels are voiced. We have no voiceless vowels. Vowels are produced with the velum raised; there are no nasal vowels in English. Occasionally, a vowel will take on some of the nasality of a neighboring /m/, /n/, or /ŋ/. Say *man* and compare the vowel to the vowel in *bat*. The first vowel should be quite nasal compared to the second production. Vowels are always produced with an open vocal tract. You should not experience any constriction along its length.

Vowels are the nuclei of syllables. Alone, they can stand as words or syllables. Words like *eye* and *a* are permissible in English; *s, p,* or *b* are not. Vowels have this unique privilege because they carry the speech power in the language. "Power" refers to the amount of sound energy that can be measured in the production of a word. Any constriction along the vocal tract results in reduced energy or loudness of a sound as it exits. Because vowels are characterized by an open vocal tract, speech energy is reduced minimally.

Vowels are different from consonants in that vowel production is usually less distinct and precise. From individual to individual, there is a lot of variation in production. Phoneticians have had a difficult time describing where the tongue is in each vowel. Vowel resonance or quality is defined traditionally by describing what the tongue, lips, and pharynx are doing. Certain factors have been identified as important in distinguishing one vowel from another.

We can talk about place and manner as we did with consonants, and we add the features tension and lip rounding. Place is used to describe the place where the tongue is highest or lowest. Try saying *real–rule* and *fail–foal* to feel the contrasting tongue movements. In the first word of each pair, you should feel the tongue bunch to the front of your mouth. As you say the second word immediately after, you will notice that the tongue moves to the back of the mouth. Manner describes the height of the tongue in the mouth. Contrast *bead–bad* and *hoot–hot* to feel the difference between high and low vowels. The relative tension of the tongue also affects the vowel. Tense, or tight, and lax, or relaxed, tongue tensions are represented by the pairs *seen–sin, aid–Ed,* and *fate–fete*. These characteristics of the tongue affect vowel resonance or quality by altering the configuration of the vocal tract. Changing lip position can also affect the shape of the oral cavity. In English, back vowels tend also to have lip rounding, as in *who, hoe,* and *hot*. As you said those words, you noticed that your lips were "pouting"; i.e., rounded and slightly protruding. Other languages have both front and back rounded and unrounded vowels.

As you did for consonants, move your tongue in your mouth and explore the positioning for each vowel. Contrast high and low, front and back, and tense and lax vowels.

Even though you know the various vowel characteristics, you still will find it difficult simply to say a vowel and classify it immediately according to place, manner, tension, and lip rounding features. We can abbreviate articulation features for vowels as PMTL (place, manner, tension, lip rounding). Remember, vowel production is less distinct and precise than consonant production. The vowel classifications that we use are, at best, approximate descriptions of tongue position. You already have suspected that the best way to associate vowel sounds and their phonetic description is to memorize them. To help in keeping vowel features clear, we use a vowel quadrilateral—a visual representation of where vowels are articulated in the vocal tract. Figure 7-2 shows a vowel quadrilateral and its anatomy.

Key words for the vowel symbols follow. "Front," "central," and "back" refer to tongue position in the oral cavity. The sounds are also arranged from high to low, and you will feel your tongue drop as you say the vowels in succession.

FRONT		CENTRAL		BACK	
Symbol	Key Word	Symbol	Key Word	Symbol	Key Word
/i/	m**ee**t	/ə/	**a**bove	/u/	c**oo**l
/ɪ/	m**i**t	/ʌ/	**a**bove	/ʊ/	c**oo**k
/e/	m**a**te	/ɚ/	murd**er**	/o/	c**oa**t
/ɛ/	m**e**t	/ɝ/	m**ur**der	/ɔ/	c**au**ght
/æ/	m**a**t			/ɑ/	c**o**t

(lax vowels are indicated by *)

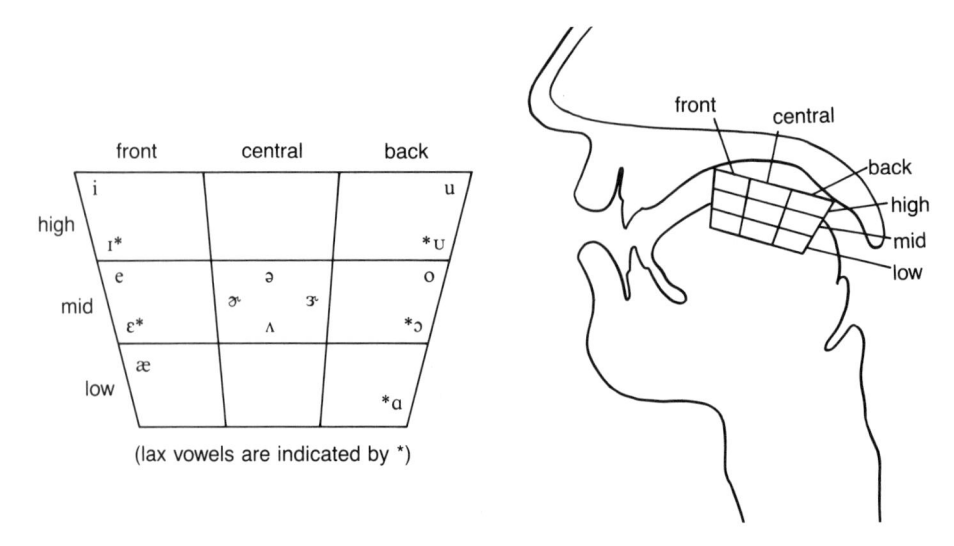

FIGURE 7-2 (A) Vowel quadrilateral and (B) its anatomic correlates

You notice that in the key words above all vowels are in stressed syllables except /ə/ and /ɚ/. These symbols are called *schwa* and *schwar*, respectively. They refer to mid-central tense vowels that appear in unstressed syllables. /ɚ/ is "retroflexed" or "r-colored," which refers to the blending of the sounds /ə/ and /r/ into one. Sometimes /ə/ and /ʌ/ are difficult to distinguish in English, but remember that /ʌ/ occurs in stressed syllables and /ə/ is seen only in unstressed contexts. *Above* is transcribed /əbʌv/. Occasionally, in careless articulation, /ə/ is omitted.

Diphthongs

The vowels that you studied above are discrete segments. Each vowel is represented by one articulator position. But some "vowels" that are familiar to you were missing. You observed that we omitted words like *eye*, *owe*, and *boy*. The vowels in these words are called more accurately diphthongs. A **diphthong** is a combination of one vowel nucleus and another vowel that glides away from the nuclear vowel. We perceive a diphthong as one unit. However, when you isolate each vowel sound in the sample words above, you notice that your tongue assumes two positions as you say each diphthong. In producing *eye*, the tongue starts at the bottom of the mouth, and then rises. The symbol for this diphthong is /aɪ/. When you say /aɪ/, the diphthong is not exactly equal to the sound of each vowel separately. Say *ah* and then say /ɪ/ as in *mitt*. As you say each vowel, make the pause between them shorter and shorter. Even though you produce the vowels practically as one, you still do not hear the exact diphthong /aɪ/. We are in the habit of considering diphthongs as really just simple vowels; you will need some training to hear the two sounds that compose a diphthong. It will help you to remember that a diphthong stands as one syllable. Figure 7-3 is the vowel quadrilateral showing the relationship of diphthongs to each other. The first vowel is the central or nuclear vowel (i.e., receives emphasis) except in /ju/. /ju/ is actually a combination of a glide and a vowel, but for our purposes, we will consider /ju/ a diphthong. In /ju/, /u/ receives the most emphasis. Elongate and emphasize the diphthongs in each of the following words to emphasize and experience the glide from one sound to another.

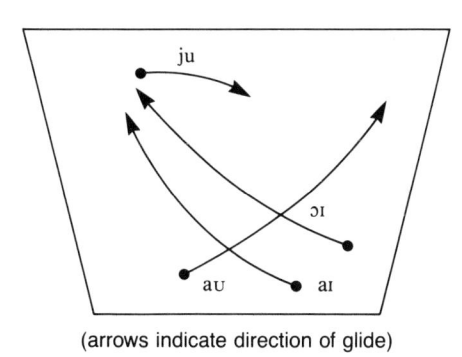

(arrows indicate direction of glide)

FIGURE 7-3 Diphthong quadrilateral

/aɪ/	**f**igh**t**, **h**eigh**t**, **t**rie**d**
/aʊ/	**f**o**w**l, **o**u**t**, **p**o**und**
/ɔɪ/	**f**oil, **t**oy, **c**oin
/ju/	**f**eu**d**, **c**u**k**e, **us**e, **you**

Words in parentheses illustrate other possible spellings for these diphthongs.

Other diphthongs are possible. These first four diphthongs we discussed are **phonemic diphthongs;** that is, changing the diphthong will change the word. However, occasionally we use **nonphonemic diphthongs** when we stress a syllable with a diphthong. /oʊ/ and /eɪ/ are nonphonemic diphthongs. When you say *mow* and *pay,* you use these diphthongs. But when you say *motor* and *paper,* the diphthongs change to /o/ and /e/, respectively. The sound is essentially the same and you do not change the meaning of the word when you add or drop the second part of the diphthong. In this text, we will consider only phonemic diphthongs in our discussions of sound production and improvement.

Consonant/Vowel Distinctions

You are prepared now to understand the distinction between vowels and consonants. The following list helps to separate their special characteristics:

CONSONANT	VOWEL
vocal tract constricted	vocal tract open
articulation features—PMV	articulation features—PMTL
airflow stopped or modified by articulators	airflow continuous
must be combined with vowel	can stand alone as syllable/word
voiced or voiceless	always voiced
velum lowered or raised	velum always raised

SUMMARY

You now have a beginning understanding of articulatory phonetics. You have been introduced to the phoneme, the crucial element of phonetics and phonology. You have been exposed to the various IPA symbols for the phonemes of English which will enable you to "sound out" English words. Your knowledge of the contribution of the various articulators to phoneme production will help you to classify phonemes into their sound families of consonants (stops, fricatives, affricates, nasals, and glides) and vowels (simple vowels and diphthongs). The nature of the phoneme as a sound that makes a difference, as a member of family of sounds and as a group of distinctive features is now clear to you. In the next chapter, we will examine each phoneme individually, along with its particular articulation features. Knowing accurate articulation will allow you to modify your production of any phoneme and to correct your pronunciation in selected words. In Chapter 8, your task is to apply this information to practice in learning the nature of specific phonemes.

STUDY QUESTIONS

1. What is articulatory phonetics? How is it different from phonology?
2. What are the three definitions of a phoneme?
3. What is the IPA? Why do we need such an alphabet?
4. What is an articulator? What is the most important articulator? Why?
5. What are the major classifications of phonemes?
6. How are consonants and vowels different? Vowels and diphthongs?
7. What are the articulation features for vowels? For consonants?

Chapter 8
The Sounds of English

At this point, you have a general, theoretical background about how phonemes are produced. This is excellent material for exams, but you could not evaluate your own articulation and pronunciation and that of your classmates with this information. To examine critically how *you* speak, you require more detailed knowledge about how you are moving the articulators and about the pitfalls of pronunciation.

INTRODUCTION

In this chapter, you will put to use considerable information from previous chapters. Concepts of place, manner, and voicing of consonants and place, manner, tension, and lip rounding of vowels have practical application. The distinction between articulation and pronunciation becomes crucial now as you begin to understand whether a problem in your speech comes from improper sound production or misunderstanding about how a sound is produced in a certain position in a word. Dialect issues will become important also as you see how your particular dialect may influence the production of certain sounds. Remember, dialect variations are simply different, not substandard. If you use a dialect variation of a sound, you may choose to use or not use the Standard English production in certain situations. When we describe certain pronunciation errors, we have strived to *not* include some "errors" that actually are becoming part of Standard English. Most of these have to do with reducing certain vowels to /ə/ in unstressed syllables. You may choose to "clean up" your articulation for formal presentations, but overcorrect speech can sound stilted in casual conversation.

Why this chapter? The ultimate purpose of this book is to provide you with a foundation of knowledge so that you can assess your voice, articulation, and pronunciation and correct it accordingly. Some of you may be asserting smugly to yourselves that your speech is just perfect. However, we expect that most of you will find many minor and perhaps some major imprecisions in your speech. Unless you have been a professional speaker, you probably have not devoted any energy listening to your speech or that of others. In our rush to express our thoughts, we often become sloppy in speech and require reminders to be clearer. This chapter provides the specific, "ideal" production of each sound and outlines possible errors and variations.

CHAPTER FORMAT

We will discuss consonants, vowels, and diphthongs. For each phoneme, we provide key words, identifying features of each phoneme, a description of production, a schematic diagram of articulation position, common errors of articulation and pronunciation, and dialect variations. Each phoneme section concludes with sample words and sentences containing the target phoneme. These words and sentences are *not* designed for practice but rather for illustration and example. Chapter 10 contains practice materials. As you read this chapter, identify your weaknesses in articulation and pronunciation. You will then be ready to move to Chapter 9, where you will design your own personal improvement program.

CONSONANTS

STOPS

/p/   pie, sipping, cup

PMV Features: bilabial/stop/voiceless
Description of Production:

Lips are pressed together, impeding the airstream; pressure is built up in the oral cavity and released in a burst with no voice.

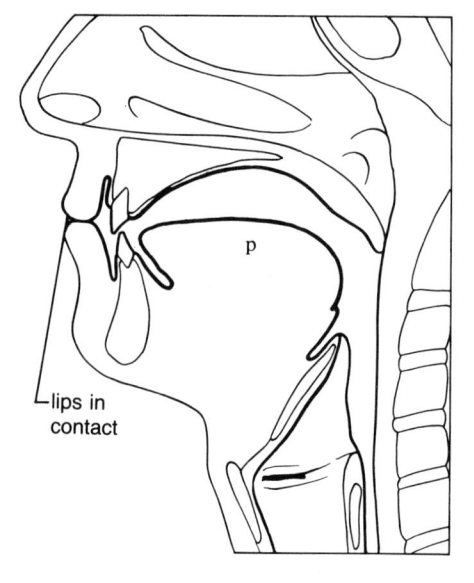

lips in contact

Common Errors

Articulation Errors

1. Incomplete closure can result in inadequate aspiration.
2. Excessive aspiration can occur.

Pronunciation Errors

1. Omission of /p/ before consonant in words such as *preempt, bumpkin, exempt*.
2. Addition of /p/ where it should be "silent" in words such as *pneumonia, pneumatic, pneumothorax*.

Dialect Variations

1. Certain foreign English dialects may confuse the degree of aspiration of /p/ and /b/ so that these phonemes sound similar: *pet–bet, pest–best, peer–beer*.

Sample Words

peace	apple	lap
pail	supper	mop
put	wrapper	hope
part	puppy	keep
pool	roping	trip

Sample Sentences

1. Peter played the piano, hoping to capture the composer's spirit.
2. Chef Pierre reprimanded the waiter for putting too much pepper on the patron's salad.
3. Polly planted purple and pink petunias in her garden.
4. Happy puppies appeal to people of all ages.
5. The plumber replaced the old lead pipes with new copper pipes.

/b/ book, rubber, web

PMV Features: bilabial/stop/voiceless
Description of Production

The lips are in the same position as for /p/; the airstream is released with voice and the "energy" of airflow is reduced.

lips in contact

Common Errors
Articulation Errors

1. Incomplete closure of the lips can result in a fricative quality to the sound.
2. Excess aspiration as the sound is released will result in a /b/ that is more like /p/.

Pronunciation Errors

1. Addition of /ə/ in final position in words such as *Bob*—/babə/; *lab*—/læbə/; *lobe*—/lobə/.

Dialect Variations

1. As in /p/, /b/ may become a fricative for some nonnative English speakers.

Sample Words

boy	flabby	ebb
bad	rubbing	tub
bunk	baby	lobe
beast	abut	mob
bill	saber	rib

Sample Sentences

1. *Bob* bought a ru*bb*er *b*all for the *b*a*b*y.
2. They placed the *b*a*b*y's cri*b* *b*eside their *b*ed.
3. *B*ill's *b*ar*b*er shop was ro*bb*ed by a masked *b*andit.
4. *B*etty and *B*ertha hoped to su*b*stitute muscle for fla*b*.
5. *B*ar*b*ara was *b*itter when her *b*oss fired her from her jo*b*.

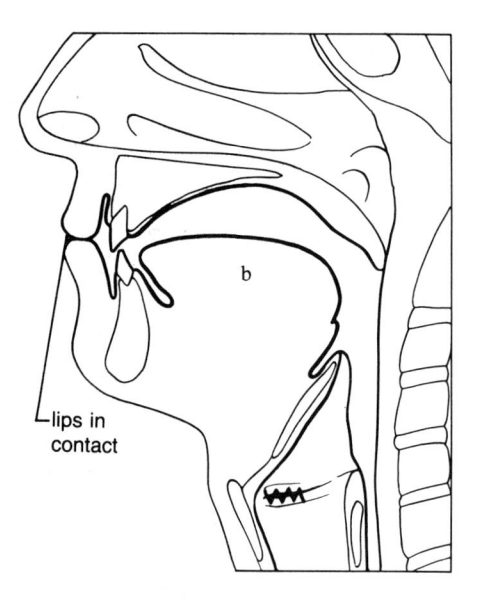

/t/   *t*ack, at*t*end, ha*t*e

PMV Features: alveolar/stop/voiceless
Description of Production

> The tongue tip and blade touch the alveolar ridge; sides of the tongue are against teeth and gums to form a seal. Pressure is built up and then released with aspiration.

Common Errors

Articulation Errors

1. Distortion of /t/ can occur when the tongue moves from the alveolar ridge to behind the front teeth.

Pronunciation Errors

1. /t/ can be overwhelmed easily and omitted when it stands before or after /s/ in words such as *mist* or *mists*—/mɪs/; *cast* or *casts*—/kæs/; *rest* or *rests*—/rɪs/.

2. Omission of /t/ will occur if it comes after a consonant and at the end of a word. Examples are *kept, fort, fault, wrapped, meant, sent.*

3. /t/ is vulnerable to omission when it is in the middle position as in words such as *letter, softball, shutter, molten, battle, mental.*

4. /d/ may be substituted for /t/ in medial position in words such as *matter, rated, putty, latter.*

Dialect Variations

1. In Black English, when /st/ or /kt/ occurs at the end of a word, the /t/ is omitted as in *best*—/bɛs/; *passed*—/pæs/; *last*—/læs/; *liked*—/laɪk/.

Sample Words

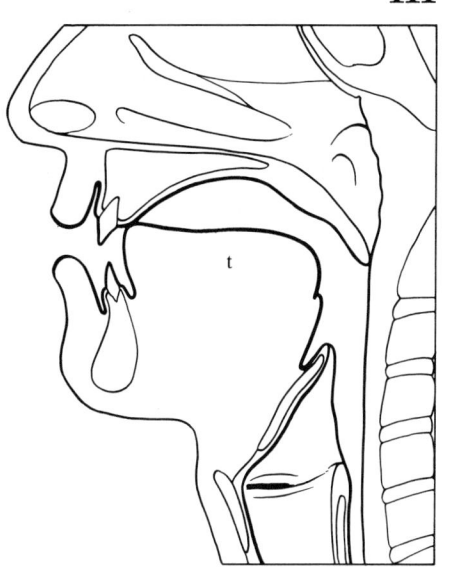

*t*ime	ta*tt*oo	ligh*t*
*t*ape	dain*t*y	sui*t*
*t*own	Oc*t*ober	ru*t*
*t*oy	fif*t*een	ra*t*
*t*ea	in*t*elligent	mee*t*

CHAPTER 8

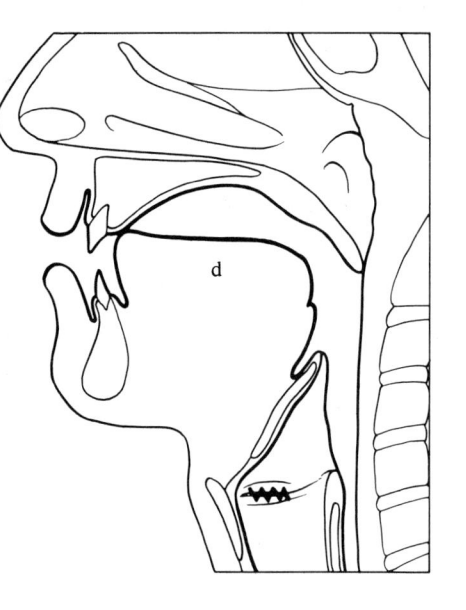

Sample Sentences

1. Terrence *t*ook *t*ime *t*o *t*ie the kno*t*.
2. Every *t*axpayer *t*rembles on April fif*t*eenth.
3. The freigh*t*er and the *t*anker *t*raversed the equa*t*or *t*ogether.
4. Pa*t* couldn'*t* subs*t*itu*t*e *t*echnique for crea*t*ivi*t*y.
5. A pho*t*ograph of the pain*t*ing highligh*t*ed i*t*s in*t*rica*t*e de*t*ail.

/d/ *d*ice, a*dd*ing, lea*d*

PMV Features: alveolar/stop/voiced
Description of Production

The tongue and blade touch the alveolar ridge; sides of the tongue are against the teeth and gums to form a seal. The voiced airstream is released with less force and aspiration than for /t/.

Common Errors

Articulation Errors

1. /d/ can be distorted to a "dental" /d/ by moving the tongue tip to the front teeth.

Pronunciation Errors

1. Omission of /d/ will occur if it comes after a consonant and at the end of a word. Examples are *held, wild, find, world.*
2. /d/ can disappear when it appears in the medial position in words such as *pudding, powder, ladder, hidden.*

Sample Words

*d*ense	bo*d*y	hi*d*e
*d*ock	ra*d*ish	brea*d*
*d*ude	sha*d*ow	hoo*d*
*d*ay	hi*d*ing	san*d*
*d*ive	to*d*ay	nee*d*

Sample Sentences

1. He wante*d* to *d*ismiss his pre*d*ecessor.
2. *D*avi*d* save*d* his *d*imes for the *d*iscount store.
3. Sha*d*e was *d*esired from the *d*esert sun.
4. The bri*d*esmaids waite*d* at the *d*oorway for the bri*d*e.
5. *D*octor Ma*d*ison planne*d* *d*isciplinary action against the resi*d*ent.

/k/   *k*iss, e*ch*o, ba*k*e

PMV Features: velar/stop/voiceless
Description of Production

The back of the tongue is brought up to the soft palate, allowing pressure to build up behind it. Air is then released with aspiration.

Common Errors
Articulation Errors

1. Distortion of /k/ can be caused by incomplete tongue-to-velar closure, changing the sound from stop to fricative.

Pronunciation Errors

1. Addition of /k/ when it should be "silent" in words such as *k*now or *k*nit.
2. Omission of /k/ in words that end in /sk/, /skt/, or /sks/. Examples are ma*sk*, ma*sks,* ma*sked.*

Dialect Variations

1. Omission of /k/ in word-final sk-blends occurs in Black English. Examples are *desk*—/dɛsk/ → /dɛs/; *risk*—/rɪsk/ → /rɪs/.

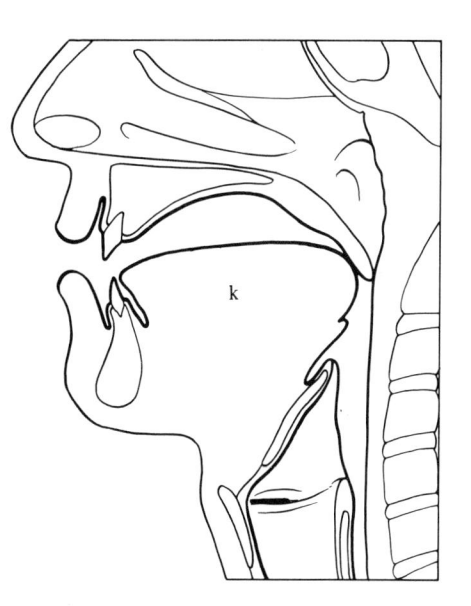

CHAPTER 8

114

Sample Words

ca*b*	buc*k*le	ba*k*e
*k*ill	ba*c*on	sin*k*
*k*ind	a*c*ne	tan*k*
*c*ane	an*k*le	do*ck*
*k*eep	ba*ck*stab	pi*k*e

Sample Sentences

1 Caroline aw*k*wardly too*k* her *c*oat and wal*k*ed out the ba*ck* door.
2 The *c*offee *c*ake *c*ompleted ba*k*ing at six o'*c*lock.
3 The pi*c*ture of the sna*k*e would ma*k*e your s*k*in *c*rawl.
4 *Ch*emicals lo*c*ated in the rail *c*ar were identi*c*al to those *k*ept in the storehouse.
5 *C*osmeti*c* aspe*c*ts of the surgery be*c*ame a primary *c*oncern.

/g/ *gh*ost, lu*gg*age, sta*g*

PMV Features: velar/stop/voiced
Description of Production

The back of the tongue is raised to the soft palate, and stops there to build up air pressure in the oral cavity. The airflow is released in a voiced airstream.

Common Errors
Articulation Errors

1 Distortion of /g/ can be caused by incomplete tongue-to-velar closure, changing the sound from stop to fricative.

Pronunciation Errors

1 If /g/ is followed by another stop consonant, such as /d/ in *bagged*—/bægd/, there is a tendency to not fully produce /g/. The /g/ is not released as in *got*, but you must make sure to make the velar contact with your tongue to create the proper sound. Examples are *hugged, slugged, big bomb, egg bagel*.

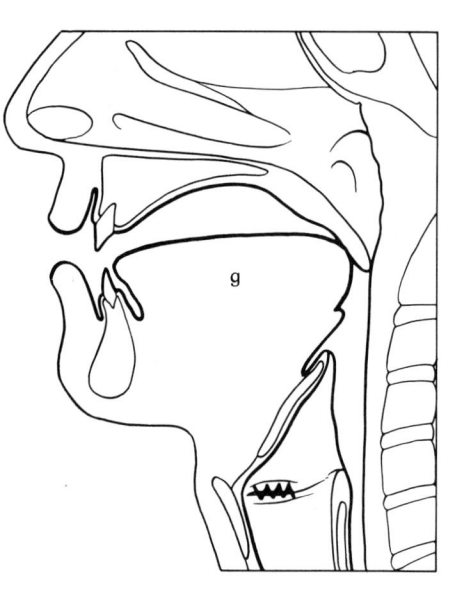

2   When the word is a "root" word—that is, is not modified by a prefix or suffix—the combination of letters "ng" must be pronounced /ŋg/. Examples are *tangle, English, hunger.*

3   Some root words + suffixes are the exception to the above rule: *longer, stronger, younger.*

Sample Words

gas	again	egg
gain	ugly	bog
gulf	target	drag
guide	begin	tug
gossip	cougar	fatigue

Sample Sentences

1   Gaye's dog lingered in the flower garden.
2   Digging into family gossip has got to end.
3   The governor vigorously gave his guarantee.
4   The legality of the rigorous negotiations was investigated.
5   Edgar gave a long monologue about gardening with fertilizer.

FRICATIVES

/f/   *f*eet, mu*ff*in, laug*h*

PMV Features: labiodental/fricative/voiceless
Description of Production

The upper teeth "bite" the lower lip and the airstream escapes laterally in a continuous fashion.

Common Errors
Articulation Errors

   1   /f/ is one of the most visible and easily articulated phonemes. Errors are rare.

Pronunciation Errors

   1   Be sure to distinguish clearly between /f/ and /v/ in words such as *few–view; fine–vine; safe–save.*

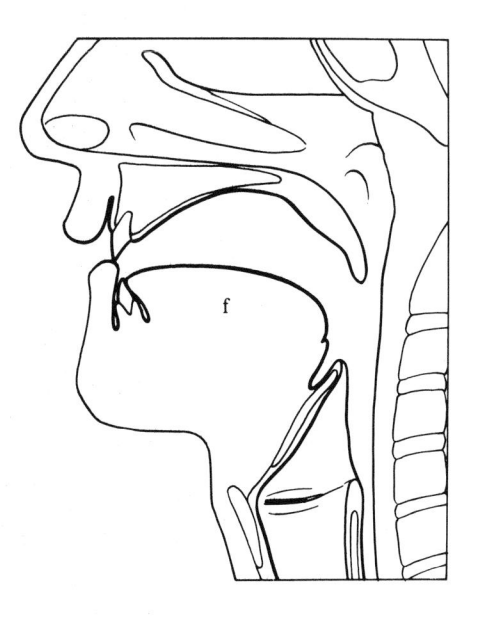

Dialect Variations
    Dialect variations are rare.

Sample Words

*f*ast	a*f*ter	el*f*
*f*ine	mu*ff*le	lau*gh*
*f*our	so*f*a	roo*f*
*f*ool	com*f*ort	tou*gh*
*f*eet	be*f*ore	gira*ff*e

Sample Sentences

1. The *f*ugitive pro*f*essed his disbelie*f* over being *f*ound.
2. Finally, the *ph*ysician signaled that he was o*ff* the tele*ph*one.
3. The *f*undamental *f*acts of the case dumb*f*ounded the tou*gh* jury.
4. Fortunately, *F*iona le*f*t the *f*ueling of rumors to So*ph*ia.
5. Sta*ff* members *f*ought *f*or the modi*f*ication of the layo*ff* plan.

/v/   *v*iew, ne*v*er, sa*v*e

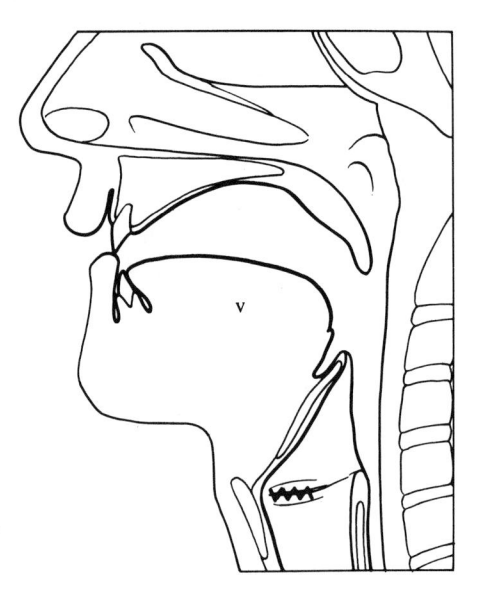

PMV Features: labiodental/fricative/voiced
Description of Production

    The upper teeth "bite" the lower lip and the voice airstream moves through the narrow gap continuously.

Common Errors
Articulation Errors
    As with /f/, errors are rare.

Pronunciation Errors

1. See under pronunciation errors for /f/.
2. Substitution for /f/ for /v/ is possible when /v/ occurs before a voiceless consonant: I *have* to go—/hæv/ → /hæf/; I *love* Tom—/lʌv/ → /lʌf/.

Dialect Variations

1. Substitution of /b/ for /v/ is common in Spanish-English dialect as in *vote*—/vot/ → /bot/; *vase*—/veɪs/ → /beɪs/.

Sample Words

*v*erb	ca*v*ity	lo*v*e
*v*at	gra*v*y	nai*v*e
*v*odka	se*v*en	ca*v*e
*v*anilla	a*v*enue	hi*v*e
*v*ote	e*v*il	do*v*e

Sample Sentences

1 Every *v*ote had been given to the former governor.
2 The *v*eteran *v*iewed his ser*v*ice with resol*v*e.
3 *V*era *v*olunteered to di*v*e off of the cliff.
4 The picnic gro*v*es will be a*v*ailable ele*v*en days in No*v*ember.
5 Gi*v*en se*v*eral di*v*erse options, her problem was sol*v*ed.

/θ/   *th*igh, au*th*or, tee*th*

PMV Features: linguadental/fricative/voiceless
Description of Production

The tongue is placed lightly under or just behind the upper front teeth. An unvoiced continuous airstream flows through the narrow slit.

Common Errors
Articulation Errors

1 It is possible to substitute a dentalized /t/ for /θ/ by allowing the tongue-teeth contact to create a stop.

Pronunciation Errors

1 Omission of /θ/ before consonant can occur in words such as *birthday, bathtub, toothpaste*.

Dialect Variations

1 In Black English, substitution for /f/ for /θ/ occurs. Examples *Ruth*—(ruθ/ → /ruf/; *tooth*—/tuθ/ → /tuf/.

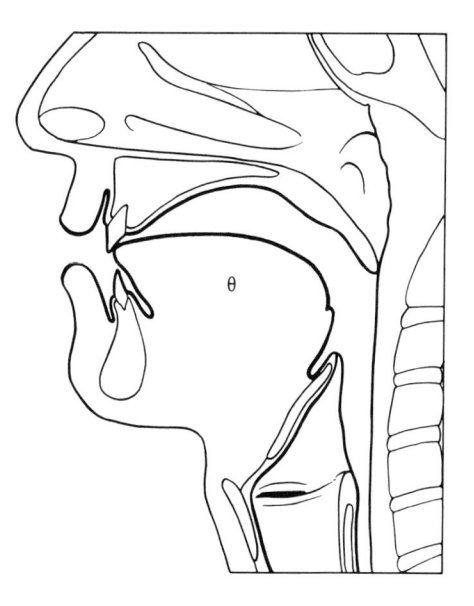

2 In Spanish-English dialect, /t/ or /s/ may be substituted for /θ/. Examples are *thigh*—/θaɪ/, /taɪ/, or /saɪ/.

Sample Words

*th*irsty	ru*th*less	mou*th*
*th*orn	too*th*brush	bo*th*
*th*ick	le*th*al	benea*th*
*th*istle	no*th*ing	zeni*th*
*th*eme	heal*thy*	tru*th*

Sample Sentences

1 The *th*ieves were a ru*th*less, cu*tth*roat bunch.
2 Edi*th* *th*ought that ari*th*metic would bring her no*th*ing but misery.
3 Ka*th*leen wi*th*held her *th*eory on the wor*th* of special training for mara*th*ons.
4 The six*th* *th*understorm was a mammo*th* one.
5 The *th*orough au*th*or lived in the nor*th* of England.

/ð/   they, bo*th*er, clo*th*e

PMV Features: labiodental/fricative/voiced
Description of Production

The tongue comes in contact with the upper teeth and voiced airflow exits through a small gap.

Common Errors
Articulation Errors

1 Substitution of /d/ for /ð/ can occur when the tongue comes in firm contact with the teeth, creating a stop.

Pronunciation Errors

1 Pronunciation errors are not common.

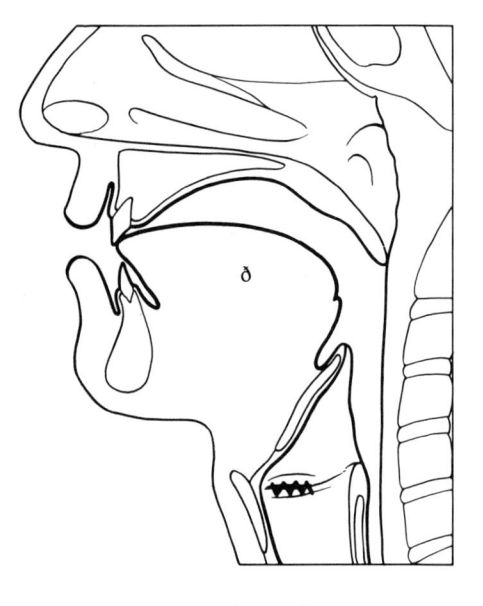

Dialect Variations

1. In Black English, /v/ is substituted for /ð/. An example is *mother*—/mʌðɚ/ → /mʌvɚ/.
2. In both Black English and Spanish-English dialects /d/ is substituted for /ð/ in words such as *then*—/ðɛn/ → /dɛn/; *these*—/ðiz/ → /diz/.

Sample Words

*th*ese	bo*th*er	ba*th*e
*th*ough	clo*th*ing	clo*th*e
*th*eir	la*th*er	soo*th*e
*th*at	hea*th*er	smoo*th*
*th*en	mo*th*er	see*th*e

Sample Sentences

1. Let's ga*th*er hea*th*er on *th*ose moors.
2. My o*th*er bro*th*er likes to bring us toge*th*er.
3. Lea*th*er clo*th*ing will brea*th*e in *th*is wea*th*er.
4. *Th*e sou*th*ernmost road is smoo*th*er *th*an o*th*ers.
5. *Th*eir ba*th*ing suits smoo*th* *th*e figure.

/s/ *s*oft, i*c*ing, fa*ce*

PMV Features: alveolar/fricative/voiceless
Description of Production

The blade of the tongue comes almost in contact with the alveolar ridge. The lateral edges of the tongue press up against the teeth. The voiceless airstream is directed through the grooved tongue.

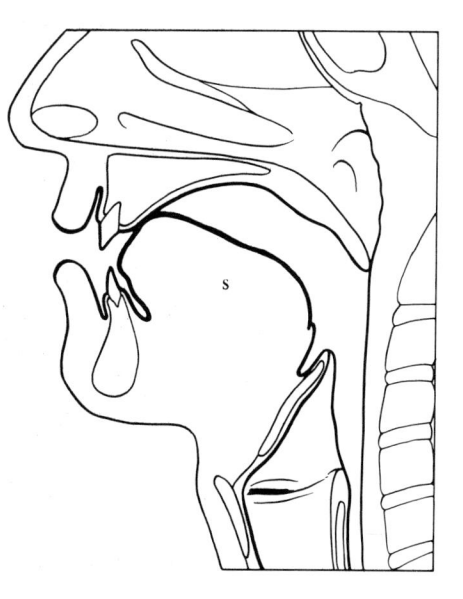

Common Errors

Articulation Errors

/s/ with its partner /z/ is one of the most frequently misarticulated sounds owing to the complex nature of its production.

1. An "interdental lisp" occurs when /θ/ is substituted for /s/. Examples are *sip*—/sɪp/ → /θɪp/; *sew*—/so/ → /θo/.

2. A "lateral lisp" occurs when air is directed to the sides of the tongue instead of down the narrow groove of the tongue.

3. A "whistling" /s/ can be caused by missing teeth, by dentures, or by the tongue tip touching the alveolar ridge.

Pronunciation Errors

1. Be careful not to substitute /ʃ/ for /s/ in phrases such as *miss you*—/mɪsju/ → /mɪʃju/; *pass you*—/pæsju/ → /pæʃju/; *kiss you*—/kɪsju/ → /kɪʃju/.

Dialect Variations

There are no common dialect variations.

Sample Words

service	gasoline	dance
signal	bracelet	jealous
safe	proceed	menace
savage	passage	glass
scenic	deceive	dice

Sample Sentences

1. Samantha sang her somber song for the audience.
2. Mistakes stand apart in a sea of excellence.
3. Her sister's sight was saved by the surgeon's skill.
4. A sudden burst of sunshine made the canals of Venice gorgeous.
5. The tortoise chased the hare across the grass.

/z/ zone, laser, rise

PMV Features: alveolar/fricative/voiced
Description of Production

The tongue blade nearly touches the alveolar ridge. The voiced airstream flows through the groove in midtongue, resulting in a buzzing turbulence.

Common Errors
Articulation Errors

1. /z/ will be lisped if /s/ is replaced by /θ/. /ð/ is substituted for /z/ as in zoo—/zu/ → /ðu/; visor—/vaɪzɚ/ → /vaɪðɚ/.

2, 3. Lateral lisps and "whistling" can occur as for /s/.

4. /ʒ/ can be substituted for /z/.

Pronunciation Errors

1. Be sure to pronounce the letter "s" as /z/ in the following verbs: *excuse, house, use*.

Dialect Variations
There are no common dialect variations.

Sample Words

zucchini	cozy	amuse
zodiac	prison	size
zebra	trouser	arouse
zenith	visit	dispose
zany	dozen	trapeze

Sample Sentences

1. The newspaper reports every disaster that spoils the cruise.
2. All zebras at the zoo were prone to frenzy in the drizzly rain.
3. Crowds enjoyed the pleasant jazz at the Brazilian resort.
4. The musician always plays that stanza with zealous enthusiasm.
5. The breeze blew the clothes on the clothesline about in the hazy afternoon.

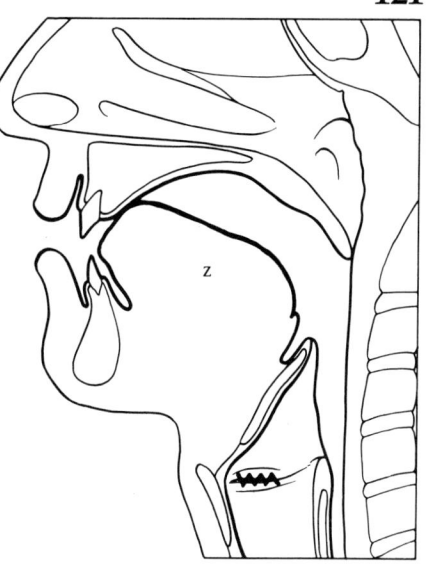

/ʃ/ shop, ashes, push

PMV Features: palatal/fricative/voiceless
Description of Production

Tongue position is quite similar to that for /s/. Make an /s/ and then slowly draw your tongue back along the hard palate. You notice that your tongue now has a broad groove in it and the voiceless continuous airflow is aimed at the palate. The sides of the tongue continue to make contact with the upper teeth, and tongue blade and tip are pointed, but not touching the alveolar ridge. Lips are rounded to some degree.

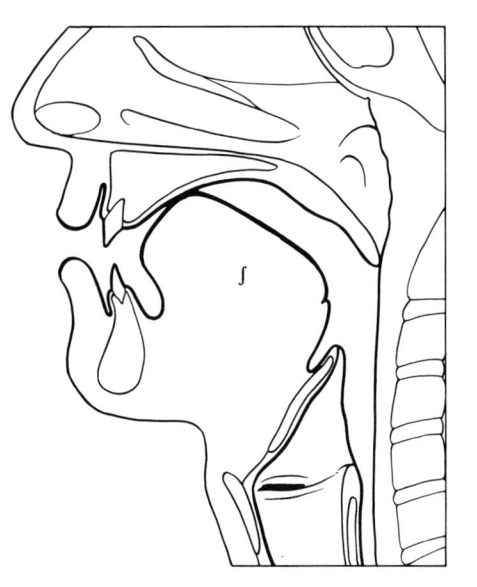

Common Errors

Articulation Errors

1 An interdental or lateral lisp can distort /ʃ/ as it does /s/.

Pronunciation Errors

1 Substitution of /tʃ/ for /ʃ/ in words with a "ch" spelling is common. Examples are *chef, chase, chalet, chagrin.*

Dialect Variations

1 In English with Spanish influence, /tʃ/ can be substituted for /ʃ/ in words such as *shine*— /ʃaın/ → /tʃaın/; *mash*—/mæʃ/ → /mætʃ/.

Sample Words

sugar	tissue	anguish
shadow	fashion	thrush
shop	cushion	sash
shelf	cashew	leash
shine	motion	fresh

Sample Sentences

1 The tension and friction between the British physician and his chauffeur caused a showdown.

2 The ushers washed the chandelier before the first show.

3 The sheperd extinguished the flash fire before it consumed the sheep near Cheyenne.

4 Ti*ss*ue paper *sh*ould be used to *sh*ield the *sh*irt from wrinkles.

5 The *sh*eriff *sh*ouldered his *sh*otgun and set out to man his *sh*ift.

/ʒ/ evasion, beige

PMV Features: palatal/fricative/voiced
Description of Production

The tongue blade is positioned behind the alveolar ridge. The sides of the tongue are against the teeth. The voiced airstream is directed through a shallow depression in the tongue.

Common Errors
Articulation Errors

1 /ʒ/ occurs very infrequently in English. As for /ʃ/, any lisp can affect the production of /ʒ/.

Pronunciation Errors

1 Occasionally, /dʒ/ is substituted for /ʒ/ in words such as *garage*, *corsage*, and *camouflage*.

Dialect Variations

1 Dialect variations are not common.

Sample Words

vi*si*on	bei*g*e
plea*s*ure	gara*g*e
deci*si*on	presti*g*e
ca*s*ual	rou*g*e
amne*si*a	camoufla*g*e

Sample Sentences

1 The reporters came to the conclu*si*on that the Hoo*si*ers were the best in their divi*si*on.

2 The cultural inva*si*on of A*si*a was viewed as subver*si*on by the people.

3 The trea*s*ure of Per*si*a was only a mira*g*e.

4 She mea*s*ured the hem of the bei*g*e dress with preci*si*on.

5 The televi*si*on crew filmed the explo*si*on and ensuing confu*si*on.

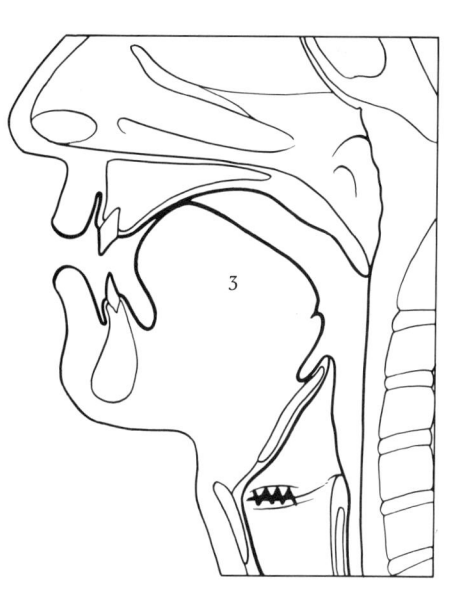

/h/ hot, keyhole

PMV Features: glottal/fricative/voiceless
Description of Production

This consonant is unique in that the articulators—tongue, lips, jaw—assume no particular position. The vocal folds are apart as in a whisper (no voice) and the airflow is in a continuous stream. In words, the articulators are positioned for the following vowel or diphthong.

Common Errors
Articulation Errors

Articulation errors are not common.

Pronunciation Errors

1. /h/ frequently is omitted in unstressed syllables or unstressed words in sentences. This is not necessarily an error; in rapid speech, a missing /h/ is not noticed, but in slower speech it would be. Examples are *fishhook, groundhog, overhaul, pothole, forehead, mishap, rehearse.*

2. You may hear /h/ omitted before /ju/. This is not acceptable. Examples are *hue, humility, human, huge, humus, Houston.*

Dialect Variations

1. Native speakers of Hebrew, Spanish, Japanese, and Greek may confuse /h/ with a fricative sound made in the back of the mouth by raising the tongue to the velum. This may be avoided by dropping the tongue to the floor of the mouth.

Sample Words

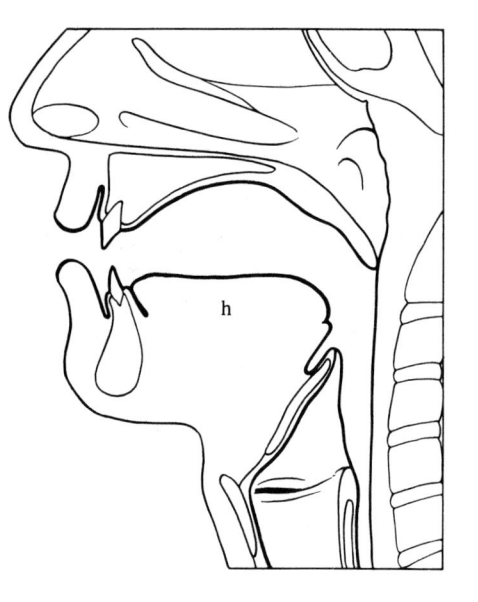

health	inhale
hoop	behavior
honey	inherit
hamster	rehearse
humor	keyhole

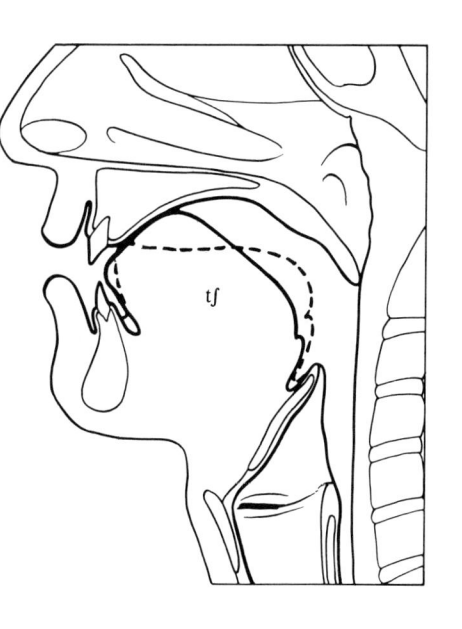

Sample Sentences

1 *H*elp me *h*old the *h*ula *h*oop.
2 *H*arry *h*oped that the *h*ard *h*at would *h*elp *h*is *h*ealth.
3 *H*ilary in*h*aled the *h*istorical atmosphere at the *H*ermitage.
4 The troupe from O*h*io re*h*earsed the *h*oliday play.
5 The *h*ormones found in the *h*owling monkey were similar to those in *h*umans.

AFFRICATES

/tʃ/ *ch*in, tea*ch*er, cou*ch*

PMV Features: palato-alveolar/affricate/voiceless
Description of Production

The tongue assumes the position for /t/ (tongue tip and blade at alveolar ridge; sides of tongue to upper teeth). Airflow is stopped. Just as the stream of air is halted, the tongue tip and blade are lowered, and the voiceless airflow is released through a shallow depression in the tongue as in /ʃ/.

Common Errors
Articulation Errors

1 Any lisp present for /s/ and /z/ may be present also for /tʃ/.

Pronunciation Errors

1 Substitution of /ʃ/ for /tʃ/ can occur in words where /tʃ/ appears after a consonant. Examples are *sculpture, structure, culture, conjecture, effectual*. Notice the "tu" spelling.

Dialect Variations
Dialect variations are not common.

Sample Words

*ch*ocolate	tea*ch*er	atta*ch*
*ch*annel	den*tu*re	prea*ch*
*ch*eer	coa*ch*es	tou*ch*
*ch*owder	lun*ch*eon	crou*ch*
*ch*oose	ri*tu*al	sti*tch*

CHAPTER 8

126

Sample Sentences

1. Under the wat*ch*ful eye of the tea*ch*er, he gave his lec*tu*re on *Ch*inese litera*tu*re.
2. Agricul*tu*re can be a risky ven*tu*re if you *ch*oose to be ri*ch*.
3. A line of white bir*ch*es lined the dit*ch* outside the *ch*ur*ch*yard.
4. The spiri*tu*al leader of the *ch*ur*ch* was also a ran*ch*er.
5. Mu*ch* to our surprise, the pit*ch*er could also pin*ch*-hit.

/dʒ/   *jeep, aging, ledge*

PMV Features: palato-alveolar/affricate/voiced
Description of Production

The tongue assumes the position for /d/ (tongue tip and blade at alveolar ridge; sides of tongue to upper teeth). Airflow is stopped. Just as the stream of air is halted, the tongue tip and blade are lowered, and the voiced airflow is released through a shallow depression in the tongue as in /ʒ/.

Common Errors
Articulation Errors

1. Any lisp present for /s/ and /z/ may be present also for /dʒ/.

Pronunciation Errors
Pronunciation errors are not common.

Dialect Variations
Dialect variations are not common.

Sample Words

*j*ar	a*g*ent	avera*g*e
*j*elly	sol*d*ier	we*dg*e
*g*entle	ob*j*ect	sie*g*e
*j*acks	re*j*oice	ca*g*e
*j*uicy	ma*j*or	ima*g*e

Sample Sentences

1. The le*g*end of the Lone Ran*g*er was told every *J*anuary at the lo*dg*e.
2. *J*anet ple*dg*ed to aven*g*e the dama*g*e to her lu*gg*age.
3. Her ma*j*or in colle*g*e was *G*erman *g*eology.
4. *J*eff acknowle*dg*ed that the practical *j*oke was not exactly an*g*elic.
5. The in*j*ection halted the almost tra*g*ic dama*g*e to *G*eorge's system.

NASALS

/m/   *m*eal, si*mm*er, ja*m*

PMV Features: alveolar/nasal
Description of Production

The lips are pressed together, closing the oral tract. The velum is lowered and the voiced continuous airflow is directed through the nose. The resonance in /m/ can be felt in the upper teeth and bones of the face.

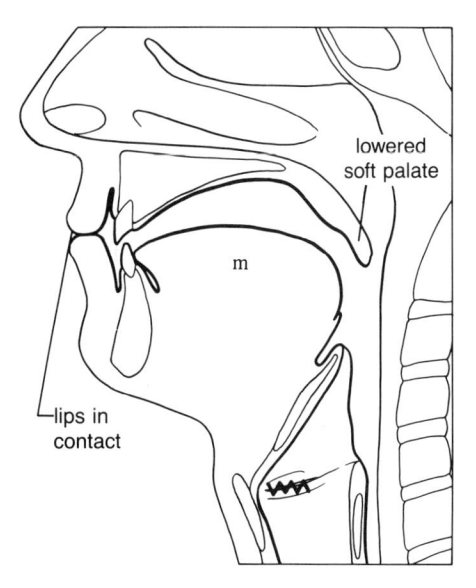

CHAPTER 8

128

Common Errors
Articulation Errors

1 /m/ is one of the easiest consonants to make because of its visibility. Articulation errors are uncommon. Occasionally, a head cold or any physical blockage of the nasal cavity will result in denasalization. All nasals will become their voiced-stop counterparts. Examples are /m/–/b/; /n/–/d/; /ŋ/–/g/.

Pronunciation Errors

1 /m/ frequently can disappear when it occurs before any consonant. Examples are *temple, impeach, scamper.*

2 If /m/ does not vanish, it may change to /n/ under the influence of any consonant that is articulated with tongue and teeth or alveolar ridge (/θ/, /t/, /d/, /l/, /n/). Examples are *warmth, sometime, streamed, comely, come now, hymnal.*

Dialect Variations
Dialect variations are not common.

Sample Words

*m*atch	strea*m*er	stea*m*
*m*achine	gra*mm*ar	pri*m*e
*m*odel	de*m*on	do*m*e
*m*uslin	fa*m*ous	syste*m*
*m*ute	tu*m*ble	ja*m*

Sample Sentences

1 *My m*other *m*akes *m*uch *m*oney.
2 A*m*y and *M*artin *m*otored up the *m*ountain to the su*mm*it.
3 *M*arvin's *m*other *m*aintained that ga*m*bling would *d*a*m*age his fa*m*ous reputation.
4 The *m*elody was familiar to choir *m*e*m*bers who had *m*e*m*orized it.
5 Pu*m*pkins beco*m*e popular in the autu*m*n season.

/n/ *n*ote, u*n*it, vei*n*

PMV Features: alveolar/nasal/voiced
Description of Production

The tongue tip/blade touches the alveolar ridge; sides of the tongue are in contact with the upper teeth. The velum is lowered, and airflow is directed through the nasal cavity.

Common Errors
Articulation Errors
Articulation errors are not common.

Pronunciation Errors
Most of the pronunciation errors occur when /n/ assimilates to another sound (that is, it takes on the characteristics of another sound).

1. /ŋ/ can be substituted for /n/ in words where /n/ comes before /k/ or /g/ (alveolar /n/ assimilates to velar feature of /k/ and /g/). Examples are *tranquil, conquer, sunglasses, mankind;* also in words with "in-", "en-", or "un-" prefixes—*income, enclose, unkind.*

2. Substitution of /m/ for /n/ will occur in words where /n/ comes before /p/ or /b/ (alveolar /n/ assimilates to bilabial feature of /p/ and /b/). Examples are *rainbow, chicken pox.* This occurs also with the prefixes "in-" and "un-" in words such as *inborn, input, unbeaten, unpack.*

3. /m/ or /ŋ/ can be substituted for /n/ when /n/ appears at the end of a word and a bilabial or velar stop appears at the beginning of the next word in combinations such as *on purpose, can be, in cahoots, open gate.*

Dialect Variations
Dialect variations are not common.

Sample Words

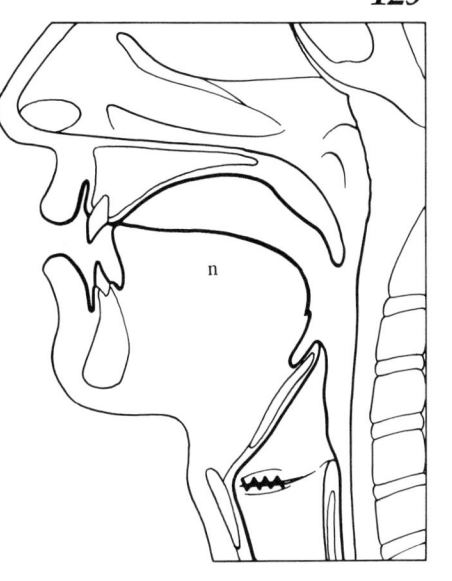

*kn*ock	ow*n*er	vei*n*
*n*oodle	ca*nn*on	balloo*n*
*n*avy	a*nn*ounce	pho*n*e
*n*inety	e*n*amel	ski*n*
*n*ow	di*n*osaur	lea*n*

Sample Sentences

1 Collee*n* complai*n*ed of pai*n* i*n* her *n*eck.
2 Dea*n* remai*n*ed behi*n*d to *n*egotiate the fi*n*al price for the *n*ecklace.
3 Britai*n*'s *N*orth Sea oil mea*n*t gai*n*ful employme*n*t for hu*n*dreds.
4 We ca*nn*ot ig*n*ore the importance of pea*n*uts to the economy.
5 Jea*n* was know*n* to be the o*n*ly sa*n*e o*n*e i*n* the bu*n*ch.

/ŋ/   ji*ng*le, wro*ng*

PMV Features: velar/nasal/voiced
Description of Production

> The body of the tongue is raised to meet the lowered velum. At this point, the airstream is directed through the nasal cavity. Almost no sound resonates in the oral cavity.

Common Errors
Articulation Errors
   Articulation errors are not common.

Pronunciation Errors

1 Addition of /g/ to words ending in /ŋ/ may occur. This error can be made by nonnative English speakers who do not know that the "ng" spelling stands for the phoneme /ŋ/. Examples are *cling, gang, pang, rung, tong.*

Dialect Variations

1 /n/ may appear for /ŋ/ in Southern dialects in words with "-ing" suffix. (Teachers will often call this "dropping the -g.") Other dialect variations are acceptable as you pursue your career, but in a Standard English-speaking business world, this sound substitution often is stigmatized. Listeners may label speech as "careless" on the basis of this sound change. Examples are *walking—walkin; jumping—jumpin; thinking—thinkin; opening—openin.*

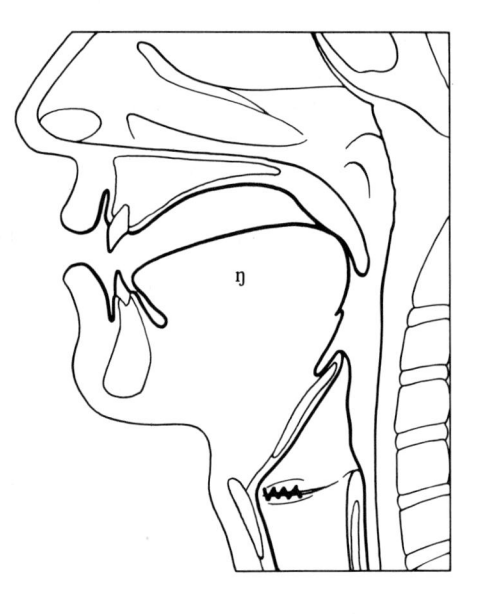

Sample Words

si*ng*er	eveni*ng*
do*n*key	wro*ng*
ha*ng*er	swi*ng*
ju*ng*le	fa*ng*
stro*ng*er	cryi*ng*

Sample Sentences

1. He was the pi*ng* po*ng* ki*ng* in Ho*ng* Ko*ng*.
2. The ju*ng*le outside Ba*ng*kok was forbiddi*ng*.
3. Si*ng*i*ng* is a rewardi*ng* and satisfyi*ng* career for the talented.
4. The fa*ng*s of a Be*ng*al tiger are terrifyi*ng*.
5. That morni*ng*, she was aski*ng* that the bells be ru*ng* on the hour.

GLIDES

/w/, /hw/   *w*and, a*w*ay

PMV Features: bilabial/glide/voiced
Description of Production

> The back of the tongue is raised to the palate. The lips are rounded. The breath is directed through the lips. The other articulators are positioned to form the following vowel. Some people optionally produce an /h/ before the /w/ in words such as *where* or *when*.

Common Errors
Articulation Errors
   Articulation errors are not common.

Pronunciation Errors

1. /w/ and /hw/ may be indistinguishable in your dialect. You may choose to include slight aspiration on the second word in this pair: *wear–where*. However, in conversation, the context is usually sufficient to differentiate such words, as in the phrase "Which witch?"

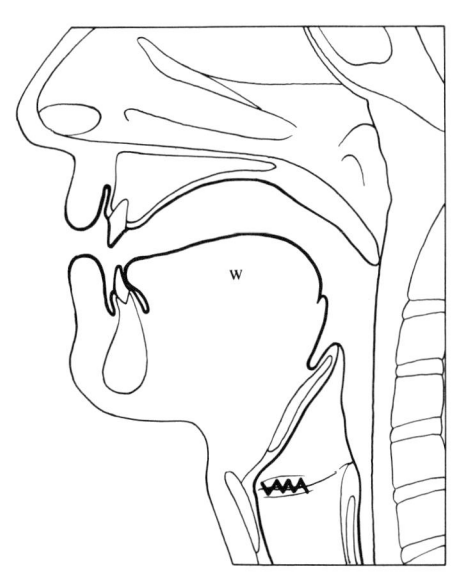

CHAPTER 8

132

us have only /w/ in our phonemic repertoires.
The power of the /h/ is minimal, and most of

Dialect Variations
Dialect variations are not common.

Sample Words

*w*ool	be*w*are
*w*ire	to*w*er
*w*illow	a*wh*ile
*w*ash	sand*w*ich
*w*eather	drive*w*ay

Sample Sentences

1 Warren *w*as a*w*are that the express*w*ay *w*as *w*et.
2 Water *w*ashed across Wanda's *w*indshield.
3 Spider *w*ebs *w*ere *w*oven in the *w*edge of *w*oodwork.
4 Hard*w*are stores are *w*orthy for *w*indow *w*eatherproofing.
5 We *w*ent to Wisconsin to *w*itness the *w*arbler migration.

/j/   *y*olk, co*y*ote

PMV Features: palatal/glide/voiced
Description of Production

The tongue tip and tongue blade are raised to the alveolar ridge. The "glide" happens as the tongue is moved into position for the following vowel. Experiment with the variants of /j/ by trying these combinations: /ji/—*y*ield; /ju/—*y*ou; /jɪ/—*y*ip; /jo/—*y*oke; /jʌ/—*y*oung; /jɛ/—*y*ellow.

Common Errors
Articulation Errors
Articulation errors are not common.

Pronunciation Errors

1 Occasionally, you will hear someone add /j/ before /u/ in such words as *stew*—/stju/; *Tuesday*—/tjuzde/; *June*—/dʒjun/. To "j" or not

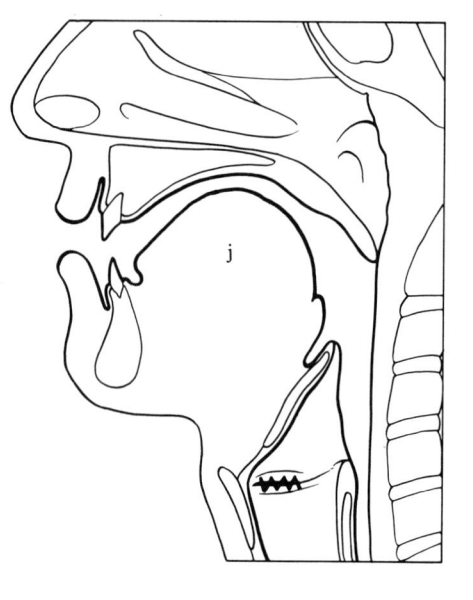

THE SOUNDS OF ENGLISH

133

is merely a matter of preference. The more common pronunciations of the above words are /stu/, /tuzde/, and /dʒun/.

Dialect Variations

1. Native speakers of Scandinavian languages will often substitute /j/ for /dʒ/, because the letter "j" represents the sound /j/ for them. Examples are *jump*—/jʌmp/; *jane*—/jen/.

Sample Words

yield	million
yelp	lawyer
yogurt	reunion
yawn	canyon
you'll	crayon

Sample Sentences

1. Coyotes are known to yowl at unfamiliar visitors.
2. The youngsters used to yell at the New York Yankees games.
3. The lawyer's genius yielded a million dollar settlement.
4. Each year, young students yearn to be at the youth hostel in Uruguay.
5. Yesterday was unique for the seniors and juniors at the university.

/r/   rock, be*rr*y, ba*r*

PMV Features: palatal/glide/voiced
Description of Production

/r/ is one of the most difficult sounds in English to discuss. Its production has no truly precise description. Across other languages, /r/ can be trilled or flapped or rolled. /r/ is usually produced by tightening the midportion of the tongue and pointing the tongue tip up to the alveolar ridge or down to the lower teeth. Because /r/ is a glide, other articulators often assume the position of the following vowel.

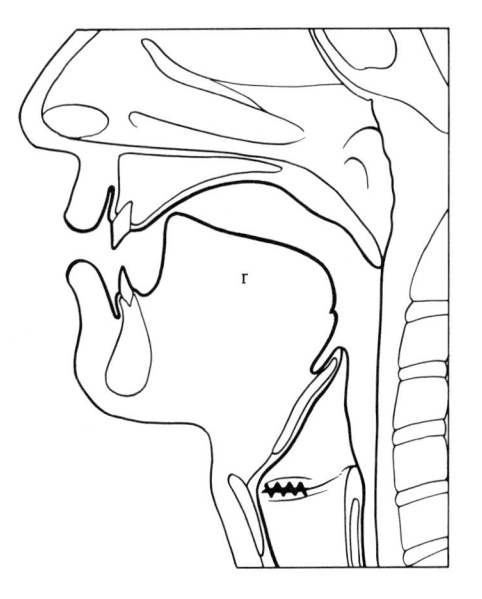

Common Errors

Articulation Errors

1. /w/ is commonly substituted for /r/. Young children who are learning /r/ often make this substitution. /r/ may not be articulated properly until age 7. While people regard this error as endearing in childhood, it loses its charm in adulthood and may become a liability.

Pronunciation Errors

Pronunciation errors are not common.

Dialect Variations

1. In Eastern and Southern dialects, /ə/ is substituted for /r/ after vowels or before consonants (except for /ɑ/, which becomes lengthened /ɑ:/ as in *car*). Examples are *cheer*—/tʃiə/; *oar*—/oə/; *tour*—/tuə/; *forgive*—/foəgɪv/; *part*—/pɑ:t/; *mar*—/mɑ:/.

2. The /r/ *is* articulated in Eastern and Southern dialects when the next word begins with a vowel in such combinations as *here or there; Dear Abby, soar above; tear out.*

3. In Eastern dialect, speakers add /r/ ("intrusive r") between words when the first word ends in a vowel and the second word begins with a vowel. (You will also hear this in British English dialect.) Examples are *saw Amy*—/sɑr emi/; *in lieu of*—/ɪn lur ʌv/; *my uncle*—/maɪr ʌŋkəl/; *know of*—/nor ʌv/.

Sample Words

*r*ope	ea*rr*ing	appea*r*
*r*ake	pa*r*ade	enco*r*e
*r*ug	co*r*al	repai*r*
*wr*eath	tou*r*ist	empi*r*e
*r*ise	pi*r*ate	insu*r*e

Sample Sentences

1. In this wo*r*ld of i*rr*ationality, *r*eason is a vi*r*tue to be t*r*easured.
2. *R*yan pu*r*chased the Pe*r*sian *r*ug from a *r*eputable dealer.
3. *R*isk does not b*r*ing *r*apid *r*ewards.

4 *Rh*onda brought a *wr*ought i*r*on chai*r* to the fi*r*e sale.

5 *R*egan made a *wr*y *r*esponse to *R*obert's *r*eprimand.

/l/ *l*eave, ga*ll*on, coo*l*

PMV Features: alveolar/glide/voiced
Description of Production

The tongue tip touches the alveolar ridge. The sides of the tongue are dropped to let the airstream pass. There are two allophones of /l/—a "clear" [l] as in *light* and *left* and a "dark" [l] that usually appears in the word-final position and usually in the word-medial position as in *pill* and *William*. Contrast the /l/ in *lip* and *pill* to feel the difference.

Common Errors
Articulation Errors

1 Substitution of /w/ for /l/ can occur. Examples are *like*—/waɪk/; *leaf*—/wif/.

Pronunciation Errors

1 [l] is often omitted before a consonant in words such as *calculate*—/kɑukulet/; *million*—/mɪjən/; *shoulder*—/ʃodɚ/.

2 Occasionally, you might hear someone add /l/ where it should be quiet in words such as *walk*—/wolk/; *chalk*—/tʃɔlk/; *calf*—/kælf/; *salmon*—/sælmən/.

Dialect Variations

1 The stereotypical portrayal of the Oriental English dialect confuses /r/ and /l/ as in "reary velly solly." Speakers who have an Oriental language as their native or home language do have a sound that is similar to both /r/ and /l/; hence the confusion when they attempt to produce either sound. To make their speech more like Standard English, Oriental speakers

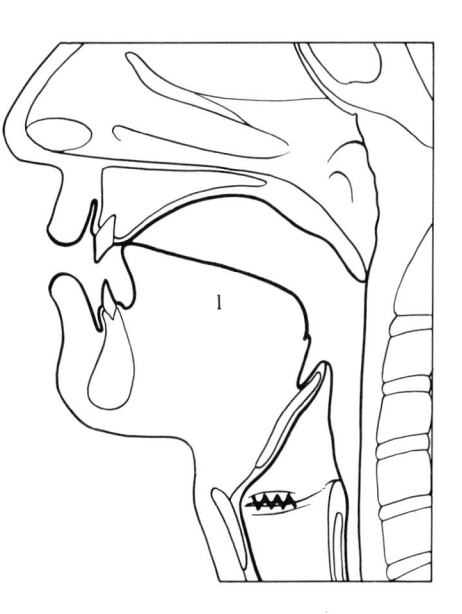

must learn to articulate /r/ and /l/ as separate phonemes.

Sample Words

*l*ight	je*ll*y	ba*ll*
*l*emon	ba*ll*oon	hi*ll*
*l*amb	fo*ll*ow	snai*l*
*l*ungs	umbre*ll*a	coa*l*
*l*oose	sa*l*ad	shove*l*

Sample Sentences

1 Laura *l*iked *l*inen and *l*ace to accent her *l*iving room.
2 Linda and Phy*ll*is fe*l*t that the i*ll*ustrations *l*ent credibi*l*ity to their writing.
3 The fie*l*d at the O*l*ympics was fi*ll*ed with hopefu*l* mi*l*ers.
4 Pau*l* fe*l*t that his bache*l*or status made Wi*ll*iam jea*l*ous.
5 Lobster has *l*ots more ca*l*ories than other she*ll*fish.

/i/ eat, keep, money

PMTL Features: high/front/tense/unrounded
Description of Production

The front of the tongue is brought up toward the hard palate, with jaws almost closed and lips spread apart, as in a smile. The sides of the tongue contact the upper teeth.

Common Errors
Articulation Errors
   Articulation errors are not common.

Pronunciation Errors

1 /iə/ may be substituted for /i/ when it appears before /l/ in words such as *feel*—/fiəl/; *meal*—/miəl/.

Dialect Variations
   Changes due to dialect are not common.

Sample Words

ether	seem	knee
equal	feast	plea
enough	mean	ski
eel	people	prairie
elope	bean	agree

Sample Sentences

1 We eat eels only when they're free.
2 Ethan feels that coffee is best with cream.
3 Willy's jeep was green with gilt leaf trimming.
4 The Court of Appeals agreed with Harry's guilty plea.
5 Harvey, the beagle, dreams of flying across fields after weasels.

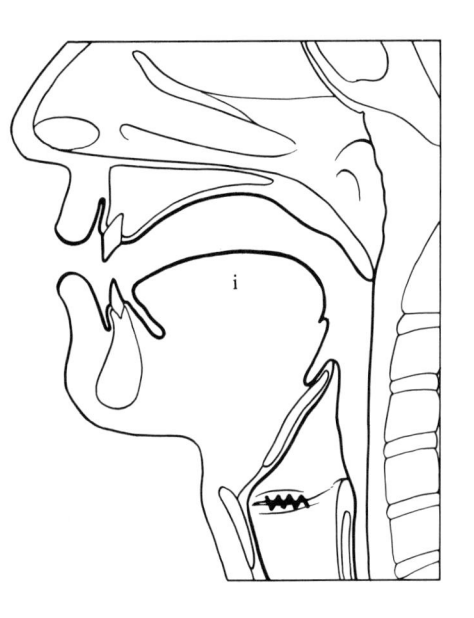

/ɪ/   *i*tch, p*i*stol

PMTL Features: high/front/lax/unrounded
Description of Production

> The tongue is raised to the palate, not quite as high as for /i/. The tongue is not tensed. The lips are spread as for a smile.

Common Errors
Articulation Errors
> Articulation errors are not common.

Pronunciation Errors

1. /ɪ/ can become /ə/ in words with prefixes such as *de-*, *be-*, *pre-*. In casual speech it is easy to allow that first vowel to drop to a central one.
2. /ɛ/ may be substituted for /ɪ/ in words such as *six*—/sɛks/; *bit*—/bɛt/; *kid*—/kɛd/.

Dialect Variations

1. Native Spanish speakers may substitute /i/ for /ɪ/. Examples are *bit*—/bit/; *with*—/wiθ/.

Sample Words

*i*diot	d*i*tch
*i*gnore	gu*i*lt
*i*ssue	kn*i*t
*i*nk	k*i*tten
*i*nch	h*y*mn

Sample Sentences

1. *I*n every *i*nstance, B*i*ll bu*i*lt the best *i*gloo possible.
2. S*i*nce S*y*lvia m*i*sses her k*i*tten, she can p*i*ck another.
3. Cher*i*sh early memories of the Sm*i*ths to call upon at s*i*xty.
4. If he *i*gnored the *i*tch, *i*t pers*i*sted *i*n annoying h*i*m.
5. L*i*z won the s*i*x m*i*llion dollar lottery.

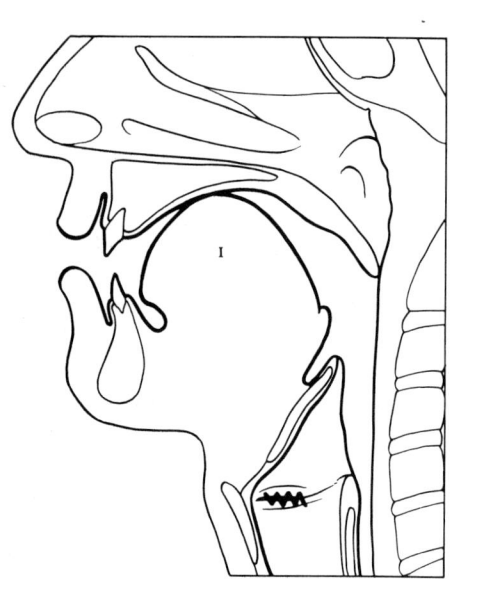

/e/ able, rage, stay

PMTL Features: mid/front/tense/unrounded
Description of Production

The front of the tongue is raised to the level of the oral cavity. The tongue is tense, and lips are not rounded.

Common Errors
Articulation Errors
   Articulation errors are not common.

Pronunciation Errors
   Pronunciation errors are not common.

Dialect Variations

1 You may be producing a single vowel, diphthong, or "triphthong" (combination of three vowels) when you say words such as *aid*, *crayon*, or *day*. In these words, /e/ comes before a voiced consonant, in an accented syllable, or at the end of the word. Possible pronunciations of *aid* are /ed/, /eɪd/, or /eɪəd/. The final production is typical for a Southern dialect.

Sample Words

acorn	stage	bay
ancient	favor	delay
eighty	gravy	clay
ail	mate	neigh
agent	lame	day

Sample Sentences

1 Amy ate way too many grapes.
2 A delay in making up sick days results in late paychecks.
3 Radiation from routine x-rays may be safe.
4 Gray days in April are commonplace in Saint Paul.
5 The gale raged after great clouds sailed into the sky.

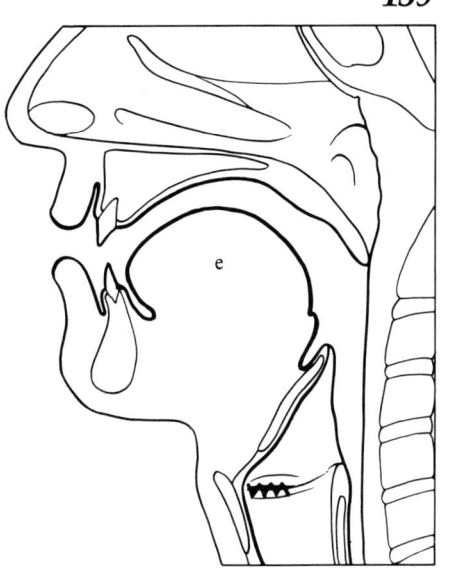

/ɛ/ end, sell

PMTL Features: mid/front/lax/unrounded
Description of Production

The tongue is slightly lower in the mouth than for /e/. The tongue is relaxed and the mouth is slightly more open than for /e/.

Common Errors
Articulation Errors
Articulation errors are not common.

Pronunciation Errors

1. /ɪ/ may be substituted for /ɛ/ in words such as *set*—/sɪt/; *men*—/mɪn/; *pen*—/pɪn/; *get*—/gɪt/.
2. /e/ commonly is substituted for /ɛ/ when /ɛ/ occurs before /g/ or /ʒ/ in words such as *egg*—/eg/; *peg*—/peg/; *measure*—/meʒɚ/.

Dialect Variations
Dialect variations are not common.

Sample Words

end	g*ue*ss
ever	s*e*nd
extreme	y*e*t
ethics	s*ays*
exercise	h*ea*d

Sample Sentences

1. *Extra eggs* were needed for the omel*et*.
2. *Every* fri*end* was pr*e*sent for the S*e*ptember w*e*dding.
3. A perc*e*ntage of the profits will be s*e*nt to all personn*e*l.
4. *Ellen* will r*e*member the *expression* on his face as he s*ai*d farewell.
5. Twelve m*e*n sat in judgment at the w*ea*lthy man's trial.

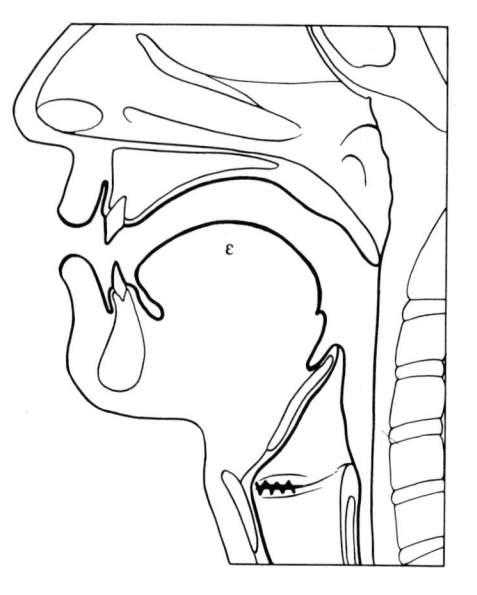

/æ/ *a*pple, bl*a*ck

PMTL Features: low/front/lax/unrounded
Description of Production

The front part of the tongue is moved upward slightly. The lips are opened and unrounded.

Common Errors
Articulation Errors
Articulation errors are not common.

Pronunciation Errors

1 /æɪ/ or /æə/ may be used instead of /æ/. This typically happens when a word with /æ/ is slowly articulated and the quality of /æ/ takes on more tenseness.

Dialect Variations
Dialect variations are not common.

Sample Words

*a*ttic	fl*a*g
*a*ttitude	s*a*nd
*a*bsent	c*a*lf
*a*fter	sn*a*g
*a*bsolute	l*au*gh

Sample Sentences

1 Practically half the class can't pass the algebra examination.
2 Frank has a passion for having his back scratched.
3 Do you plan to have the actors stand on that platform in the last act?
4 Damaged lamps can be had at half price on Saturday.
5 The champion has answered Max's demands for a rematch.

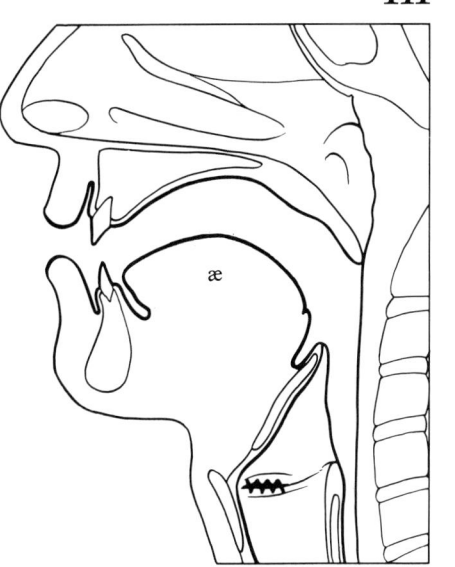

/ə/ (schwa) *a*mount, stom*a*ch, stigm*a*

PMTL Features: mid/central/lax/unrounded (unstressed)
Description of Production

The front of the tongue remains on the floor of the mouth while the middle portion of the tongue moves only slightly toward the hard palate. Lips are unrounded, and the mouth is open slightly.

Common Errors
Articulation Errors
/ə/ is one of the easiest vowels to produce; it is rarely misarticulated.

Pronunciation Errors

1 /ə/ is easily omitted. Because it appears only in unstressed syllables, it is often ignored in pronunciation. Examples are *different*—/dɪfrɪnt/; *camera*—/kæmrə/; *liberal*—/lɪbrəl/.

2 Addition of /ə/ can occur when a speaker is being too cautious. Examples are *business*—/bɪzənɪs/; *bracelet*—/bresəlɪt/.

Dialect Variations
Dialect variations are not common.

Sample Words

*a*lone	m*a*chine
*a*nother	rec*e*ive
*o*ccur	giv*e*n
*a*ttempt	t*o*day
*a*dvance	bas*i*s

Sample Sentences

1 The ch*a*meleon has *a*n *a*mazing *a*bility to *a*void movem*e*nt.
2 Sev*e*n pand*a*s were tak*e*n to North Americ*a*n reserv*e*s for protecti*o*n.
3 Don't *a*ttract *a*ttenti*o*n by *a*nnouncing your presence.
4 Par*e*nts *a*gree that s*u*pport increas*e*s perform*a*nce.
5 The *a*dults fell *a*sleep *a*fter fixing th*e* cause of the flood fr*o*m the batht*u*b.

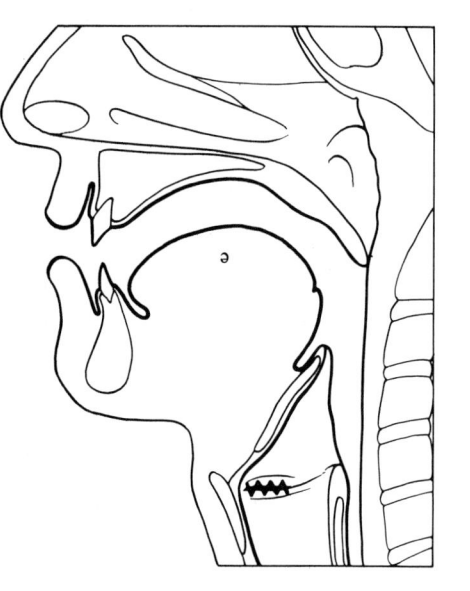

/ʌ/ under, duck

PMTL Features: mid/central/lax/unrounded (stressed)
Description of Production

> The midportion of the tongue is raised slightly to the palate; the remainder of the tongue lies at the floor of the mouth. /ʌ/ and /ə/ are very similar—/ə/ is shorter and weaker.

Common Errors
Articulation Errors
> Articulation errors are not common.

Pronunciation Errors

1. Occasionally, /ɪ/ or /ɛ/ may be substituted for /ʌ/. Examples are *just*—/dʒɪst/ or /dʒɛst/; *such*—/sɪtʃ/ or /sɛtʃ/.

Dialect Variations

1. Various speakers of other languages will substitute the back vowels /u/, /ɔ/, or /ɑ/ for /ʌ/ in words such as *cut, rub, does, come*.

Sample Words

*u*ncle	*o*nce
*u*p	s*u*ffer
*o*ther	*co*me
*u*s	g*u*n
*u*tter	fr*o*nt

Sample Sentences

1. One hundred ducks fluttered over the nests.
2. The puppies were hungry for biscuits from the cupboard.
3. Nothing is better on an empty stomach than peanut butter fudge.
4. Justine's husband was under the weather after supping on her custard.
5. Chuck wants mustard on his hamburger bun.

CHAPTER 8

144

/ɝ/   ea*r*n, thi*r*st, occ*ur*

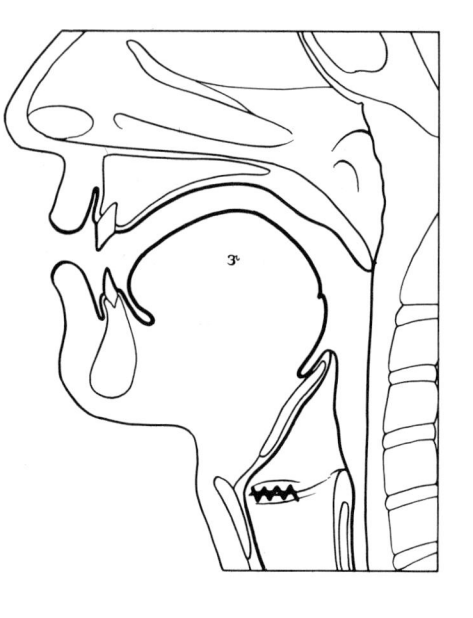

PMTL Features: mid/central/tense/rounded (stressed)
Description of Production

The midportion of the tongue is raised halfway to the palate. The tongue tip is behind the lower teeth or raised to just behind the alveolar ridge. Lips are slightly rounded and open.

Common Errors
Articulation Errors

1 Individuals who misarticulate /r/ will often omit the "r-coloring" of /ɝ/. The resulting vowel /ɜ/ is produced with lip rounding in words such as *hurt*—/hɜt/; *dirt*—/dɜt/. (If the speaker uses a New York, Eastern, or Southern English dialect, this is *not* an error.)

Pronunciation Errors

1 Confusion between /ɝ/ and /rɪ/ can happen through inattention to word spelling, which guides pronunciation. These reversals are common:

correct	*incorrect*
perfect—/pɝfəkt/	*prefect*—/prɪfəkt/
prevail—/prɪvel/	*pervail*—/pɝvel/

Dialect Variations

1 /ɝ/ can change to /ɜ/ in New York, Eastern, or Southern English dialects. This is often referred to as "dropping the r-coloring." /ɜ/ is a more lax and lower version of /ɝ/. However, the lip rounding remains the same. Examples are *serve*—/sɜv/; *first*—/fɜst/; *bird*—/bɜd/.

Sample Words

ea*r*th	p*ur*pose	p*urr*
ea*r*ly	sk*ir*t	f*ir*
ea*r*n	ve*r*ge	b*urr*
ea*r*l	h*ur*t	st*ir*
*ur*ge	te*r*m	he*r*

Sample Sentences

1. Tige*rs* and beave*rs* w*er*e h*er* fav*or*ite animals.
2. F*er*ns flo*ur*ish in moist *ear*th.
3. *Ir*ving *ear*nestly courted *Er*ma, his form*er* n*ur*se.
4. Thi*r*ty bi*r*ds w*er*e out *ear*ly s*ear*ching for w*or*ms.
5. Our f*ur*niture became di*r*ty in the *ur*ban setting.

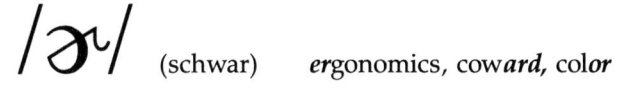

/ɚ/ (schwar) e*r*gonomics, cow*ard*, col*or*

PMTL Features: mid/central/tense/rounded (unstressed)

Description of Production

The position for /ɚ/ is similar to that for /ɜ˞/. The tongue is more relaxed and lower. Production of /ɚ/ may be shorter.

Common Errors
Articulation Errors

1. If you have difficulty producing /r/, you may substitute /ə/ for /ɚ/. Examples are *sugar*—/ʃugə/; *cover*—/kʌvə/; *brother*—/brʌðə/.

Pronunciation Errors

1. If you do not pay attention to spelling, you may confuse /ɚ/ with /rɪ/ in words such as

correct	incorrect
children—/tʃɪldrɪn/	*childern*—/tʃɪldɚn/
entrance—/ɛntrɪns/	*enternce*—/ɛntɚns/
pretend—/prɪtɛnd/	*pertend*—/pɚtɛnd/

Dialect Variations

1. Speakers of New York, Eastern, and Southern dialects drop the r-coloring of /ɚ/ as they do for /ɜ˞/. If you do this as part of your dialect, be sure not to convert /ɜ/ or /ə/ into diphthongs /ɜɪ/ or /əɪ/. Examples are *permit*—/pəmɪt/ (verb); *dancer*—/dænsə/; *offered*—/ɑfəd/.

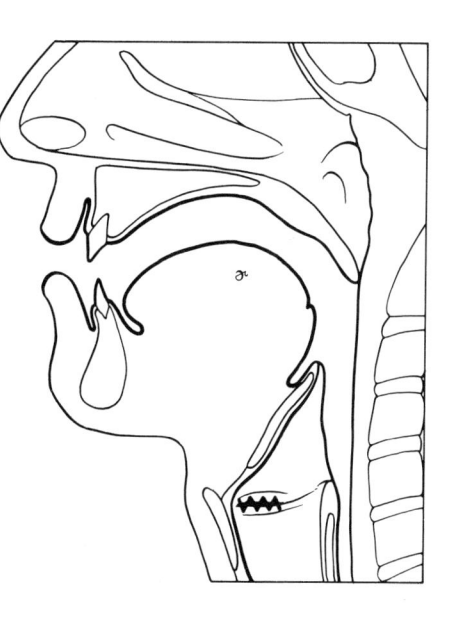

CHAPTER 8

146

Sample Words

pe*r*spire	off*er*
diffe*r*ence	gath*er*
cow*ar*d	togeth*er*
rese*r*vation	popul*ar*
info*r*mation	dinn*er*

Sample Sentences

1 The inte*r*national lab*or* union met eve*r*y Decemb*er*.
2 Teach*er*s all over the district looked forw*ar*d to Septemb*er*.
3 The last item required to f*ur*nish his bedroom was a mirr*or*.
4 H*er* mem*or*y for the dress patt*er*n was dist*ur*bed.
5 Fath*er* worked up a rath*er* stiff lath*er* before he used the raz*or*.

/ɑ/   h*o*nest, cl*o*ck, hurr*ah*

PMTL Features: low/back/lax/unrounded
Description of Production

The tongue remains on the floor of the mouth and the jaw is lowered. The back of the tongue raises slightly. The mouth is open wide and the lips are unrounded.

Common Errors
Articulation Errors

1 Occasionally, [a] is substituted for /ɑ/. [a] is an allophone for /ɑ/—halfway between /æ/ and /ɑ/. Glide from a /æ/ (*at*) to /ɑ/ (*off*). [a] will occur between these two vowels. As you practice these words, make sure you are producing /ɑ/: *autumn, almond, hot, sock, bottle.*

Pronunciation Errors

1 Take care to avoid producing [a] in words such as *car, start, park, sharp.*

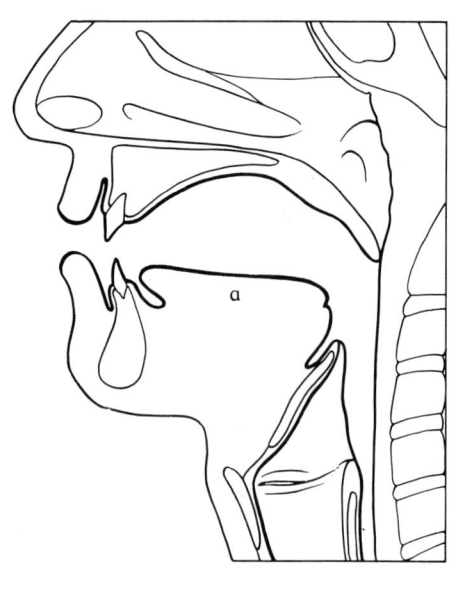

THE SOUNDS OF ENGLISH

Dialect Variations

1 In Eastern dialects, /ɔ/ and /ʌ/ may be used for words such as *hot, chop, knock*.

Sample Words

*au*tumn	rock	Sh*ah*
*au*to	f*a*ther	hurr*ah*
*aw*kward	b*o*ttle	bl*ah*
*al*mond	b*o*x	
h*o*nest	d*o*t	

Sample Sentences

1 Bob's father went to Harvard.
2 The box of rocks was locked for a dollar.
3 Mark parked his car near the garbage can.
4 The marchers marched to the park to block the draining of the pond.
5 The locket in the shape of a heart fit into his pocket.

/ɔ/   *off, taught, claw*

PMTL Features: low/back/lax/rounded
Description of Production

The back of the tongue is raised halfway to the palate while it remains relaxed. The lips are rounded.

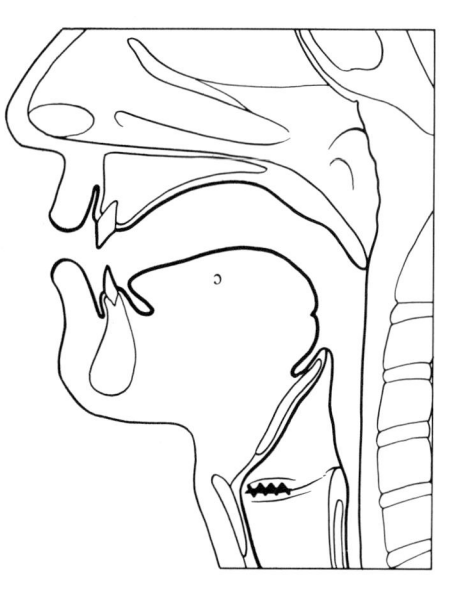

CHAPTER 8

148

Common Errors
Articulation Errors

1. Occasionally, you might hear speakers who do not produce /ɔ/. Instead, they use /ɑ/ for all vowels. These word pairs will sound similar.

/ɑ/	/ɔ/
barn	born
pond	pawned
tart	torte

   You can easily alter the misarticulation by rounding your lips and raising the back of the tongue.

Pronunciation/Dialect Variations

1. /ɔ/ can be an unstable sound. Some dialects do not have it at all. Other dialects honor it in some contexts. Still other dialects will use /ɔ/ in all possible instances. In the following pairs of words, check your production.

/ɑ/	/ɔ/
barn	born
farm	form
car	corn
mar	more
nod	gnawed
cot	caught
knotty	naughty
pod	pawed

Sample Words

*o*ften	t*au*ght	p*aw*
*aw*ful	w*a*lk	s*aw*
*a*ll	f*aw*n	str*aw*
*ou*ght	m*au*l	cl*aw*
*o*ffice	c*au*ght	r*aw*

Sample Sentences

1. The *au*dio signal f*o*r that s*o*ng *o*n the radio was *aw*ful.
2. She sprinkled s*a*lt *o*n the sidew*a*lk after the snowf*a*ll.
3. He y*aw*ned so hard that his j*aw* got c*au*ght.
4. We were t*au*ght to n*o*t g*aw*k at b*a*ld men.
5. D*aw*n b*ou*ght an *au*tomobile at the *au*ction last *au*tumn.

/o/ open, nose, narrow

PMTL Features: mid/back/tense/rounded
Description of Production

The back of the tongue is raised to the midpoint between the floor of the mouth and the palate. The tongue is tense and lips are rounded.

Common Errors
Articulation Errors
Articulation errors are not common.

Pronunciation Errors

1. /o/ in unstressed syllables should not be further reduced to /ə/ in words such as *yellow, hotel, obey*.
2. /o/ can easily become /oə/ before /l/ and /n/ in words such as *poll, foal, loan, cone, old*.

Pronunciation Variations

1. /o/ can become a nonphonemic diphthong—/oʊ/—in stressed syllables in words such as *open, over, ocean, only*.

Dialect Variations
Dialect variations are not common.

Sample Words

open	bowl	dough
oak	moat	arrow
odor	nose	though
oval	choke	toe
occasion	flown	shallow

Sample Sentences

1. Olaf received a standing ovation after his piano solo.
2. She made the shore with only one oar.
3. The boat floated on the ocean with a dead motor.
4. Tomorrow, we'll go through the whole show.
5. She wrote him a note asking for the money owed her.

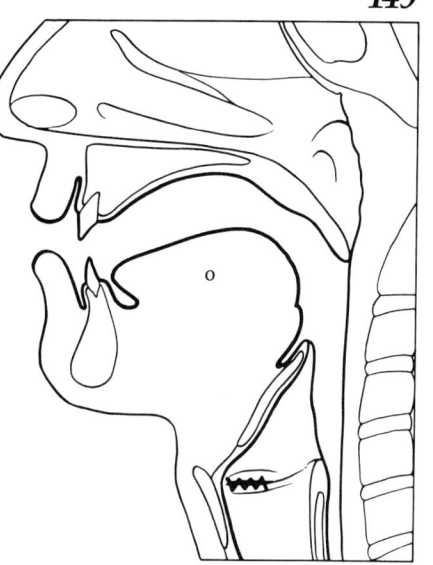

/ʊ/ st**oo**d

PMTL Features: high/back/lax/rounded
Description of Production

> The tongue is raised in the back, although not as high as for /u/. Lips are rounded, less than for /u/. The tongue is relaxed.

Common Errors
Articulation Errors
> Articulation errors are not common.

Pronunciation Errors

1. /ʊ/ can transform into /ʊɪ/ or /ʊə/ if you do not take care to produce a pure vowel in words such as *put, book, push, should*.
2. It is also possible to substitute /u/, /ʌ/, or /ə/ for /ʊ/ in words such as *cookie, look, could*.

Dialect Variations
> Dialect variations are not common.

Sample Words

    r**oo**f
    st**oo**d
    w**o**man
    w**ou**ld
    l**oo**k

Sample Sentences

1. Every t**ou**rist knew that she sh**ou**ld visit the neighborh**oo**d.
2. His horse c**ou**ld raise his h**oo**ves high enough to cross the br**oo**k.
3. We read b**oo**ks on how to h**oo**k a br**oo**k trout.
4. It was underst**oo**d that c**oo**kies, p**u**dding, and tea with s**u**gar were the afternoon snack.
5. The b**u**ll p**u**lled the load of w**oo**d to the f**oo**t of the mountain.

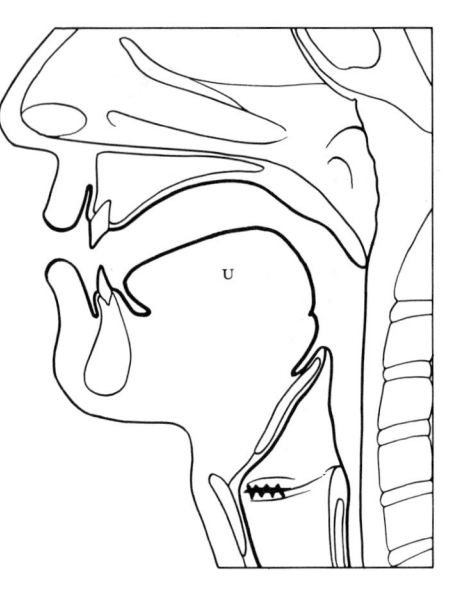

/u/   *oo*ze, sp*oo*n, cl*ue*

PMTL Features: high/back/tense/rounded
Description of Production

> The back of the tongue is raised high and the lips are rounded.

Common Errors
Articulation Errors

1. In producing /u/, some speakers tend to create a diphthong—/uə/—in stressed syllables.

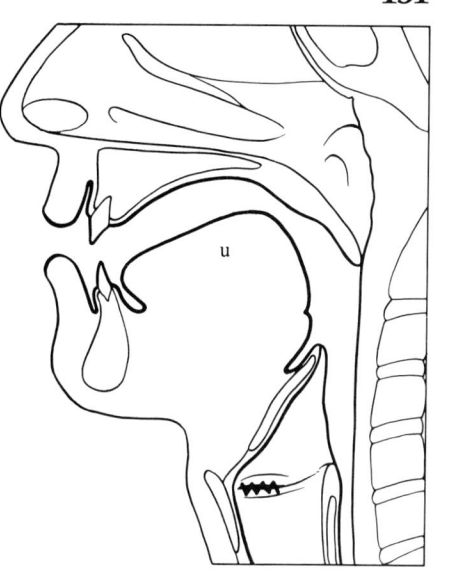

Pronunciation Errors

1. Several words may be pronounced with /u/ or /ʊ/. Dictionaries list /u/ as the first choice, but that does not mean that using /ʊ/ is nonstandard. Examples are *root, roof, hoof, hooves, whoop, room, soot, coop, hoop*.

Dialect Variations

1. Many foreign languages do not have both /u/ and /ʊ/ vowels. Consequently, if you are not a native speaker of English, you may confuse /u/ and /ʊ/. When producing /ʊ/, the lips are less rounded and the tongue is less tense.

/u/	/ʊ/
stewed	stood
pool	pull
shoed	should
cooed	could
Luke	look

152

Sample Words

*oo*dles	b*oo*t	wh*o*
*oo*ps	f*oo*d	ch*ew*
*oo*ze	r*oo*f	thr*ew*
	c*oo*p	r*ue*
	dil*u*te	z*oo*

Sample Sentences

1. The r*u*thless cr*ew* of the sl*oo*p thr*ew* the fr*u*it overboard.
2. Bab*oo*ns at the z*oo* used sp*oo*ns to eat their f*oo*d.
3. Watson hoped to f*oo*l Holmes with a n*ew* cl*ue*.
4. R*u*th added n*oo*dles t*o* the chicken st*ew*.
5. The n*ew* d*u*ke preferred b*oo*ts over sh*oe*s.

DIPHTHONGS

In this section, we will discuss the phonemic diphthongs. As you recall, these are produced by changing quality and articulation in one sound. PMTL features for each diphthong will be a combination of the features for each of the two vowels contained in it. The description of production will always add a glide as the tongue slides into the second component of the diphthong.

/ju/ *united, future, review*

PMTL Features: high/front/tense/unrounded to high/back/tense/rounded

Description of Production

The tongue moves from a position high and front in the mouth to a high-back position. The tongue is tense, and, at the end of production, the lips are rounded.

[lips rounded]

Common Errors
Pronunciation Errors

1. Avoid adding a /ə/ before /ju/ in these words: *view*—/vəju/; *cute*—/kəjut/; *feud*—/fəjud/.

2. In unstressed syllables, /ju/ should not be reduced to /ə/. (Occasionally, /ju/ sounds like /jʊ/—this is acceptable.) Examples are *fabulous, accurate, ridiculous*.

Sample Words

union	refuse	few
use	human	you
utilize	beauty	yew
unit	cube	view
university	music	new

Sample Sentences

1. Hugh refused to remain in the humid climate.
2. The union was popular at the huge university.

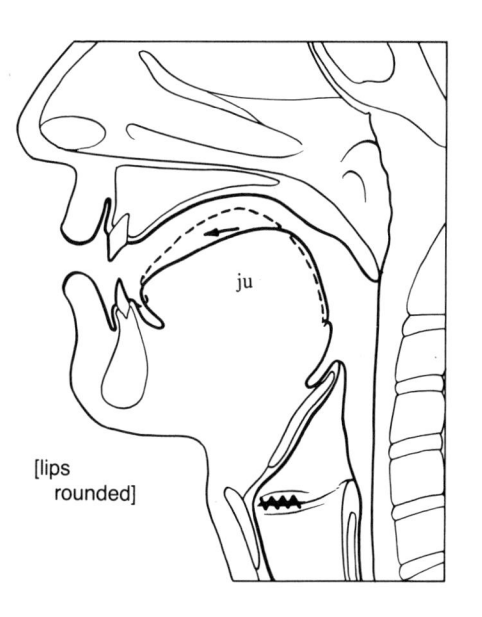

3 The teacher v*iew*ed the p*u*pil's m*u*sic with h*u*mor.

4 The *u*tility company *u*sed uranium to f*ue*l its plant.

5 Let's contin*ue* this debate with *you* about *eu*genics in the f*u*ture.

/aɪ/ *i*dea, wh*i*te, h*igh*

PMTL Features: low/central/lax/unrounded to high/front/lax/unrounded

Description of Production

The tongue is in a relaxed position on the floor of the mouth. It moves to a high front position as in /ɪ/. The lips remain unrounded.

Common Errors
Dialect Variations

1 In Southern English, /aɪ/ is usually produced as /aə/. If you wish to change this, try to move from *tying*—/taɪɪŋ/ to *tie*—/taɪ/ by dropping /ɪŋ/. Examples are *flying–fly; sighing–sigh; buying–buy.*

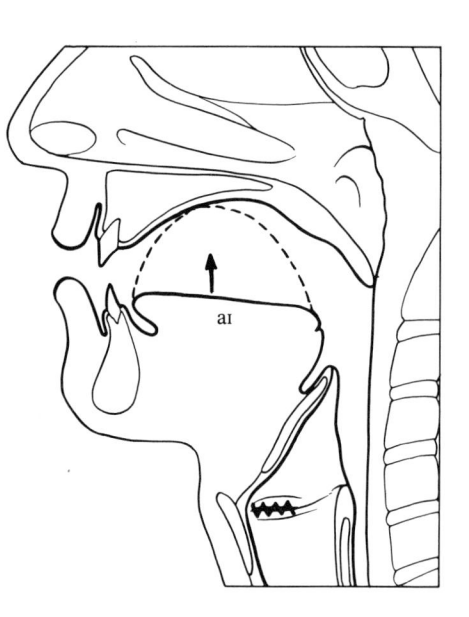

Sample Words

*i*ce	n*i*ght	b*uy*
eye	disg*ui*se	sh*y*
*i*sland	b*i*ke	fr*y*
*i*tem	st*y*le	sk*y*
*i*dle	s*i*de	tr*y*

Sample Sentences

1 M*i*ke adm*i*red the he*igh*t of the k*i*te in the sk*y*.

2 D*i*nah descr*i*bed the cr*i*me at the l*i*brary with a s*igh*.

3 D*i*ane s*igh*ed at the s*igh*t of another d*i*nosaur fossil from the *i*sland.

4 Ch*i*na sought to *i*solate itself and rel*y* on its fores*igh*t.

5 The *i*ris cl*i*mbed h*igh* next to the p*i*le of t*i*res.

/aʊ/ *ou*tside, p*ou*nce, h*ow*

PMTL Features: low/central/lax/unrounded to high/back/lax/rounded

Description of Production

The tongue begins at the floor of the mouth in a relaxed position. Then, it moves to /ʊ/—a high, back, relaxed, and rounded position.

Common Errors
Articulation/Dialect Variation

1 If you are from New York City or other areas of the East, you may produce /aʊ/ as /æʊ/ or /ɛʊ/. If you remember the PMTL features of /æ/ and /ɛ/, you recall that these vowels are higher and more tense than /a/. You can change the nonstandard diphthongs to /aʊ/ by opening your mouth wider and by lowering your tongue.

Sample Words

*ou*t	sh*ow*er	pl*ough*
*ou*ch	c*ou*nty	c*ow*
*ow*l	m*ou*se	n*ow*
*ou*r	am*ou*nt	br*ow*
h*ou*r	gr*ou*nd	all*ow*

Sample Sentences

1 The cat p*ou*nced on the m*ou*se with a l*ou*d me*ow*.
2 The *ow*l hooted from the b*ough* on the h*ou*r.
3 He pl*ow*ed the gr*ou*nd using the best c*ow* in the c*ou*nty.
4 The pr*ow*ler made no s*ou*nd as he crept over the gr*ou*nds ar*ou*nd the h*ou*se.
5 The kangaroo m*ou*se has a p*ou*ch that reaches d*ow*n to the gr*ou*nd.

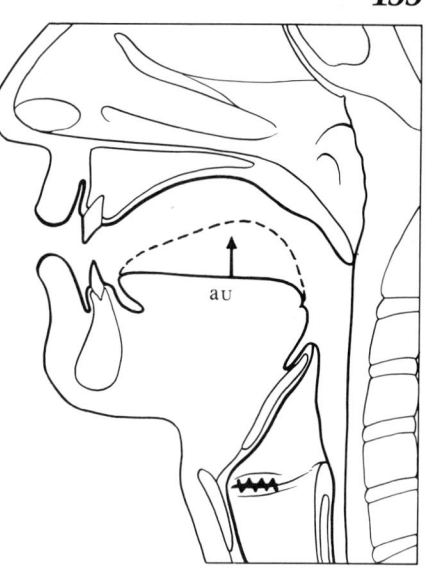

/ɔɪ/ oil, voice, joy

PMTL Features: mid/back/lax/rounded to
high/front/lax/unrounded
Description of Production

The tongue is raised in the back to the middle position and glides to the high-front position, where it remains relaxed and becomes unrounded.

Common Errors
Articulation Errors

1. Be sure to lip-round at the beginning of /ɔɪ/ to avoid producing /ɛɪ/ or /əɪ/. Examples are *coy–coin–coil; boy–boil–broil; toy–toil–toys.*

Sample Words

ointment	royal	toy
oil	join	destroy
oyster	poise	decoy
oink	choice	soy
oily	point	enjoy

Sample Sentences

1. Freud enjoyed pointing out Roy's avoidance of joy.
2. That moist soil was best for growing soybeans.
3. Joyce's choice was to put ointment on the horse's loin.
4. Lloyd destroyed his voice by speaking over noise.
5. Detroit toiled to prepare for the royal voyage.

STUDY QUESTIONS

1. What are common articulation errors for /r/ and /s/?
2. Are consonants or vowels more easily misarticulated? Why?
3. What happens to sounds adjacent to /m/, /n/, or /ŋ/?

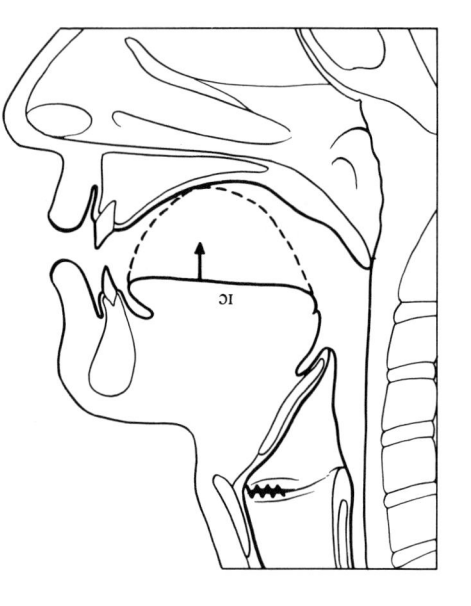

Chapter 9
Assessing Your Articulation

You are ready to begin the process of assessment of your articulation and pronunciation. You have devoted a significant amount of your education to assessment. In every instance, you were being tested for your knowledge of a particular subject; the ultimate goal was a grade. We are using assessment in a different sense here. In this chapter, you will learn to evaluate your production of each of the phonemes we discussed in Chapter 8. After you assess your articulation and pronunciation, you will be ready to design your own program for improvement.

BACKGROUND INFORMATION

Assessment is only the first step in the process of improving your articulation and pronunciation. After you have identified your problem areas, you must decide which errors are interfering most with your speech. Do you reduce all unstressed vowels to /ə/? Do you have a lisp? Do you substitute /n/ for /ŋ/ in words like *running* or *laughing*? Often you must rely on the judgments of your classmates to assist you in choosing the most significant errors. Prioritizing your errors will help you to set goals. Goals can be of two types. Long-term goals that you set for articulation and pronunciation improvement are general objectives, such as "improve my articulation of /s/ phoneme" or "improve my pronunciation of /p/ in words where it should be silent or present." Long-term goals such as these cannot be accomplished immediately. You will break each long-term goal into a series of steps, or short-term goals. Each long-term goal that you achieve is the result of completing several short- term goals. If you had set this long-term goal—"Improve my articulation for /r/"—your short- term goals might be (1) correctly produce /r/ in the middle of words, (2) correctly produce /r/ in word-final position, and (3) correctly produce /r/ at the beginning of words. Each of these three short-term goals will bring you closer to better articulation of /r/ in every word where it appears.

There are two reasons for separating the task of improvement into steps. First, you can be overwhelmed by the idea of "fixing" your errors for /r/. This is analogous to saying "I'm going to be better at math." Where do you begin? You may be discouraged before you can start. Second, you can measure your improvement much more effectively if you take each of your short-term goals and consider them individually. A short-term goal such as "Correct my pronunciation of *ch* words of French origin (*chaperone, chef*)" will allow you to gauge your improvement toward the long-term goal of "Improve my pronunciation of problem words."

Evaluating Articulation and Pronunciation

Suppose you receive a term paper with a grade of C from your instructor. As you leaf through the pages, you expect to see some red-inked notations about spelling or grammar or organization. There are no comments! How can you be expected to improve your next assignment for a better grade? You confront the same type of situation when someone says to you that your speech isn't clear or that you mispronounce words. To aid you in your quest to improve your speech, we have separated errors of articulation and pronunciation into error types. Armed with the knowledge of how your speech or your classmates' speech has gone wrong, you will be prepared to structure an improvement program.

Types of Articulation Errors

There are four types of articulation errors—substitutions, omissions, distortions, and additions. A substitution is a replacement of one sound for another. Common substitutions are /w/ for /l/ or /r/ phonemes. /θ/ may be substituted for /s/. We often represent such errors as "w/r"; this means /w/ was substituted for /r/. Vowel sounds may be substituted for each other; this usually occurs when a diphthong is created—/uə/ may be substituted for /u/ in words such as *threw* and *who*.

An omission is a substitution of a kind. When you omit a phoneme, you are, essentially, replacing that sound with nothing. Omissions are quite rare in adult articulation. By the time you have reached adulthood, you are a capable producer of all English phonemes. Occasionally, you may come across someone who consistently omits the middle sound of a word or omits /s/ at the end of a word when a consonant precedes it (not as part of a dialect variation). Children make such errors more frequently than adults.

Sound distortions are more common. When you produce a phoneme that is "off-target"—that is, it is not the proper sound, yet it is not another phoneme—then you have made a distortion. Incomplete or excessive aspiration for /p/, dentalizing a /t/ (moving place of articulation to the teeth), and creating a fricativelike sound from /k/ are considered to be distortions. Your listener will probably recognize these sounds as the intended phoneme, but he will realize also that you have made an error in production.

Phoneme additions, like omissions, are not commonly found in adult articulation. Children do not usually make addition errors either. An addition error is exactly what it seems—a sound is always added to another phoneme. Some might classify the addition of /ə/ to /i/ in stressed syllables (such as *me*—/miə/ or *convenient*—/kʌnviənjənt/) as addition errors. However, we generally consider such changes to be diphthongs and would call these substitutions errors.

Articulation Errors and Articulation Disorders
At this point, we must consider what makes a series of articulation errors an articulation disorder. We discussed various types of articulation errors in the previous section. When these errors are made consistently and interfere with the intelligibility of your speech, then you have disordered articulation. Individuals who consistently substitute /w/ for /r/ or /θ/ for /s/ have an articulation disorder. Such errors may not make speech completely unintelligible, but they do disrupt communication. Articulation errors such as diphthongization of certain vowels in stressed syllables usually do not constitute disorders because diphthongs are not created for *all* vowels. This type of error does not affect intelligibility greatly. If you determine that you have an articulation disorder, you should seek assistance from a speech-language pathologist. He or she can design a therapeutic program to correct your problem.

Articulation Imprecision
Occasionally, you will hear someone whose speech sounds indistinct or "mushy." You know that his voice is loud enough, and you understand what he is saying. Many of the articulatory contacts, however, appear "off-target." Persons who are deaf often may have speech that sounds imprecise, as might persons who have cerebral palsy affecting their speech. Deaf or hearing-impaired individuals have never heard speech fully and must rely on their estimates of how to produce phonemes. Cerebral palsied persons have muscle weakness or rigidity that impairs their ability to move the articulators in smooth sequence. However, most imprecise articulation that is heard is due to careless, casual sound production. Evaluating this type of speech is difficult to do on a sound-by-sound basis. Most errors would be marked as distortions. Often this type of speech is most easily corrected by slowing speech rate and by making the effort to make all points of articulation contact.

Types of Pronunciation Errors
Articulation errors and pronunciation errors are easy to confuse. As you remember, an articulation error occurs when a phoneme is consistently misproduced. A pronunciation error occurs when a sound is omitted or is misproduced in some way inconsistently or in a certain position in a word. You know how to make a sound properly, but in certain contexts, often through the influence of neighboring sounds, the target phoneme is changed in some manner. The standard errors that we see in pronunciation are substitutions, omissions, additions, sound confusions, use of inappropriate stress, and syllable reduction or deletion.

Substitution errors in pronunciation are very common. You may substitute /d/ for /t/ in *matter* or *better*. /z/ may become /s/ in the verbs *excuse, house,* or *use*. You may substitute /ɛ/ for /ɪ/ in *six, kit,* or *bid*. Such changes typically take place because the target phoneme is next to another and it takes on some of its neighbor's characteristics. In *better* and *matter*, the /t/ becomes voiced like its neighborhood vowels. Often the speaker confuses a word with another, as in *excuse*. Words from a foreign source, such as *chef* or *chauffeur*, may keep their original pronunciation while we try in vain to change them to match English spelling rules.

Pronunciation omissions occur in words such as *preempt* or *exempt*, where /p/ is overwhelmed by /m/ and disappears. Similar errors are possible for /t/ in words like *mist, cast, mists,* and *casts*. /s/ is a more "powerful" sound; that is, it emits more sound energy than /t/. Omissions take place in rapid, casual conversation when the speaker does not make all articulatory contacts for all sounds and words such as *mist* and *mists* will sound similar.

Phoneme additions usually come about as a result of not knowing how a certain word is pronounced. *Pneumonia, knowledge,* and *bracelet* may be produced with the addition of /p/, /k/, and /ə/, respectively. Typically, you may mispronounce a word with an addition if you read the word and do not consult a dictionary for the appropriate pronunciation.

Most of us have been guilty of using inappropriate stress in pronouncing a particular word. You may know exactly how a certain word is pronounced, but in the execution of articulation, you may misprogram your articulators and produce, for example, *mischiévous* instead of *míschievous*. *Omnípotent* may become *omnipótent*. The best way to improve your ability to place word stress appropriately is to practice problem words until your ear becomes "trained" to hear the correct production. Generally, when you mispronounce a word by not stressing syllables properly, you tried to follow rules for pronouncing words and came across a word that was an exception.

Syllable reduction or deletion often results in a word that sounds half-"swallowed." In syllable reduction, you have "reduced" the vowel in a syllable to /ə/. Now, this is a natural process, and it usually becomes active in unstressed syllables. However, when *electoral* is pronounced /əlɛktərəl/ instead of /ilɛktərəl/, then you have lost some of the flavor of the word. Syllables may be lost in *terrible*—/tɛrbəl/ and *probably*—/prɑbli/.

When you carefully consider each sound as you pronounce a word, you will give each phoneme its proper emphasis in the word.

Dialect Variation

When you read Chapter 8, you noted that we included a section on dialect variation. We purposely used the term "variation" rather than "error" to avoid stigmatizing your dialect, if you have one, and to emphasize that differences in articulation and pronunciation based on dialect are acceptable. A dialect variation may be one of the "errors" we have mentioned above—substitution, omission, addition, syllable reduction/deletion, or stress change. We will take this opportunity to reconsider dialect issues.

Dialect Revisited

We must discuss dialect again because at this point you may be asking yourself, "What about *my* dialect?" "Do I have to change *my* speech?" We have attempted to present "Standard" English articulation and pronunciation in the main body of our discussion on sound production. "Nonstandard" English became the errors that were possible for each sound. Dialect variations are nonstandard in that they do not correspond to the Standard English pronunciation as described by dictionaries.

We have not included all possible dialect variations; certainly, we may have missed some of your sound differences. How do you determine if differences in your speech are dialect variations or errors? Listen to people around you in your community, if that is your native dialect area. If your compatriots speak as you do, then your sound differences *are* dialect variations. However, if you do *not* hear changes similar to your own, then you are probably making articulation or pronunciation errors.

The decision to change certain signature, distinctive characteristics of your dialect can be made only by you. We can discuss the relative attributes of standard and nonstandard dialects; the business world may not be so unbiased. If the profession you choose to enter places a high premium on Standard English usage, then you may decide to alter your speech accordingly for business situations. A dialect adds character and richness to the communication of its speaker. Dialect is a very real part of your social and cultural heritage and identity. Speech homogeneity has its disadvantages.

Coarticulation Errors

Errors related to coarticulation generally come about as a result of assimilation. As you remember, coarticulation happens when the articulators move simultaneously to produce two sounds. Consonants and vowels are coarticulated frequently. When you say *toe* or *cool*, the lips are rounding as you produce the consonant in anticipation of the vowel. Lip-rounding is not a consonant feature for /t/ or /k/, but the feature has "assimilated" to those two phonemes. Other examples of coarticulation that result in phoneme substitution are *rainbow* (/n/ becomes /m/); *miss you* (/s/ becomes /ʃ/ under influence of palatal glide); *I have to go* (/v/ becomes /f/ before voiceless consonant). Correction of coarticulation errors is possible if attention is directed to those sound combinations where it might occur. You will be able to anticipate some of the sound substitutions when you realize the adjacent phonemes differ only slightly in place of articulation. You can concentrate on making full articulator contacts.

ASSESSMENT

Using the Student Pronunciation/Articulation Test (SPAT)

You are ready now to evaluate your articulation and pronunciation. The SPAT (Appendix 4 in the back of this book) has been designed to test your production of all sounds of English in every position that they appear. Words with the target consonant phoneme are listed by manner of articulation (stop, fricative, nasal). Words containing the vowel phoneme are listed also by manner of articulation (front, mid, back). After word lists for assessing articulation, there is a word list for testing pronunciation. Finally, we have included a paragraph to evaluate phoneme production in running speech. Phonemes tend to be produced more accurately when they occur in a single word than when they are part of a sentence or paragraph. The test form, or "answer sheet," has spaces for recording errors. Target sounds are highlighted in the paragraph to make it easier to focus attention on articulation and pronunciation of the speaker.

You are already familiar with most of the terminology used on the test form. The words *initial, medial,* and *final* refer to the beginning, middle, and end positions, respectively, in each word in which a sound can appear. Several "blends" or consonant-consonant combinations are presented because some speakers tend to omit part of a blend.

Test Administration Procedures

The SPAT is most effective when used in a small group of three to four persons. One person elects to be the speaker and the remaining persons in the group serve as judges. As the speaker reads the word lists, judges mark errors as they happen—substitution, omission, distortion, addition. If you are acting as a judge, it is important that you focus only on the target phoneme. You can become easily distracted if you attempt to score all the phonemes in the word. For the pronunciation word lists, circle words that are mispronounced. If you are the speaker, do not try to be overcorrect as you read the pronunciation word lists. You want to produce words in the most representative way possible to assure that you know your pattern of errors.

After the word lists have been scored, the speaker should read the paragraph. On the judge's test form, you will notice that target phonemes have been highlighted. If you are a judge, focus your listening skills on that sound. After the speaker has read the paragraph, transfer errors to the appropriate space on the word list test form. Also note any other observations about sound errors that you happen to notice.

Analyzing Results

When everyone in your group has completed the testing process, you are ready to examine your articulation and pronunciation errors. List each of your errors, along with its error type (substitution, distortion, etc.). Separate the errors into articulation and pronunciation errors, consulting Chapter 8 if necessary. Your group members may be able to help you with other errors that they have observed in your speech. When you have completed your tally, you are prepared to move on to the real work of the evaluation process.

A PLAN FOR IMPROVEMENT

You are ready to enter the final phase of assessment. You are prepared to design your own program to correct your misarticulations and mispronunciations. The first step is to locate your strengths and weaknesses. We include strengths here because you can use your good articulation and pronunciation of sounds and words to carry over into those areas that are problematic for you. When you are listing your errors as well as your strengths, use your classmates to help you identify them. They may have noticed other problems that were not tested on the SPAT. Their objectivity can be useful to you. For example, you may have consistently distorted /s/ and /z/ in the medial position in the paragraph, but your production of those sounds in isolated words was good. To further assist you in selecting your good and bad sound productions, you may want to tape yourself reading the word lists and paragraph to listen for other positive and negative aspects of your articulation/pronunciation that the judges missed.

Now you can begin to target your priority areas for improvement. How do you decide what is important? You can apply several criteria while you examine your errors. Those errors that fulfill the most criteria should be tackled first. Factors you should consider are consistency of error, contribution to intelligibility, and ease of correction. An error is consistent when it occurs in all usages—in both words and paragraphs and in all word positions. You can use your judges to determine if the sound error measurably influenced the "understandability" of the word. Finally, you want to concentrate first on those sound errors that you can correct with fair ease. If you can rank your phoneme production errors along these criteria, you will be ready to move to the next step.

Setting goals, as we have discussed, will allow you to narrow your focus for improvement and to see measurable change. Choose one major goal, such as "Improve ability to distinguish between /f/ and /v/." Break this task into manageable parts: (1) Improve /f/–/v/ distinction in word-initial position, (2) improve /f/–/v/ distinction in word-final position, and (3) improve /f/–/v/ distinction is word-medial position. This approach may appear simplistic, but you have a real chance to change your articulation if you can see the possibility to easily accomplish part of your larger goal.

Finally, you are ready to get down to business. Choose one short-term goal. Gather your materials—word lists, sentences, paragraphs. You may find it helpful to create some of your own practice materials for your particular goal. For example, you may want to make up contrastive word pair lists for distinguishing between /f/ and /v/.

> feud—viewed
> file—vial
> feel—veal

You can always create nonsense words if that is helpful. As you collect practice materials, be sure to start with the easiest stimuli. Syllable and word practice will enable you to stabilize your sound before you move to sentences and paragraphs. Finally, you are ready to practice. Schedule approximately 20 to 30 minutes of practice three to four times per week. You may be able to give yourself less time. Tape your practice sessions. You may even choose to enlist someone to listen to you. After you feel confident that you can correct your target error, you might try some "negative" practice; that is, try to produce your phoneme the "old" way and contrast it with the "new," correct production.

If you follow these steps systematically, you will accomplish successfully your goals for correct phoneme production. Remember that other persons can assist you in being objective about your articulation and pronunciation. They will be your judges for sound improvement!

Chapter 10 will guide you in selecting goals and practice materials. Using it with Chapter 9, you will have the foundation to create articulation and pronunciation success.

TEST FORMAT

There are three tear-out sheets in Appendix 4. One is a stimulus sheet with a listing of target words and the phonetically balanced paragraph. The second is a test form, and the third is the answer key with target sounds highlighted. The paragraph has target sounds highlighted also to direct judges' listening skills.

STUDY QUESTIONS

1. What are four types of articulation errors?
2. What are the six possible pronunciation errors?
3. How do you differentiate between articulation errors and articulation disorders?
4. Are dialect variations articulation or pronunciation errors?
5. How do articulation errors and pronunciation errors differ?

Chapter 10

Articulation and Pronunciation Improvement

In Chapter 9, you assessed your articulation and pronunciation. By now, you have identified your weak areas and you are ready for the final step in this process. You are prepared now to improve your articulation and pronunciation. This chapter is designed so that you may take your specific goals and choose exercises that will help you to accomplish those goals. We have provided an outline for improvement; you will develop other word lists, sentences, and paragraphs as you need them for more practice.

USING THIS CHAPTER

You may have set your goals for improvement after reading Chapter 9. You can use objectives listed in this chapter. After you draw up your list of goals, you are ready to practice. Be sure to set a schedule for yourself that is realistic; an hour a day of practice is unnecessary and an impossible schedule to keep. Twenty to thirty minutes three times per week is a manageable amount of time. Start with production of your sound in syllables—for example, /bi/, /bɪ/, /bu/, /bæ/—and then move to practice with words, sentences, and finally paragraphs. Set aside some time during your day when you will practice your sound in the "real world"—e.g., really concentrate on good phoneme production for the first 15 minutes after lunch. After three to four weeks of concentrated attention and practice with your sound, you will find your new sound production becoming more natural and easy to make.

To improve pronunciation of specific words, we suggest that you read aloud through all the pronunciation lists at the end of the chapter, matching your pronunciation to the standard or nonstandard transcription. Add mispronounced words to your goals for improvement and practice, saying them until you have the "sound" of the word firmly in your memory.

IMPROVING LISTENING SKILLS

One benefit of learning about articulation and pronunciation and taking steps to improve your communication is that you become a better listener. Your listening skills increase as you begin to pay attention to various aspects of your speech. You may notice that some of your classmates seem to "listen" better than you do; that is, they can identify articulation errors and variations more quickly. This listening skill is not an inborn talent. They have learned to focus their attention and listen for specific sounds. They learned to listen better by listening!

It may be easier for you to begin your listening improvement by listening to others. Gradually, you can begin to rate the speech of others and compare it to your own production. Do you speak like other persons in your community of speakers? You may be helped by choosing someone whose speech you particularly admire. "Take apart" their speech and decide just what elements make it exemplary speech to you. Exercises such as this one will help you to analyze better your articulation and pronunciation and set specific goals for improvement.

WHEN TO ASK FOR HELP

While you have the ability to change and improve your speech, there are some errors that may not be possible for you to correct. If you have some poor articulation as a result of an "organic" problem—that is, muscle weakness, malformation of the oral structures (e.g., cleft palate), or teeth malocclusion—then you may require more assistance to help you compensate for these impairments. You may wish to change your foreign or nonstandard dialect to a standard one. Although we provide specific examples of dialect variations, these are not grouped by dialect. You may choose to seek help in designing a systematic program in changing your dialect.

The person who can best assist you with these improvements and changes is a speech-language pathologist. You may be more familiar with the term "speech therapist." This person is trained specifically in the anatomy and physiology of speech and in techniques to improve speech production. You can locate speech-language pathologists by looking in the yellow pages under that heading; by contacting your local university, if they have a speech pathology or communication disorders department; or by calling the American Speech-Language-Hearing Association (ASHA) at 1-800-638-8255. ASHA will be able to provide you with a listing of certified speech-language pathologists in your area.

DESIGN OF THIS CHAPTER

This chapter, like Chapter 8, follows a sound-by-sound format. We review the PMV (for consonants) and PMTL (for vowels) features, correct production, and description of errors. We have taken each of the possible articulation and pronunciation errors and written improvement objectives that you can use to set your own long- and short-term goals. We then present practice materials—specific exercises for each improvement objective and general word and sentence lists for each phoneme. At the end of this section, you will find passages for practice. Finally, we have collected words that are commonly mispronounced and arranged them by type of pronunciation error.

You are ready to go. Set your goals, design a practice schedule, and choose your practice materials. You may develop some practice materials of your own with your problem sound. Keep your goals realistic and your practice consistent and you will become an effective communicator—a goal within reach of all of us.

CONSONANTS

STOPS

SOUND: /p/

PMV Features: bilabial/stop/voiceless
Correct Production

> Lips are together. Pressure builds up in the oral cavity and is released in a silent burst.

Articulation Errors

1. Incomplete closure
2. Excessive aspiration

Pronunciation Errors

1. Omission of /p/ before consonants (*contempt*)
2. Addition of /p/ where it should be silent (*pneumonia*)
3. Confusion with /b/ as to degree of aspiration (foreign dialect)

Improvement Objectives

1. Make sure lip closure is adequate.
2. Avoid excessive aspiration—should be slight puff.
3. Be sure to make articulatory contact before consonants, although it is not necessary to release /p/.
4. Remember that /p/ is silent in *pneu-* prefix.
5. Make a clear distinction between /p/ and /b/. /b/ is *not* aspirated.

Practice Materials

Objective 3

Emphasize /p/:

kept	except	adapt
slept	intercept	disrupt
prompt	attempt	corrupt
adept	adopt	script

Objective 4

pneumonia   pneumograph
pneumothorax pneumogastric
pneumatic

Objective 5

pie	buy	park	bark
poll	bowl	pound	bound
peak	beak	pin	bin
peat	beat	Perth	berth
pill	bill	pout	bout
pass	bass	pounce	bounce

Words

pin		chop
peach		drip
pie		ship
pea		loop
pay		sheep
peck		ape
pole		help
push		nap
pine		soap
pen		jump

postage	papoose	scallop
penny	stupid	bishop
pilot	leopard	elope
powder	puppet	footstep
parade	happy	flagship
pocket	teapot	turnip

poem	popcorn	eavesdrop
portrait	report	ketchup
propeller	capital	membership
position	opinion	cantaloupe
postulate	supervise	citizenship
proponent	episode	periscope
passenger	capacity	cinemascope
possibility	superior	lollipop
potential	appearance	rattletrap
patented	octopus	fingertip

Sentences

1. The disappearance of the politician from Pittsburgh, Pennsylvania, was a puzzle to the police.
2. The pointer and the poodle slipped under the drainpipe and escaped.
3. Perhaps the purchase of the piano was inappropriate since I happen to be penniless.
4. The vice-president of the company was disappointed that the policy-holder pulled out of the contract.
5. Practically all the parishioners in the Protestant church paid for a part of the new chapel.
6. Patients staying in the hospital over a long period of time are provided only partial payment.
7. The apartment appeared to have been lived in by a pair of mice.
8. In her opinion, the value of the piece would drop significantly since the paint was chipped in several places.
9. The disappearance of the pearl drop earrings was kept quiet in the department store.
10. The recipe called for pumpkin, allspice, and ginger.
11. Please put your peach pits in the paper bag.
12. The police found the escapee sleeping against the mountain slope.
13. The couple eloped by slipping down the fire escape.
14. Apparently, Paul missed his appointment to feed the penguins at the animal park.
15. She shopped for slippers, diapers, and a special soap.

SOUND: /b/

PMV Features: bilabial/stop/voiceless
Correct Production

> Lips are together. The voiced airstream is released with a burst, but with less energy than /p/.

Articulation Errors

1. Incomplete lip closure
2. Excess aspiration (with resulting /p/-like sound

Pronunciation Errors

1. Addition of /ə/ in word-final position
2. Can distort to fricative (foreign dialect)

Improvement Objectives

1. Make sure lip closure is adequate.
2. Avoid excessive aspiration; /b/ is fully voiced.
3. Avoid overvoicing final /b/ so much that /ə/ is present.

Practice Materials

Objective 3

Produce /b/ only at the end of these words:

bib	grab	nab
cab	hub	rob
cub	job	rub
ebb	lab	sob
fib	mob	tab

Words

bag	club
bear	robe
booth	knob
bomb	cube
bite	snub
both	ebb
best	crab
bait	sob

ARTICULATION AND PRONUNCIATION

beam		web
badge		rib
budget	cowboy	sparerib
butcher	bubble	describe
bother	cabbage	bathrobe
ballot	blackboard	earlobe
billow	subway	cobweb
bison	bobbin	ice cube
before	obey	kabob
beauty	habit	proverb
banana	fabulous	
bulletin	hamburger	
burglary	somebody	
beginning	cucumber	
barnacle	hibernate	
beverage	nobody	
benefit	liberty	
bachelor	remember	

Sentences

1. The binding on the book was about to split.
2. The baritone singer from Abilene performed with the Boston Symphony.
3. The baby on the billboard bore a strange resemblance to my brother.
4. Rabbits love to nibble cabbage in Bob's garden.
5. The robber drew his saber and rode bareback into battle.
6. Bavarian blueberry cobbler is best with cream on the bottom.
7. Bananas from Colombia are a good buy this December.
8. Beverly wrote books on botany for a Broadway publisher.
9. Debbie and Bob remembered gambling in Bermuda.
10. Bonnie's back bent under the weight of boxes of balloons.
11. My brother bandaged the bruise on the beagle's forepaw.
12. The lumberjacks bedded down in the cabin during November while cutting timber.
13. Our cupboard had a number of beautiful blue dishes.
14. Build me a boat with billowing sails.
15. Bill learned the basics of baseball in his backyard.

SOUND: /t/

PMV Features: alveolar/stop/voiceless
Correct Production

> The tongue tip and blade make contact with the alveolar ridge. Pressure is built up behind the teeth and released with aspiration.

Articulation

1 Distortion when tongue moves to behind teeth

Pronunciation Errors

1 Omission when adjacent to /s/
2 Omission after a consonant in word-final position
3 Omission in medial position
4 Substitution of /d/ for /t/ in word- medial position

Improvement Objectives

1 Make the tongue contact firmly at the alveolar ridge.
2 Clearly pronounce /t/ when next to /s/.
3 Pronounce /t/ in word-final position.
4 Pronounce /t/ in word-medial position.
5 Use /t/ instead of /d/ when it appears in word-medial position.

Practice Materials
Objective 2

baste	host	rest
boost	just	toast
chest	least	west
east	most	wrist

Objective 3

craft	shift	except
gift	sift	corrupt
lift	adopt	erupt
raft	concept	subscript

Objectives 4, 5

cottage	gutter	mutter
better	flutter	putty
button	glitter	shatter
flatten	jetty	written
baited	grater	patent

Words

tan		boot
team		coat
talk		got
tame		mate
tea		gnat
toil		wheat
top		sweat
tool		put
tin		newt
time		eat

termite	cotton	narrate
topple	guitar	promote
temper	floating	faucet
tonsil	hotter	walnut
teaspoon	clutter	salute
today	pattern	repeat
toaster	sweater	sailboat
turkey	mitten	sunset

tentacle	compute	coconut
tornado	monitor	execute
tapestry	hospital	patriot
tuition	rattlesnake	ventilate
typewriter	delighted	apricot
technical	theater	celebrate
tangerine	rotation	thermostat
tablecloth	vitamin	destitute

Sentences

1 Take time to tackle the difficult problem.
2 Don't stop talking on my account.
3 There are too many trees in the forest.

4 Write the letter before it's too late.
5 He was too tall to fit in the seat.
6 Saturday will fit well into my time schedule.
7 It would be better at a different time.
8 My tonsils were taken out when I was twelve.
9 He wanted me to teach him to tell time.
10 She tripped up the last step.
11 It's against the law to litter.
12 Twilight is my favorite time.
13 Talk to the tall man on the left.
14 My little sister is a tattletale.
15 Twenty-two tall trees were cut to make that bridge.

SOUND: /d/

PMV Features: alveolar/stop/voiced
Correct Production

The tongue tip and blade make contact with the alveolar ridge. Pressure is built up behind the teeth and voiced air is released.

Articulation Errors

1 Distortion by moving tongue behind upper teeth

Pronunciation Errors

1 Omission of /d/ after consonant in word-final position
2 Omission of /d/ in word-medial position

Improvement Objectives

1 Make a clear production of /d/ by keeping tongue at alveolar ridge.
2 Pronounce /d/ after consonants in word-final position.
3 Pronounce /d/ in word-medial position.

Practice Materials
Objective 1
Pronounce these words:

ARTICULATION AND PRONUNCIATION

duel	dot	dupe
do	doe	duke
dawn	donate	dock
daunt		

Now try these:

deep	Dan	din
deal	day	deed
dip	date	dim
Dick		

Objective 2

cold	bagged	child
mild	sagged	grabbed
scold	rigged	buzzed
wild	ribbed	merged

Objective 3

chowder	ridden	Sweden
hidden	wedding	kidding
sadden	maiden	ladder
sudden	Eden	deaden

Words

day		pad
dice		head
dance		slide
duck		hand
dog		food
deep		wood
dine		head
deer		send
dart		lid
door		paid

demon	body	arcade
discuss	cider	salad
dozen	cadet	painted

diamond	vandal	ahead
dentist	lady	reviewed
dollar	feeding	railroad
danger	today	lemonade
defeat	radar	expected
daffodil	federal	fishing rod
diagram	rodeo	Robin Hood
diminish	nobody	Galahad
denial	medial	bodyguard
delicate	radio	leotard
decision	spider web	overboard
disorder	adequate	
dialect	moderate	

Sentences

1. The paddlewheel steamed into the Mississippi Delta with Dan aboard.
2. Dr. Donovan deemed it necessary to delay Mrs. Randall's scheduled delivery date.
3. Glazed doughnuts were Donald's delight.
4. The deputies altered the documents to avoid detection.
5. Edwina faced the fact that she was destined to develop the abandoned property.
6. Sandy's desire is to undermine Don's command of the children.
7. Donations were offered in the name of Mr. McDougall.
8. The condition of the deserted property offended those who wished to rent it.
9. Diamonds and emeralds hold a tremendous fascination for devoted collectors.
10. We wanted to postpone a definite decision.
11. Can you determine the difference between the two duets?
12. The residents of the building defended its dilapidated condition.
13. Diane and Derek hoped to be first on the deck for dancing.
14. My confidence was eroded after I received a D on the final.
15. Directors and producers met to discuss contract proceedings.

ARTICULATION AND PRONUNCIATION

SOUND: /k/

PMV Features: velar/stop/voiceless
Correct Production

The back of the tongue contacts the soft palate. Pressure is built up behind the tongue and the voiced airstream is released.

Articulation Errors

1. Distortion of /k/ from incomplete closure against soft palate

Pronunciation Errors

1. Addition of /k/ in words where it should be silent
2. Omission of /k/ when it follows /s/

Improvement Objectives

1. Make closure complete between tongue and soft palate.
2. Do not pronounce k in words beginning with *kn*.
3. Pronounce a clear /k/ when it follows /s/.

Practice Materials
Objective 2

knead	knee	knight	knapsack
kneel	knot	knit	knock
known	knuckle	knife	knew
knell	know	knave	knob

Objective 3

exhale	aches	mix	cracks
excite	coax	ox	rocks
expert	fix	six	jokes
boxer	fox	tax	hooks
mixer	hoax	cakes	lynx

Words

king		duck
cow		creek
cat		steak

CHAPTER 10

kiss		hook
cup		pick
key		sock
kite		black
kick		like
cake		wreck
comb		lack
candy	accept	critic
cabin	because	heartache
coffee	bobcat	shamrock
custom	bookcase	traffic
kindle	locust	antique
cushion	package	halfback
consume	vacant	basic
copper	income	public
canopy	accident	fantastic
cardinal	encourage	atomic
colorful	vacation	artichoke
kangaroo	calico	volcanic
cucumber	bakery	motorbike
courteous	decorate	gigantic
concentrate	pelican	buttonhook
casual	bicycle	storybook

Sentences

1. I simply can't cope with that color of carpet.
2. Could you carry my makeup in your case?
3. Can't you copy that character more clearly?
4. Please lock your bike wheel before you leave.
5. Look for the package in your locker.
6. I would like a cup of black coffee.
7. She locked her keys in the trunk of her car.
8. It looks like the blacktop is sticky.
9. The king's crown located in the castle was fantastic.
10. The local bookstore couldn't keep enough books.
11. Could you soak the dirty clothes for me?
12. Horseback riding cannot compete with hiking as my favorite sport.
13. We came right away because Kevin called us.

14 The kids peeked at the packages under the Christmas tree.

15 They talked back and forth on their walkie-talkies.

SOUND: /g/

PMV Features: velar/stop/voiced

Correct Production

The back of the tongue contacts the soft palate. Pressure is built up behind the tongue and the voiced airstream is released.

Articulation Errors

1 Distortion of /g/ from incomplete closure against soft palate

Pronunciation Errors

1 Distortion of /g/ when followed by stop consonant

2 Omission of /g/ in root words with *ng* spelling

3 Omission of /g/ in certain root words + suffixes

Improvement Objectives

1 Make closure complete between soft palate and tongue.

2 Pronounce /g/ fully when followed by stop consonant.

3 Pronounce /g/ in root words with *ng* spelling.

4 Pronounce /g/ in these words: *longer, stronger, younger.*

Practice Materials

Objective 2

hugged	chugged	rug burn
slugged	big bomb	tugboat
bagged	egg bagel	rag doll
bragged	big toe	vague twinge
sagged	stag dance	tag team

Objective 3

| angle | tangle | finger |
| linger | English | Bengal |

Chapter 10

mangle	hunger	England
wrangler	tingle	anguish

Words

goat		leg
game		dog
gate		big
gun		gag
gown		bug
golf		bag
guilt		frog
ghost		egg
give		stag
got		rogue
gallop	buggy	bulldog
garden	disguise	eggnog
govern	baggage	washrag
given	meager	nutmeg
gather	figure	hotdog
garlic	tugboat	fatigue
gaily	dugout	colleague
golden	wagon	intrigue
gasoline	recognize	dialogue
guardian	dignify	monologue
guarantee	begonia	catalog
gorilla	regulate	carpetbag
governor	vinegar	chili dog
gardenia	eagerly	polliwog
garrison	agony	moneybag
gallery	pentagon	underdog

Sentences

1 Groups of fans gathered to watch the golf match.
2 Mountain guides galloped to the borders of Mongolia.
3 Gaping gashes were gouged in the hillside.
4 The ghostly figure hugged the walls of the gorge.
5 Gandolf hid the dagger from the dragon.
6 Gulliver felt ragged from the slugging he had received.
7 The sugar bowl is against the garbage bags.

8   We garnished the goulash with gobs of sour cream.
9   The golden sun was gone in a glorious flash.
10 His haggard and gaunt appearance frightened the guests.
11 Can you guess that beagle's response to your signal?
12 A group of little girls giggled at the saga of Raggedy Ann.
13 Guessing games made Garfield disgusted.
14 Gone are the muggy days in the gaslight district.
15 Hugo had to walk on eggshells near the magnolias.

FRICATIVES

SOUND: /f/

PMV Features: labiodental/fricative/voiceless
Correct Production

   The upper teeth bite the lower lip. The voiceless airstream flows continuously.

Pronunciation Errors

   1   Distortion to /v/

Improvement Objectives

   1   Distinguish clearly between /f/ and /v/.

Practice Materials
   Objective 1

few	view	fend	vend
fine	vine	foul	vowel
safe	save	fuse	views
ferry	very	feud	viewed
fast	vast	folly	volley
fear	rear	fan	van

   Words

   foot   laugh
   fade   cough

five		thief
fast		safe
fight		beef
four		off
fate		roof
fat		tough
fine		elf
foal		graph
famine	coffee	belief
funny	defy	layoff
finger	enforce	kerchief
favor	comfort	sheriff
fairy	awful	cutoff
forget	effort	penknife
future	sofa	takeoff
follow	stuffing	rainproof
factory	artifact	waterproof
follower	official	telegraph
pharmacy	pacify	phonograph
festival	buffalo	bulletproof
federal	professor	handkerchief
fantasy	microphone	disbelief
physician	suffocate	hunting knife
faculty	telephone	weatherproof

Sentences

1. Follow those folks to the festival.
2. Felix enjoyed the comfort of an overstuffed sofa.
3. Officials made an effort to enforce safe driving regulations.
4. Laughter was heard from the pharmacy to the furniture store.
5. Photography was effective in the campaign to beautify the forest.
6. The family picnic ended with fireworks and a fantastic bonfire.
7. The snowfall covered the field with a fluffy powder.
8. The infantry defended the fort from a herd of foraging buffalo.
9. Jeff felt safe with a lifeguard at the pool.
10. Do you prefer French fries or corn fritters?
11. Fred fired up the furnace after hearing the frigid forecast.
12. The fireflies flitted in the fading light.

ARTICULATION AND PRONUNCIATION

13 I think you've had enough decaffeinated coffee.
14 Fran suffered from heartburn after eating fast food.
15 Her offer of favors belied her fickle nature.

SOUND: /v/

PMV Features: labiodental/fricative/voiced
Correct Production

    The upper teeth bite the lower lip. The voiced airstream escapes continuously.

Pronunciation Errors

1 Confusion of /f/–/v/ sounds
2 Substitution of /f/ for /v/ when /v/ is before voiceless consonant
3 Substitution of /b/ for /v/

Improvement Objectives

1 See first objective for /f/.
2 Emphasize voiced feature of /v/ when before voiceless consonant.
3 Avoid substituting /b/ for /v/.

Practice Materials
  Objective 1
    See exercises for /f/.

  Objective 2

I have to go.	roll of tape
I love Tom.	You've taken it.
I've taught that.	leave tonight
We've promised him.	live catch
You give to them.	slave trader

  Objective 3
    Contrast these words:

vote	boat	vest	best
vase	base	vane	bane
van	ban	vale	bail
vise	buys	vague	beg

Words

vat		save
vote		hive
verb		heave
van		stove
vet		love
vest		have
vast		sieve
vein		solve
void		five
vex		cave
villain	favor	behave
valley	seven	naive
velour	beaver	relieve
veto	oven	captive
velvet	gravy	above
varnish	river	archive
vacuum	clover	remove
vocal	evil	festive
vanilla	November	abusive
visual	discover	effective
violin	flavorful	positive
victory	adventure	relative
vehicle	boulevard	expensive
ventilate	elevate	negative
vitamin	average	decisive
vacation	provider	offensive

Sentences

1. David discovered the cave when he ventured down the beach.
2. I crave the heavenly flavor of vanilla ice cream.
3. In late November, a velvet snow covered the river valley.
4. Our victorious volleyball team was invited to several tournaments.
5. It was evident that investors in the invention would never make a profit.
6. Several mountain visitors vanished into the crevices after the avalanche.
7. The evil villain stuffed five little elves into his oven.
8. The vampire rose from the grave every evening at seven.
9. We ventured across the vast desert with the native caravan.

10 Harvey placed his beehives in a field by clover and violets.
11 The beaver with a cavity behaved very strangely.
12 Every time the Senate voted, the president threatened a veto.
13 Evelyn warmed the gravy on the stove while she rinsed the vegetables in the sieve.
14 Vanessa loved the valentine she received from Victor.
15 Soviet parents viewed television videos with disapproval.

SOUND: /θ/

PMV Features: linguadental/fricative/voiceless
Correct Production

　　The tongue lightly touches the upper teeth. A voiceless airstream escapes continuously.

Articulation Errors

　　1 Distortion of /θ/ to dentalized allophone

Pronunciation Errors

　　1 Omission of /θ/ before a consonant
　　2 Substitution of /f/ for /θ/
　　3 Substitution of /t/ or /s/ for /θ/

Improvement Objectives

　　1 Make sure tongue tip rests under upper teeth.
　　2 Produce /θ/ when it occurs before a consonant.
　　3 Produce /θ/ instead of /f/ for *th*.
　　4 Produce /θ/ instead of /t/ or /s/ for *th*.

Practice Materials
　Objective 2

fifth grade	faithful	birthday
bathmat	Kathleen	toothpaste
bath towel	mothball	withstand

CHAPTER 10

Objective 3

thirst	first	death	deaf
thought	fought	loath	loaf
thin	fin	myth	miff
think	fink	Ruth	roof
thigh	fie	lath	laugh

Objective 4

thick	tick	sick	cloth	clot	
thigh	tie	sigh	both	boat	
thug	tug		broth	brought	
thorn	torn		math	mat	mass
thing		sing	path	pat	pass

Words

thumb		tooth
thick		with
thorn		south
thaw		myth
thin		mouth
third		bath
thought		both
thing		teeth
three		wealth
thirst		earth
thimble	nothing	cheesecloth
thousand	healthy	mammoth
thunder	author	outgrowth
thermos	ethnics	dishcloth
thirty	toothpaste	birdbath
thistle	bathtub	beneath
Thursday	faithful	zenith
thirsty	earthquake	phone booth
therapy	stethoscope	tablecloth
thunderstorm	anything	underneath
thickening	cathedral	aftermath
thoroughbred	mythical	arrowsmith
thematic	pathetic	cottonmouth

Thanksgiving	faithfully	voting booth
thunderous	authorize	fortieth
thirty-three	marathon	twentieth

Sentences

1. The trees withered to nothing in the thin soil.
2. Think through the math problem thoroughly.
3. He thought their themes quite uncouth.
4. One fifth of all myths and rumors come through Ruth.
5. The wrath of his kith and kin caught Theodore without warning.
6. We thought that the tooth fairy brought thimbles for our thumbs.
7. Keith mourned the death of his third canary.
8. The thunder rumbled from north to south.
9. There's a marathon the third Tuesday of every month.
10. Athens was threatened with thundershowers on Thanksgiving.
11. The theater thrived on profits from the mammoth movie.
12. Thirteen thirsty players drank from the icy thermos.
13. His method of therapy was ruthless and unethical.
14. Wealthy patrons rebuilt the cathedral after the earthquake.
15. Beth chipped her tooth when she fell in the bathtub.

SOUND: /ð/

PMV Features: linguadental/fricative/voiced
Correct Production

The tongue lightly touches the upper teeth. A voiced airstream escapes continuously.

Articulation Errors

1. Substitution of /d/ for /ð/

Pronunciation Errors

1. Substitution of /v/ for /ð/
2. Substitution of /d/ for /ð/

CHAPTER 10

Improvement Objectives

1. Make sure that the tongue comes under the teeth and that airflow is continuous.
2. Produce /ð/ instead of /v/ for *th*.
3. Produce /ð/ instead of /d/ for *th*.

Practice Materials

Objective 1

than	Dan	thy	die
then	den	thence	dense
they	day	their	dare
those	doze	thee	Dee

Objective 2

than	van	clothe	clove
thy	vie	swathe	suave
thee	vee	loathes	loaves

Objective 3

See exercises for Objective 1.

Words

the	loathe
this	teethe
that	soothe
thus	smooth
their	clothe
thine	breathe
these	bathe
though	scythe
those	writhe
them	scathe

thereby	weather	bequeath
therein	feather	unclothe
thyself	lather	
themselves	although	
thenceforth	bother	
thereto	other	
thereof	mother	
therewith	either	

ARTICULATION AND PRONUNCIATION

189

thereabout
thereafter
thereunder
thereupon

another
together
weatherman
bathing suit
otherwise
withdrawal

Sentences

1. Neither mother nor father could soothe the teething baby.
2. The hunting knife was sheathed in smooth leather.
3. Don't breathe a word about their torn clothing.
4. My grandmother lives farther up the northern shore.
5. My brother loathes tight-fitting clothing.
6. Although he bequeathed his fortune to them, the heirs were unhappy.
7. Together they withdrew their entry into the featherweight boxing class.
8. The children enjoyed bathing by themselves, although Mother worried about their safety.
9. They walked farther up the hillside to gather heather for their mother.
10. In this seething summer weather, either bathing suits or shorts are acceptable.
11. Few of the others could withstand the incessant drum rhythms.
12. Theodore didn't bother to lather his face, thereby irritating it when shaving.
13. I gather that breathing is difficult for you in this weather.
14. The children smoothed their clothing after writhing and wrestling in the grass.
15. He could use neither one nor the other.

SOUND: /s/

PMV Features: alveolar/fricative/voiceless
Correct Production

   The tongue blade lightly contacts the alveolar ridge. Sides of the tongue touch the upper teeth. Continuous voiceless airstream leaves oral cavity through groove in tongue.

Articulation Errors

1. Substitution of /θ/ for /s/
2. Lateral lisp (air escapes through sides of tongue)
3. Distortion of /s/ by contacting alveolar ridge too firmly

Pronunciation Errors

1. Substitution of /ʃ/ for /s/

Improvement Objectives

1. Produce /s/ instead of /θ/. First, produce /θ/. Gradually pull tongue into mouth until tongue blade touches alveolar ridge. You should hear /s/.
2. Eliminate lateral /s/. (1) Try putting a straw in your mouth and direct /s/ through it. (2) Hold your finger in front of your nose and direct /s/ to that target.
3. Eliminate "whistling" /s/ by relaxing tongue contact with alveolar ridge.
4. Make clear, precise /s/, being sure to keep tongue forward.

Practice Materials
Objective 1

Contrast these words:

seem	theme	song	thong
sigh	thigh	pass	path
sin	thin	sick	thick
sum	thumb	mass	math

Objective 4

Produce clear /s/:

miss you	race you
pass you	less young
kiss you	crease your pants
chase your cat	dress your child

Words

soap	miss
sail	rice
sand	bus
sock	mouse
safe	face

ARTICULATION AND PRONUNCIATION

suit		dance
sew		geese
sink		dice
seal		goose
sort		kiss
simple	pencil	mattress
seven	whistle	famous
Sunday	seesaw	menace
sandal	castle	caboose
severe	bracelet	office
sailor	icing	process
city	baseball	vicious
cider	descent	reduce
civilian	casserole	generous
cinema	courtesy	infectious
satellite	classify	various
suitable	recipe	octopus
sensible	disable	humorous
solitude	jealousy	enormous
sympathy	producer	cleanliness
souvenir	episode	happiness

Sentences

1 Suddenly Sara sat upright on the sofa.
2 The scene ended slowly with a kiss.
3 The serpent slinked and slithered through the slime.
4 My boss sounded disgusted with the entire situation.
5 The missile whistled as it passed overhead.
6 Gus sought mussels by the sea.
7 The hideous moss draped the trees at sunset.
8 Let's settle this issue once and for all.
9 We saw the soldier on Independence Square.
10 Isometric exercise is excellent for your muscles.
11 Some people say society is sick.
12 The citizens sought sanctuary in the castle.
13 Listen closely to what I have to say.
14 The geese rested at sunset during their southern sojourn.
15 The mass media are responsible for explaining so many different issues.

SOUND: /z/

PMV Features: alveolar/fricative/voiced
Correct Production

> The tongue blade lightly contacts the alveolar ridge. Sides of the tongue touch the upper teeth. A continuous voiced airstream leaves the oral cavity through groove in tongue.

Articulation Errors

1. Substitution of /ð/ for /z/
2. Lateral lisp
3. Distortion of /z/ by contacting alveolar ridge too firmly
4. Substitution of /ʒ/ for /z/

Pronunciation Errors

1. Substitution of /s/ for /z/ in verbs

Improvement Objectives

1. Produce /z/ instead of /ð/. See first objective for /s/ for suggestions to produce /z/.
2. Eliminate lateral /z/. See second objective for /s/.
3. Eliminate "whistling" /z/. See third objective for /s/.
4. Make clear, precise /z/ by keeping tongue forward.
5. Produce *s* as /z/ in verbs in practice section.

Practice Materials

Objective 4

Produce clear /z/:

excuse you	because you
denies you	whose you
seize you	praise you

Objective 5

house /s/	(noun)	house /z/	(verb)
excuse /s/	(noun)	excuse /z/	(verb)
use /s/	(noun)	use /z/	(verb)
close /s/	(adjective)	close /z/	(verb)
abuse /s/	(noun)	abuse /z/	(verb)
refuse /s/	(noun)	refuse /z/	(verb)

ARTICULATION AND PRONUNCIATION

Words

zip		buzz
zinc		wise
zero		size
zoo		nose
zeal		hose
zest		ease
zap		says
zoom		phase
zone		has
czar		is

zipper	busy	amuse
zebra	frozen	arise
zero	laser	disguise
zither	razor	series
zenith	crazy	trapeze
zealous	visit	suppose
zip code	dozen	surprise
zany	cozy	oppose

xylophone	horizon	advertise
zeppelin	composer	exercise
zucchini	amazing	paralyze
zodiac	resume	tomatoes
zinnia	refusal	immunize
zinc oxide	embezzle	dramatize
Zambia	advisor	emphasize
Zanzibar	misery	memorize

Sentences

1 Maize is the word Indians used for corn.
2 The zoning laws protect the property of citizens.
3 Please grease the hinges, but don't lose the pins.
4 Classical jazz is my favorite form of music.
5 My cousin auditioned for a Broadway musical.
6 The ladies of the club were amazingly pleasant.
7 It was one of those hazy, lazy, crazy days of summer.
8 The bindings on his skis caused him to fall.
9 Please meet me at the zoological gardens.
10 I was amazed by the Lippizan stallions in Vienna.

11 The zany activities of the zebras amused the crowd.

12 A dozen prisoners were visited by their families.

13 The newspaper reported the score as zero to zero.

14 The buzzard scours the desert for carrion.

15 Please dispose of these less than desirable old trousers.

SOUND: /ʃ/

PMV Features: palatal/fricative/voiceless
Correct Production

The body of the tongue almost meets the palate. The tongue tip and blade are pointed to the alveolar ridge. The sides of the tongue touch the upper teeth and the voiceless airstream is directed through a shallow groove in the tongue.

Articulation Errors

1 Distortion of /ʃ/ by an interdental or lateral lisp

Pronunciation Errors

1 Substitution of /t/ for /ʃ/ in words with *ch* spelling

2 Substitution of /t/ for /ʃ/ in Spanish-English dialect

Improvement Objectives

1 Produce a clear /ʃ/. Use techniques similar to those for /s/ for centralizing your airflow and eliminating a "slushy" sound.

2 Correctly produce words with *ch* spelling (of French origin).

3 Produce /ʃ/ instead of /t/. Do not allow your tongue to make contact for /t/.

Practice Materials

Objective 2

These words should be produced with initial /ʃ/:

chaise	champagne	chaperone
chef	chartreuse	chivalry
chic	chauffeur	
chagrin	chevron	
chalet	chiffon	
chamois	chandelier	

ARTICULATION AND PRONUNCIATION

Objective 3

Contrast these words:

chair	share	cheer	sheer
cheap	sheep	chew	shoe
cheat	sheet	chin	shin
choose	shoes	chose	shows
chop	shop	chore	shore
matches	mashes	batch	bash
leech	leash	much	mush
watch	wash	witch	wish

Words

ship		dish
shoe		brush
shade		leash
shell		ash
shop		hush
sheep		bush
shape		fresh
share		wish
sharp		lash
shelf		push
shallow	cashew	English
shovel	cushion	goulash
shingle	lashes	paintbrush
shadow	tissue	eyelash
sugar	ocean	finish
shoulder	issue	ambush
shiny	lotion	publish
shudder	mission	selfish
Chicago	attention	establish
Chevrolet	musician	licorice
chaperone	parachute	astonish
chandelier	fisherman	demolish
chivalry	nourishment	replenish
sheepherder	official	accomplish
sugar cane	emotion	underbrush
shuffleboard	fishing pole	extinguish

Sentences

1. A hush fell on the freshman class when the principal issued a sharp warning.
2. This machine can crush the cans and push them toward the trash can.
3. The shadows shade the sheep under the sugar maple.
4. The fishermen saw the sharp fin of a shark in the shallow shoals.
5. Sharon was sure that an admission of guilt would be issued.
6. The blushing bride wiped tears from her lashes with a tissue.
7. I was wishing we had shopped for shells instead of buying shirts at Sherman's T-Shirt Shop.
8. The shortcake recipe called for marshmallows and crushed cashews.
9. We sat in the shade, enjoying the fresh ocean breeze.
10. The shape of an old Spanish mission was used for the brochure.
11. You buy insurance to shield your possessions.
12. The shallow freshman wished fashion was a course of study.
13. In a flash, the bottle of lotion had fallen from the shelf.
14. Sherry wished that Marsha would brush the ashes from the grate.
15. The patient was in shock with a concussion and blood gushing from a sharp wound.

SOUND: /ʒ/

PMV Features: palatal/fricative/voiced
Correct Production

The body of the tongue almost meets the palate. The tongue tip and blade are pointed to the alveolar ridge. The sides of the tongue touch the upper teeth and the voiced airstream is directed through a shallow groove in the tongue.

Articulation Errors

1. Distortion of /ʒ/ by an interdental or lateral lisp

Pronunciation Errors

1. Substitution of /dʒ/ for /ʒ/

Improvement Objectives

1. Produce a clear /ʒ/. Use techniques similar to those for /s/ for centralizing your airflow and eliminating "slushy" sound.
2. Produce /ʒ/ instead of /dʒ/ in appropriate words.

Practice Materials
Objective 2
Final *g* should be pronounced /ʒ/:

garage	massage	rouge
corsage	prestige	sabotage
camouflage	beige	mirage

Words

	rouge
	beige
	loge
leisure	garage
vision	corsage
seizure	massage
fusion	mirage
treasure	prestige
version	
pleasure	
measure	
decision	camouflage
hosiery	sabotage
evasion	
conclusion	
amnesia	
explosion	
casual	
persuasion	

Sentences

1. A glazier is a most usual craftsman.
2. Their decision about anesthesia was based on her seizure problems.
3. Her azure blue and beige Persian rug was her greatest treasure.
4. The collision resulted from his casual attention to the road.

5 The dictator and his entourage went into seclusion after the regime collapsed.

6 Usually, I believe that children's television viewing should be under supervision.

7 The invasion in Asia resulted in division of the territory.

8 Corrosion of the rock and erosion from wind and rain created a fissure.

9 My vision of a clean garage was a simple mirage.

10 His illusion of prestige was destroyed by a beige leisure suit.

SOUND: /h/

PMV Features: glottal/fricative/voiceless
Correct Production

The articulators assume no special position. Vocal folds are apart and the airflow exits continuously.

Pronunciation Errors

1 Omission of /h/ in unstressed syllables or words
2 Omission of /h/ before /ju/
3 Distortion of /h/ to fricative

Improvement Objectives

1 Pronounce /h/ where it occurs in unstressed positions.
2 Pronounce /h/ when it occurs before /ju/.
3 Keep production of /h/ free of any contribution from articulators, especially tongue and pharynx.

Practice Materials
  Objective 1
    Emphasize /h/:

| groundhog | fish hook | keyhole | beehive |
| overhaul | forehead | dollhouse | bellhop |

ARTICULATION AND PRONUNCIATION

Objective 2

hue	human	humiliation
huge	Houston	
humility	humus	

Words

hat
house
hot
hair
hole
hog
hill
hose
heart
hop

happy	beehive
hotel	lighthouse
harness	behold
hollow	keyhole
hockey	behind
human	tree house
hungry	sweetheart
handle	inhale

hamburger	behavior
history	tomahawk
happiness	grasshopper
however	anyhow
holiday	inherit
whoever	overhaul
harmonize	inhibit
helium	unhappy

Sentences

1 Hazel used henna to dye her hair.
2 One chorus rehearsed the harmony for the concert at city hall.
3 Helen hurried to the hockey rink for practice.
4 Hollyhocks and hyacinths grew side by side near the house.

5   Happiness is grilled hot dogs and hamburgers.
6   The halfback also competed in the high jump in high school.
7   You'll find my handkerchiefs on a shelf behind the hangers.
8   Herb was unhappy when his rocking horse and hula hoop disappeared in the move to Hawaii.
9   He hit a home run in his bid for the Hall of Fame.
10 Henry and his sweetheart dressed as hobos for Halloween.
11 The foghorn at the lighthouse warned the ships of the approaching hurricane.
12 The helicopter landed behind the hothouse and hurried the heart attack patient to the hospital.
13 Harvey gathered honey from the beehives he kept near his house.
14 The hog looked hilarious trying to hide in the mouse hole.
15 The whole chorus sang the hymn to herald the season.

AFFRICATES

SOUND: /tʃ/

PMV Features: palato-alveolar/affricate/voiceless
Correct Production

   The tongue assumes position for /t/. Airflow is stopped briefly, then released as for /ʃ/.

Articulation Errors

   1   Distortion of /tʃ/ by a lisp

Pronunciation Errors

   1   Substitution of /ʃ/ for /tʃ/ after a consonant

Improvement Objectives

   1   Correct your lisp as mentioned for /s/.
   2   Make /t/ contact in /tʃ/ after a consonant.

ARTICULATION AND PRONUNCIATION

Practice Materials
Objective 2
Produce /tʃ/ after consonant:

actual	picture	rapture
conjecture	structure	puncture
fixture	sculpture	texture
exchange	culture	rupture

Words

chair		teach
chew		bench
church		watch
cheese		witch
change		couch
check		wretch
chin		catch
chip		preach
chain		march
chore		etch

chamber	kitchen	approach
chapter	matches	detach
cheetah	preacher	impeach
chowder	catcher	sandwich
chicken	pitcher	ostrich
chimney	patches	dispatch
chatter	ditches	attach
checkmate	teacher	enrich

champion	actual	avalanche
charity	fluctuate	butterscotch
chimpanzee	furniture	pocket watch
chewing gum	anchovy	
checkerboard	ritual	
changeable	treacherous	
chicken pox	adventure	
cheerily	amateur	

Sentences

1 We sat on a bench at the beach munching chocolate chip cookies.
2 Each March our church has a chicken dinner.

3   The aroma of chicken frying and cherry pies baking poured from the kitchen.
4   The preacher clutched at his chest to capture their attention.
5   The witches hatched a plan to cast a charm on Rachel.
6   Charlie and Chuck each cheated at checkers.
7   A woodchuck chewed notches in our birch tree.
8   A cultural exchange is planned between the two cello virtuosos.
9   The discouraged pitcher and catcher watched the rest of the game from the bench.
10 The teacher gave each child a chore and charted their success.
11 His wretched cat, Patches, scratched my chin.
12 We purchased a couch and chair with checkered upholstery.
13 We munched cheddar cheese and watched "Charlie and the Chocolate Factory" on the children's channel.
14 He chose to eat brunch and skip the cheesecake.
15 Chet was not exactly enchanted with his lunch of anchovy sandwiches.

SOUND: /dʒ/

PMV Features: palato- alveolar/affricate/voiced
Correct Production

   The tongue assumes position for /d/. Airflow is stopped briefly, then released as for /ʒ/.

Articulation Errors

   1 Distortion of /dʒ/ by any lisp

Improvement Objectives

   1 Correct your lisp as suggested in objectives for /s/.

Practice Materials
Words

   jam   fudge
   judge   bridge
   gem   badge

ARTICULATION AND PRONUNCIATION

just		cage
jet		siege
June		bulge
jar		age
jeep		merge
job		ledge
juice		rage
gentle	eject	cabbage
genius	adjust	garbage
July	enjoy	allege
jelly	banjo	manage
ginger	adjourn	passage
jewel	soldier	hostage
jungle	hedges	image
journal	angel	voyage
janitor	adjective	average
genuine	engagement	advantage
general	gingerbread	heritage
juniper	educate	foliage
jovial	digestion	privilege
juvenile	majestic	discourage
gigantic	agency	pilgrimage
genetic	oxygen	percentage

Sentences

1. Your average gentle giant just lacks courage.
2. The aging soldier felt dejected and discouraged.
3. Janet was jilted by George but refused to return her gem of an engagement ring.
4. We enjoyed jelly rolls, gingerbread, and fudge at the January bake sale.
5. Jimmy amused the jet set crowds with his banjo.
6. Jewels bulged from the pockets of his jeans.
7. I just don't understand how Jello congeals.
8. In June and July, educators take a break.
9. The major and general enjoy games of cribbage and bridge.
10. The judge denied the objection and the jury adjourned to deliberate.
11. Junior's job was to adjust the jars on the ledge.
12. Ginger and Eugene badgered each other throughout their marriage.

13 A majority of geologists judged the age of the fossil to be 3 million years.

14 Only a genius can recover his luggage and emerge unscathed at the baggage claim center.

15 The savage blaze and raging flames only singed the badger's tail.

NASALS

SOUND: /m/

PMV Features: bilabial/nasal/voiced
Correct Production

Lips are pressed together. The velum is lowered and voiced airflow exits through the nose.

Articulation Errors

1 Substitution of /b/ for /m/

Pronunciation Errors

1 Omission of /m/ before consonant
2 Substitution of /n/ for /m/ next to alveolar consonant

Improvement Objectives

1 Make sure that /m/ is fully nasal. No air should escape through the mouth.
2 Produce /m/ before consonants.
3 Do not let influence of alveolar consonant change /m/ to /n/.

Practice Materials
Objective 1
Contrast these words:

mail	bail	melt	belt	muss	bus
mall	ball	mare	bare	mite	bite
mash	bash	man	ban	mob	Bob
mile	bile	more	bore	mug	bug
mill	bill	mold	bold	my	by

ARTICULATION AND PRONUNCIATION

Objective 2
Emphasize /m/:

temple	lumber	whimsical
thimble	preempt	insomnia
amnesia	September	amphibian
cumbersome	November	limber

Objective 3

warmth	hymnal	homely
sometime	hemlock	admonition
streamed	himself	timed
comely		

Words

mint		ham
mail		fame
math		crumb
meal		cream
may		lamb
mask		dumb
mate		plum
mike		comb
mad		clam
mine		steam
market	amount	become
mother	summer	esteem
machine	farmer	boredom
manner	famous	atom
marry	mailman	random
mirror	someone	album
muscle	comic	phoneme
medal	summer	system
magician	animal	accustom
manual	camera	helium
motorboat	ceramic	stadium
microphone	cinnamon	calcium
melody	domestic	realism
magazine	ambulance	sodium
moccasin	admiral	diagram
medium	dominate	overtime

CHAPTER 10

Sentences

1. Martin ran a tree trimming and mowing service every summer.
2. The famous comedienne imitated Mae West.
3. The team's mascot is a mutt named Marvin.
4. Most of my money made some interest.
5. The symptoms of boredom are finger drumming and mindless humor.
6. The famished guests enjoyed clam chowder, baked ham, and crumb cake.
7. Martha's mouth moved in time to the music.
8. Many movie stars are expected to meet at the ceremony.
9. He claimed he would move mountains to make his dream come true.
10. Michelle's moments as a rock musician were fleeting; she couldn't manage to make the manager's audition.
11. The committee member made a motion to dismiss the meeting.
12. Each summer the mothers maintain a lemonade and limeade stand.
13. The Maine coast was teeming with mussels of prime quality.
14. The famous musician's amplifier had symptoms of malfunction.
15. The monastery bells chimed each Monday before mass.

SOUND: /n/

PMV Features: alveolar/nasal/voiced
Correct Production

The tongue tip and blade touch the alveolar ridge. The velum is lowered and voiced airflow exits through the nose.

Pronunciation Errors

1. Substitution of /ŋ/ for /n/ before /k/, /g/
2. Substitution of /m/ for /n/ before /p/, /b/

Improvement Objectives

1. Do not let /n/ take on place features of bilabial or velar consonants.

ARTICULATION AND PRONUNCIATION

Practice Materials
Objective 1

inborn	tranquil	income
input	conquer	enclose
unbeaten	sunglasses	unkind
unpack	mankind	unkempt

Words

nut		vein
nail		brown
name		phone
nap		inn
knife		noun
nose		stone
nest		frown
net		green
nine		rain
note		chin

nation	vanish	airplane
navy	union	contain
nickel	pony	fortune
normal	unit	human
knuckle	cannon	lion
narrow	minute	raccoon
noisy	dinner	motion
notice	tennis	machine

nectarine	canary	aspirin
notary	mineral	determine
nursery	opener	location
natural	scenery	submarine
nautical	banana	hurricane
nocturnal	benefit	magazine
nobody	general	collision
nitrogen	prisoner	skeleton

Sentences

1 The novelty of the dragon puppet had worn off by the end of the show.
2 Linda poured chlorine into the cistern to disinfect the rain water.

3 The northern Nevada boundary lands are known for their unique terrain.
4 Neil vowed never to knuckle under pressure from subordinates.
5 The night nurse supervisor for the nursery never neglected to turn the newborn infants.
6 Nicole's nephew went to Phoenix to hunt his fortune.
7 Sheldon sought sunshine to enhance his prized suntan.
8 I wound the thread around the bobbin of the sewing machine.
9 Affection between Aileen and Calvin deepened in the remaining days.
10 Bonnie was found innocent of all charges pertaining to the incident.
11 Several Italian immigrants came from Naples to settle in New York City.
12 November is the month when elections become the high point of most news programs.
13 Robin resigned from the company after finding a new job.
14 Mr. Edison's inventions are renowned for their contributions to humanity.
15 Erin explained to her parents that she intended to determine her own future.

SOUND: /ŋ/

PMV Features: velar/nasal/voiced
Correct Production

The body of the tongue is raised to meet the lowered velum. Voiced airstream is directed through the nose.

Pronunciation Errors

1 Addition of /g/ to *ng* words ending in /ŋ/
2 Substitution of /n/ for /ŋ/ in Southern dialect

Improvement Objectives

1 Remember the *ng* spelling stands for /ŋ/ in word-final position.
2 Pronounce *-ing* as /ŋ/.

ARTICULATION AND PRONUNCIATION

Practice Materials

Objective 1

Practice these words, being sure *not* to make the stop /g/ at the end:

bring	ring	swing
cling	sing	thing
fang	spring	wrong
long	strong	tongue

Objective 2

Say these words:

king	sing
ding	ring

Now, practice these sequences:

park	king	parking
make	king	making
find	ding	finding
load	ding	loading
pass	sing	passing
kiss	sing	kissing
color	ring	coloring
care	ring	caring

Words

sing
fang
bring
long
ring
bang
wrong
hang
king
prong

angle	belong
hanger	morning
sink	being

CHAPTER 10

single	asking
finger	finding
lengthy	crying
junk	sharing
singer	trying
fingernail	collapsing
elongate	coloring
belonging	promoting
lingering	rewarding
fingertip	wedding ring
angora	motoring
fingerprint	settling
hungering	lingering

Sentences

1. The bee sting got me running to the nearest spring.
2. Mother always detested cutting my bangs.
3. A single shingle was absent from the roofing materials.
4. The English king went to Hong Kong, viewing other kingdoms along the way.
5. One of the kangaroo's endearing qualities is its jumping skill.
6. Evening was falling as Mr. Harding returned to the jungle.
7. The length of the snake's fangs was frightening.
8. The mongoose came charging across the angle of the field to attack the cobra.
9. Sailing and jogging are among my favorite outdoor activities.
10. Angus was listening for the marauding gangs from the hilltop.

GLIDES

SOUND: /w/

PMV Features: bilabial/glide/voiced
Correct Production

The back of the tongue is raised to the palate. Lips are rounded. Breath exits through the lips.

Pronunciation Errors

   1 Some words may be produced with aspiration.

Improvement Objectives

   1 You may choose to produce /w/ with aspiration in certain words.

Practice Materials
Objective 1
Produce /w/ with aspiration:

where	while	wheel
why	whale	white
when	wheat	

Words

word
witch
wave
world
wool
wolf
web
wash
war
walk

waffle	towel
window	flower
weather	away
water	awhile
wagon	cobweb
walrus	reward
welcome	someone
windshield	hallway

wallpaper	Halloween
waterproof	fireworks
wonderful	ferris wheel
wintergreen	spider web
woodpecker	rainwater
Washington	hideaway
waterfall	unaware
wilderness	unwilling

Sentences

1. Wayne waved at Wilma as he walked down the highway.
2. Weather on Waikiki is affected by the trade winds.
3. Warren may qualify for the work program if he waits.
4. Walter wanted to water ski just to the point where the waves break.
5. Wanda waged a weary battle to win approval of the water bill.
6. Wind storms were a regular feature of winter in Wichita.
7. Wallace works on Wall Street, specializing in West German stock quotes.
8. Gwen languished on a beach in the West Indies.
9. The heat wave on Key West wore out the weary tourists.
10. Mr. Wagoner was an eyewitness to the freeway accident.
11. If you look toward the square, you may catch a quick glimpse of the queen as her motorcade swings around the corner.
12. Twenty squirrels walked along the wire above Washington Square.
13. The waitress brought some chocolate wafers at the end of the wonderful meal.
14. Mr. Wilson desperately wanted his daughter's wedding to occur next week.
15. The woodpecker made a worrisome sound as it sought worms in the willow.

SOUND: /j/

PMV Features: palatal/glide/voiced
Correct Production

> Tongue tip and blade are raised to alveolar ridge. The tongue glides into position for the following vowels.

Pronunciation Errors

1. Addition of /j/ before /u/ as alternative production
2. Substitution of /j/ for /dʒ/ in Scandinavian English

Improvement Objectives

1. Produce /u/ without /j/.

ARTICULATION AND PRONUNCIATION

2 Remember that the alphabet letter *j* represents /dʒ/.

Practice Materials
Objective 1
Practice /u/ without /j/:

stew	June	dilute
steward	food	spoon
Tuesday	tune	new

Words

yolk
yarn
yawn
yes
yell
you
yam
yeast
yet
yacht

union	million
unique	onion
yearbook	crayon
yellow	lawyer
yogurt	senior
yourself	canyon
yardstick	amuse
youngster	value

uniform	abusive
utensil	behavior
yesterday	monument
utilize	royalty
unicorn	stimulate
eulogy	transfusion
unity	familiar
Yellowstone	annual

Sentences

1 The youngest member of the royal family remained loyal to his governess.

2 *Tom Sawyer* was a regular feature of each school year's reading assignments.
3 The lawyer yearned to yodel in the midst of a court session.
4 Amelia made a valiant effort not to cry when slicing onions.
5 Mr. York dreamed of visiting the Himalayas, the Yucatan, and Tokyo.
6 Julian found a herd of stallions in the Grand Canyon.
7 Young coyotes yelped for their mothers on the borders of Yosemite National Park.
8 Yesterday, Yolanda went to the yard sale to find some old yearbooks.
9 The Mayans refused to remain loyal to the Europeans.
10 Prince William mounted a rebellion against the Duke of York.
11 The Yale sailing crew yelled in victory as their yacht crossed the finish line.
12 In this recipe, you use yogurt instead of yeast.
13 Yorkshire yields some of the best yearlings annually.
14 Each New Year's Eve, we celebrate with fireworks in the front yard.
15 Mr. Sawyer prepared a unique concoction using tortillas, egg yolks, and papayas.

SOUND: /r/

PMV Features: palatal/glide/voiced
Correct Production

The midportion of the tongue is tightened. Tongue tip is pointed up or down. The sides of the tongue contact the upper teeth.

Articulation Errors

1 Substitution of /w/ for /r/

Pronunciation Errors

1 Substitution of /ə/ for /r/ after vowels or before consonants
2 Addition of /r/ between words that end and begin with a vowel

ARTICULATION AND PRONUNCIATION

215

Improvement Objectives

1. Produce /r/ correctly. As you attempt /r/, raise and curl the tongue. You might try making the /ʒ/ sound, then tightening the tongue and dropping tongue tip slightly.
2. Produce /r/ when *r* occurs in word-final position.
3. Do not add /r/ between words.

Practice Materials

Objective 2

Practice making a clear, final /r/:

hour	clear	tire	year
hair	floor	your	leer
gear	hire	stair	sour
star	oar	smear	core

Objective 3

Make a clear separation between the two words:

saw Amy	stay away	chew on
in lieu of	gray afternoon	see over
my uncle	tray of cookies	free of it
know of	zoo animal	go away

Words

red		air
rope		shore
rock		steer
rye		far
run		four
rain		gear
rake		scar
rose		tear
read		war
right		flair
rainbow	berry	appear
radish	carrot	despair
robin	borrow	umpire
razor	caress	adore

rabbit	daring	desire
robot	syrup	guitar
raisin	earring	before
rattle	arrow	entire
rodent	parade	sincere
reaction	arrival	engineer
radio	area	hemisphere
resemble	narration	sycamore
restaurant	kerosene	souvenir
recital	faraway	seminar
recognize	director	pioneer
radical	paradise	disappear
robbery	century	reservoir

Sentences

1 Remember to write down your area code when you give me your phone number.
2 Harry was required to register for the course in arithmetic.
3 Rebecca remained at a respectful distance from the reigning dignitary.
4 Rick realized that it was redundant to receive two daily newspapers.
5 Roxanne's roommate rented her car to a neighboring sophomore.
6 Harriet always dreams of traveling to the Orient to view its archaeological treasures.
7 Hurricane Martin threatened the Florida coastal region with driving rains and high tides.
8 Carol cherished her grandmother's rocking chair.
9 Ron rubbed his wrist after spraining it during racquetball.
10 Rhonda was reluctant to erase her answer even though she was uncertain it was correct.
11 The soldier was afraid that his parachute wouldn't open when necessary.
12 The Roosevelt reunion occurred every year during September.
13 The florist arranged the flowers and greenery in an attractive display.
14 Rose and Arthur braved the rugged terrain to revisit the Roman ruins.
15 Rodney rode his tricycle down the street to his friend's driveway.

ARTICULATION AND PRONUNCIATION

SOUND: /l/

PMV Features: alveolar/glide/voiced
Correct Production

> The tip of the tongue touches the alveolar ridge. The sides of the tongue drop to let the voiced airstream pass.

Articulation Errors

> 1 Substitution of /w/ for /l/

Pronunciation Errors

> 1 Omission of /l/ before consonants
> 2 Addition of /l/ when it should be silent
> 3 Confusion of /r/ and /l/ phonemes in Oriental English

Improvement Objectives

> 1 Produce /l/ correctly; no /w/ substitution. To produce /l/ properly, say /ɑ/, then raise tongue tip slowly to alveolar ridge—/ɑ/, /lɑ/, /ɑ/, /lɑ/. Then practice making /l/ contact without vowel.
> 2 Pronounce /l/ before consonants.
> 3 Do not add /l/ when it should be silent.
> 4 Learn the articulation distinction between /r/ and /l/.

Practice Materials
Objective 2
Pronounce /l/:

gulp	help	false	talc
help	bolt	else	self
scalp	belt	elk	golf
yelp	salt	hulk	shelf
told	melt	milk	mild

Objective 3
Don't pronounce /l/:

| walk | calf | almond |
| chalk | salmon | |

Objective 4
Contrast these words:

lace	race	lip	rip	lug	rug
lack	rack	lob	rob	low	row
lag	rag	loot	root	lime	rhyme
leak	reek	loom	room	lead	read
lice	rice	lush	rush	law	raw

Words

love
lamp
lass
land
lip
lake
laugh
leaf
lobe
lie

tail
coal
ball
bull
stool
hole
pill
hill
nail
small

ladder
lettuce
lemon
little
lion
lather
launder
loser

alive
jolly
balloon
yellow
salad
follow
silly
eyelid

airmail
cancel
football
exile
recall
vowel
motel
symbol

ladybug
limousine
lemonade
lavender
lottery
lifesaver
lieutenant
leadership

gorilla
popular
skeleton
violet
illusion
regulate
telescope
celery

aerial
annual
factual
buttonhole
mutual
manual
initial

Sentences

1 Gail feels that learning Latin would appeal to Louise.
2 Sally liked all melons, but especially canteloupes.

3 The ecology movement would not allow development of the nuclear plant.
4 Lilly wanted a silver polish that would clean her silver completely.
5 Luke, the collie, howled when he was left alone on the landing.
6 Lowland gorillas like secluded hollows in the hills below Mt. Kilimanjaro.
7 The girls' high school volleyball team won the regionals.
8 Melinda was notified of the congratulatory telegram by telephone initially.
9 The scholar found it difficult to be tolerant of misspellings in his son's schoolwork.
10 Evelyn believed, as a child, that Disneyland was a true fairyland.
11 As you look down the alley, you'll see the pile of trash that must be hauled away.
12 Oil drilling near the North Pole was felt to have caused early melting of the polar ice cap.
13 The college football rally was the highlight for the cheerleaders.
14 Wallace likes to broil halibut, sole, and flounder for his family.
15 Lockers lined the length of the hallway on the high school's first floor.

VOWELS

FRONT

SOUND: /i/

PMTL Features: high/front/tense/unrounded
Correct Production

  The front of the tongue rises toward the hard palate. Lips are spread apart and the sides of the tongue touch the upper teeth.

Pronunciation Errors

  1 Substitution of /lə/ for /i/ before /l/

Improvement Objectives

  1 Do not create a diphthong before /i/.

Practice Materials
Objective 1
Keep /i/ pure:

keel	feel	congeal
peel	teal	seal
meal	real	shield
zeal	deal	field

Words

eat	beet	see
eve	mean	bee
eel	read	key
east	seem	tree
eke	bean	me
ear	feet	fee
ease	teeth	she
each	green	plea
equal	people	prairie
either	belief	agree
erase	fifteen	eerie
Easter	reason	Marie
emit	receive	
ether	teacher	
easy	machine	
ego	increase	

Sentences

1. Three people believed that treatment should be free.
2. *East of Eden* was Lee's favorite James Dean movie.
3. The mean dentist dreamed of the damage ice cream could do to teeth.
4. She was elated that, on Easter eve, they would eat eels.
5. She stayed for the evening meal because we served green peas.
6. The plumber fixed not only the leaky faucet, but also where the water had seeped under the sink.
7. The fleas had a feast on the beagle.
8. He may be able to achieve more by breathing slowly and evenly.
9. Jean skied into a tree in the first heat.
10. Dee was covered with green paint from her knees to her feet.

SOUND: /ɪ/

PMTL Features: high/front/lax/unrounded
Correct Production

The tongue is raised to the palate, almost as high as for /i/. The tongue is lax; lips are spread apart.

Pronunciation Errors

1   Substitution of /ə/ for /ɪ/ in prefixes
2   Substitution of /ɛ/ for /ɪ/

Improvement Objectives

1   Do not reduce syllable with /ɪ/ in prefixes.
2   Clearly produce /ɪ/.

Practice Materials
Objective 1
Pronounce prefixes with /ɪ/:

behave	defend	prefer
become	describe	prevent
before	demand	pretend

Objective 2
Contrast /ɪ/ and /ɛ/:

bit	bet	been	Ben
six	sex	kid	Ked
sit	set	did	dead
win	when	if	"f"

Words

it	hid
in	kid
if	guilt
inch	win
is	sit
ill	witch
ink	been
itch	hip

instant	pistol
insist	kitten
income	system
include	women
increase	until
imply	simple
ignore	river
issue	history

Sentences

1. Try not to drop a stitch when knitting that simple quilt.
2. Liz was impressed with Tim's Persian kitten.
3. Mick will hike up the hill if you insist.
4. Every issue of *Atlantic Monthly* is filled with new fiction.
5. Sid was the new kid in his economics class.
6. His sister has been satisfied with her visit to Cincinnati.
7. The subordinate reported his mistake and the incident to his commanding officer.
8. If you miss his wit and smile, wait until his next visit.
9. His skin's reaction to the medicine makes him itch.
10. Did you ignore his wish for a plastic hip cast?

SOUND: /e/

PMTL Features: mid/front/tense/unrounded
Correct Production

The front of the tongue is raised to the midpoint of the oral cavity. The tongue is tense and lips are unrounded.

Articulation and Pronunciation Errors
Errors are not common.

Practice Materials
Words

ate	great	pay
aim	fade	hay

ARTICULATION AND PRONUNCIATION

age	bait	clay
ail	lame	lay
aid	mate	stay
ache	faith	day
ape	veil	may
ace	page	ray
angel	major	delay
acorn	crayon	relay
ancient	favor	repay
eighteen	gravy	
agent	vacate	
April	railway	
able	nation	
apron	labor	

Sentences

1. Ray lost his way when he left the main road.
2. Water in the basement saturated the packing crates, ruining the antique lace.
3. Reneé was unable to evaluate the maid's performance.
4. David's display of courage gave us the inspiration to write this play.
5. Mabel trained the rats to run the maze without mistakes or hesitations.
6. Fay found it painful to lie on the x-ray table.
7. Amy suffered facial cuts and a broken leg when her car veered from the center lane.
8. The Asiatic apes favored acorns for their daily snack.
9. April's great imagination made the play's debut a success.
10. Our faith in the major league baseball team's ability stayed strong during the game.

SOUND: /ɛ/

PMTL Features: mid/front/lax/unrounded
Correct Production

The tongue is slightly lower in the oral cavity than for /e/. The tongue is lax and the mouth is more open than for /e/.

Pronunciation Errors

1 Substitution of /ɪ/ for /ɛ/
2 Substitution of /e/ for /ɛ/ before /g/ or /ʒ/

Improvement Objectives

1 Produce /ɛ/ when appropriate.
2 Pronounce /ɛ/ when indicated before /g/ or /ʒ/.

Practice Materials

Objective 1

Contrast these words:

set	sit	when	win
met	mitt	send	sinned
let	lit	head	hid
pen	pin	bet	bit

Objective 2

Produce /ɛ/ before /g/ or /ʒ/:

egg	regulate	pleasure
peg	keg	leisure
leg	treasure	beg
Meg	measure	

Words

egg	head
end	said
else	red
	yet
	led
	till
	debt
	guess

ever	heather
elbow	question
edit	ahead
extra	direct
excite	better
letter	itself

enter	second
extreme	method

Sentences

1. Extreme exercise and exertion never fail to make me exhausted.
2. Ellen's broken leg was set by Dr. Emmett.
3. Heather was so excited about sleeping in a feather bed.
4. Vendors were selling ethnic food at the street festival.
5. Emily wore her new red dress on her dinner date with Evan.
6. We were entertained by exotic dancers and rode the elephants on our trip to India.
7. Tell Peggy to dress warmly and bring extra blankets on the camping trip.
8. The Sherpa guides led the expedition to climb Mt. Everest.
9. The unfortunate family fell deeper in debt after Mr. Webb's death.
10. The editor said it is essential to change the ending to fit the story.

SOUND: /æ/

PMTL Features: low/front/lax/unrounded
Correct Production

 The front part of the tongue is moved upward slightly. The lips are open; tongue is lax.

Pronunciation Errors

 1 Substitution of /æɪ/ or /æə/ for /æ/

Improvement Objectives

 1 Do not tense tongue for /æ/; produce it at a normal rate.

Practice Materials
 Objective 1
  Don't produce diphthong for these words:

at	sad	fat
ad	cat	sat
bad	mat	tag
lad	rat	rag

Words

add	had
at	rat
am	laugh
and	flat
aft	calf
as	sand
an	shall
ask	black
after	captain
atlas	grammar
attic	happy
ankle	standard
anguish	battle
absent	began
advent	value
action	practice

Sentences

1. Adam, who can add and subtract at the age of six, has an advantage over the other children.
2. As long as I've known her, Agnes has behaved admirably.
3. After a morning of factual meetings, I'll enjoy my afternoon with Chad and Matt.
4. Children should learn to clean their feet on the mat and hang up their coats and hats.
5. Were many people adamantly opposed to the use of the atom bomb?
6. That actor's performance was actually overrated.
7. School administrators reacted hesitantly to the radical student's activities.
8. An Acme moving van attracted much attention at the accident scene.
9. The unsuspecting animals were attacked by the advancing army of ants.
10. I purchased an amethyst ring and a rattan chair while vacationing at Cape Hatteras.

CENTRAL

SOUND: /ə/

PMTL Features: mid-central/lax/unrounded (unstressed)
Correct Production

    Only the midportion of the tongue raises slightly to the palate. Lips are unrounded, tongue is lax.

Pronunciation Errors

    1 Omission of /ə/

    2 Addition of /ə/

Improvement Objectives

    1 Do not omit syllables with /ə/.

    2 Do not add /ə/ in these words: *business, bracelet*

Practice Materials
Objective 1

Produce /ə/ in these words:

different	cruel	jewelry
liberal	poetry	mystery
camera	poem	quilt
violent	similar	riot

Words

	above	control
	amount	correct
	about	machine
	agree	receive
	allot	today
	arrange	combine (verb)
	afraid	compose
	adult	supply

Sentences

See sentences for /ʌ/.

SOUND: /ʌ/

PMTL Features: mid-central/lax/unrounded (stressed)
Correct Production

The mid-portion of the tongue is raised slightly to the palate. The remainder of the tongue is on the floor of the mouth.

Pronunciation Errors

1. Substitution of /ɪ/ or /ɛ/ for /ʌ/
2. Substitution of any lax back vowel for /ʌ/

Improvement Objectives

1. Do not move /ʌ/ to front lax vowel.
2. Do not move /ʌ/ to back lax vowel.

Practice Materials

Objective 1

Produce /ʌ/ in these words:

just	some	luck
must	much	but
such	duck	cut

Objective 2

Contrast these words:

/ʌ/	/ʊ/	/ɔ/	/ɑ/
cut			cot
dull			doll
done		dawn	Don
putt	put		pot
buck	hook	hawk	

Words

up	hut
us	blood
	cut
	luck
	rub
	bus
	love
	does

under   butter
utter   cupboard
oven   stomach
ugly   hunter
umpire   husband
usher   mother
upright   country
upward   trouble

Sentences

1 Lisa just wanted to see a puppy from Santa under her Christmas tree.
2 The doctor assured us that the blood loss from Sara's cut was minimal.
3 Stomach aches can be caused by an allergic reaction to some food products.
4 "I'm afraid you're out of luck!" our tax accountant announced.
5 The district attorney alleged that the bus driver was under the influence.
6 Tanya rubbed cocoa butter on her rough, reddened hands.
7 Does it make you afraid to be alone in that hut?
8 Hannah saved the puppy as the flood waters rose above the roof tops.
9 The speaker held the attention of the adults, but the children were unimpressed.
10 The stigma of unrequited love left its ugly mark on Leah.

SOUND: /ɝ/

PMTL Features: mid-central/tense/rounded (stressed)
Correct Production

The middle part of the tongue raises halfway to the palate. Sides of the tongue meet the upper teeth. Lips are rounded slightly; tongue is tense.

Articulation Errors

1 Substitution of /ɜ/ (/ɛ/ with lip rounding) for /ɝ/

Pronunciation Errors

1 Substitution of /rɪ/ for /ɝ/ or /ɝ/ for /rɪ/
2 Substitution of /ɜ/ for /ɝ/ (dialectal)

Improvement Objectives

1 Produce /ɝ/ instead of /ɜ/.
2 Pronounce stressed *er* as /ɝ/; *re* (in prefixes) as /rɪ/.

Practice Materials
Objective 1

her rug	burr ring
fur wrap	were right
Sir Richard	sure road

Objective 2
Pronounce these words with the appropriate phonemes:

/ɝ/	/rɪ/
perfect	premise
permit	predicate
person	prevent
perjure	
permeate	

Words

earn	hurt	her
earth	burp	sir
urge	work	fur
irk	nurse	purr
urn	serve	spur
earl	bird	stir
	church	were
	heard	fir

early	furnish
urgent	turtle
earnest	worry
urban	dirty
earning	curtain
ermine	perfect
Irving	purpose
Erwin	thirty

Sentences
See sentences for /ɚ/.

SOUND: /ɚ/

PMTL Features: mid-central/tense/rounded (unstressed)
Correct Production

   The position for /ɚ/ is similar to /ɜ/. The tongue is more relaxed and lower.

Articulation Errors

   1 Substitution of /ə/ for /ɚ/

Pronunciation Errors

   1 Substitution of /rɪ/ for /ɚ/ or /ɚ/ for /rɪ/
   2 Substitution of /ə/ for /ɚ/ (dialectal)

Improvement Objectives

   1 Produce /ɚ/ instead of /ə/.
   2 Produce unstressed *er* as /ɚ/; *re* as /rɪ/.

Practice Materials
   Objective 1
      To add *r*-coloring, link *er* with *r* in these phrases:

better ring	ever ready
other runner	labor rights
never rude	never relax
sister Rose	never rule
color red	December race

   Objective 2
      Pronounce these words with the appropriate phoneme:

/ɚ/	/rɪ/
perhaps	children
percent	entrance
perform	hundred
persist	apron
perceptive	pretend
pertain	prevent
pervade	preserve
perverse	present

Words

perspire	proper
coward	rather
modern	under
percent	older
surprise	gather
standard	future
worker	finger
further	measure

Sentences

1 Her mother and father pooled their earnings to furnish the house.
2 Labor is cheaper in rural areas than in urban centers.
3 I heard that your brother began work as an editor.
4 The nurse accurately measured the dose for her patient.
5 My vision was blurred through the dirty windshield.
6 The fighter was underweight for the welterweight class.
7 I'm discouraged by my lack of earnings after long years of work.
8 Irving's manners were always perfect during church services.
9 Her thirst was quenched by the celery soda.
10 Homer was certain to serve mock turtle soup at the dinner party.

SOUND: /ɑ/

PMTL Features: low/back/lax/unrounded
Correct Production

>   The back of the tongue raises slightly while most of the tongue remains on the floor of the mouth. Lips are unrounded and opened wide.

Articulation Errors

1 Substitution of /a/ for /ɑ/

Pronunciation Errors

1 Substitution of /a/ for /ɑ/ before /r/
2 Substitution of /ʌ/ or /ɔ/ for /ɑ/ (dialect)

ARTICULATION AND PRONUNCIATION

Improvement Objectives

1. Make sure that raised part of your tongue is back in your mouth.
2. Keep production of /ɑ/ low in mouth.

Practice Materials

Objective 1

Practice /ɑ/:

autumn	honest
auto	almond
awkward	aqua

Practice /ɑr/:

car	far
park	tar
mar	ajar
sonar	candy bar

Objective 2

Contrast these words:

/ɑ/	/ɔ/	/ʌ/
hock	hawk	Huck
star	store	stir
not	naught	nut
car	core	cur
cot	caught	cut

Words

odd	stock	Shah
	drop	blah
	hot	
	not	
	dock	
	box	
	clot	
	bomb	
honest	father	
auto	bottle	
opera	beyond	

awkward	college
almond	promise
otter	follow
object	topic
obsess	doctor

Sentences

1. Would you ever buy a used auto from Honest Ron?
2. The clock marked the passing of time on the dot.
3. We awarded a mock Oscar to our favorite zombie movie.
4. Bob received a box of almonds from his father in Ottumwa, Iowa.
5. Arnold locked the ship's cabin and promptly left the dock.
6. The Shah was not honored at the benefit concert.
7. Lonnie and Roger got free tickets for the rock concert.
8. Robbie felt blah and weak from his rotten cold.
9. The fox found the rotten garbage under the rock.
10. It was awkward to be honest about dropping Dottie's bottle of perfume.

SOUND: /ɔ/

PMTL Features: low/back/lax/rounded
Correct Production

The back of the tongue raises halfway to the palate. The tongue is relaxed; lips are rounded.

Articulation Errors

1. Substitution of /ɑ/ for /ɔ/

Pronunciation Errors

1. Substitution of /ɑ/ for /ɔ/ (dialectal)

Improvement Objectives

1. Produce /ɔ/ in appropriate words. You can create /ɔ/ from /ɑ/ by raising the back of your tongue and rounding your lips.

ARTICULATION AND PRONUNCIATION

Practice Materials
Objective 1

Contrast these words:

/ɑ/	/ɔ/
barn	boon
bond	pawned
tart	torte
farm	form
mar	more
nod	gnawed
knotty	naughty
pod	pawed
cot	caught
collar	caller
star	store

Words

all	taught	paw
off	talk	saw
on	hawk	law
awe	ball	draw
awl	cause	straw
ought	false	claw
	haul	jaw
	cost	flow
often	exhaust	withdraw
awful	snowfall	
audio	assault	
office	across	
awning	appall	
auction	recall	
author	bawdy	
always	water	

Sentences

1 Grandma always wears her shawl on chilly autumn nights.
2 The cat's paw got caught in a ball of string.
3 The children love to draw with chalk on the sidewalk.
4 We walked back to the office after meeting with the lawyers.

5. You ought to raise the awnings in the fall.
6. Just before dawn, we walked to the summit and saw the sunrise.
7. It was an awful sight to see the cougar maul the fawn.
8. Little Audrey loves to turn the lights off and on.
9. We often feed our horse stalks of celery and raw carrots.
10. The off-Broadway show failed to draw a sizable audience in Boston.

SOUND: /o/

PMTL Features: mid/back/tense/rounded
Correct Production

The back of the tongue raises midway between the floor of the mouth and the hard palate. The lips are rounded; tongue is tense.

Pronunciation Errors

1. Substitution of /ə/ for /o/ in unstressed syllables
2. Addition of /ə/ to /o/ before /l/

Improvement Objectives

1. Do not reduce /o/ to /ə/ in unstressed syllables.
2. Do not create diphthong /oə/ before /l/.

Practice Materials
Objective 1

Be sure to produce /o/ in these words:

yellow	fellow	tomorrow
hotel	follow	narrow
obey	project (verb)	pillow
Chicago	provide	shallow

Objective 2

Be sure not to add /ə/:

coal	mole	scroll
pole	dole	stole
roll	parole	unroll
hole	role	North Pole

ARTICULATION AND PRONUNCIATION

Words

own	goes	blow
oaf	note	toe
oak	choke	though
oh	phone	sew
ode	bowl	dough
oar	soak	mow
oath	coat	show
old	rose	grow
open	motion	narrow
omit	domain	pillow
over	hotel	swallow
omen	program	Jello
ocean	suppose	fellow
odor	moment	window
oval	control	tallow
only	chosen	solo

Sentences

1 Rhoda found rolled oats on the floor when she opened the kitchen door.
2 Morton wrote his story over and over before court.
3 Joe mowed the oval of grass near the ocean shore.
4 The shallow moat around the castle was surrounded by goats.
5 Flo wrote a note to José concerning the overpopulation problem.
6 The aroma of fresh sourdough bread filled our noses.
7 The ocean breeze was blowing through the open window.
8 The Pristine rose was voted best of show in the Brownsborough rose show.
9 Our boat had to be towed from the shallows owing to the low tide.
10 Lauren hoed the narrow rows of yellow tomatoes.

SOUND: /ʊ/

PMTL Features: high/back/lax/rounded
Correct Production

>   The tongue is raised almost to the palate. The tongue is relaxed; lips are rounded.

Pronunciation Errors

1 Addition of /ɪ/ or /ə/ to /ʊ/ in stressed syllables
2 Substitution of /u/ or /ʌ/ for /ʊ/

Improvement Objectives

1 Produce a pure /ʊ/ in stressed syllables.
2 Do not reduce /ʊ/ or tense its production.

Practice Materials
Objective 1
Keep production of /ʊ/ short and lax as you practice the single-syllable words.
Objective 2
Contrast these words:

/ʊ/	/ʌ/	/u/
book	buck	cooed
could	cud	Luke
look	luck	stewed
stewed	stud	wooed
wood		
put	putt	
took	tuck	

Words

hood
would
wool
good
bull
soot
took
should

sugar
woman
output
cookie
bullet
tourist
bushel
manhood

Sentences

1. I took a warm woolen blanket and a good book with me to the cabin.
2. The Goodmans took a vacation to Mt. Hood National Park.
3. You should look at the hooves of a horse before you ride it.
4. Students should know the accomplishments of Booker T. Washington.
5. The chimney sweep also cleaned the soot from the roof.
6. It took long hours for Butch to hook the bullhead.
7. Would you be good enough to look after my dog Woofer?
8. Could we ask that woman to sell her woolen hooked rug?

SOUND: /u/

PMTL Features: high/back/tense/rounded
Correct Production

> The back of the tongue raises high to the palate. The tongue is tense; lips are rounded.

Articulation Errors

1. Addition of /ə/ in stressed syllables

Pronunciation Errors

1. Alternation of /ʊ/ and /u/ in some words
2. Confusion between /u/ and /ʊ/ (dialectal)

Improvement Objectives

1. Do not create /ʊə/ diphthong.
2. Make pronunciation consistent in the following words:

root	hoof	whoop	soot
roof	hooves	room	coop

3. Contrast between /ʊ/ and /u/.

Practice Materials
Objective 1

Do not add /ə/ in these words:

drool	fool	food	whose
cool	rule	soon	tool

Objective 3

Contrast these words:

/u/	/ʊ/
stewed	stood
pool	pull
shoed	should
Luke	look
cooed	could
fool	full

Words

ooze	boot	who
	food	chew
	ride	blue
	group	do
	flute	threw
	whose	crew
	fruit	coo
	spoon	shoe
oops		
oodles	baboon	bamboo
	balloon	unscrew
	dilute	Hindu
	gloomy	undo
	movement	renew
	include	redo
	produce (noun)	unto
	duty	regrew

Sentences

1 Elaine wore a dark suit and a maroon blouse for her job interview.
2 It was so difficult to choose between the macaroons and the brownies offered at the afternoon tea.
3 Would you classify Kentucky burgoo as a soup or a stew?
4 Mr. Magoo and Pepe LePeuw are my favorite cartoon characters.
5 At the zoo the children saw a moose, a kangaroo, and two baboons eating fruit.
6 In lieu of imprisonment, the foolish duke slew his enemies.
7 The mutinous crew set the cruel captain adrift without water or food.

8   The pooch chewed a hole in his master's new shoes.
9   Blue balloons were released and flew into a group of trees.
10 Dilute the fruit juice with a few drops of food coloring.

DIPHTHONGS

SOUND: /ju/

PMTL Features: high/front/tense/unrounded to high/back/tense/rounded
Correct Production

The tongue moves from high and front in the mouth to high and back. The tongue is tense and lips are rounded.

Pronunciation Errors

1   Addition of /ə/ before /ju/
2   Reduction of /ju/ to /ə/

Improvement Objectives

1   Only /ju/ should come after a consonant in appropriate contexts.
2   Do not reduce /ju/.

Practice Materials
Objective 1

Avoid adding /ə/ before /ju/ in these words:

cute	cube	mute
few	feud	fuel
view	fuse	muse

Objective 2

Produce a clear /ju/ in these words:

| value | accurate | continue |
| fabulous | ridiculous| popular |

Words

| you | fuel | view |
| youth | cube | few |

CHAPTER 10

use	cute	new
used	feud	
yew	mule	
	huge	
	mute	
unit	refuse	value
uses	beauty	review
usual	amuse	renew
union	pupil	askew
	human	
	music	
	humid	
	future	

Sentences

1. We refused to play musical chairs by mutual consent.
2. The beauty salon's volume of business increased after moving to the commuter mall.
3. The mural of the Danube River continued to amuse the visitors.
4. The beautician returned to her cubicle after vacuuming the floor.
5. The butane lighter required pure fuel.
6. Hugh viewed the fugitive mules with amusement.
7. The humorist debuted at Music Hall in a preview performance.
8. The documents on human rights are required to complete the manual.
9. A pewter finish will hold up well in this humidity.
10. I refuse to order barbecued ribs from that menu.

SOUND: /aɪ/

PMTL Features: low/central/lax/unrounded to high/front/lax/unrounded
Correct Production

From a relaxed position on the floor of the mouth, the tongue moves to a high front position. The tongue remains relaxed.

Pronunciation Errors

1. Substitution of /aə/ for /aɪ/ (dialectal)

ARTICULATION AND PRONUNCIATION

Improvement Objectives

1 Move tongue to high front position; do not reduce /ɪ/.

Practice Materials
Objective 1
Say these pairs of words, keeping /ɪ/ in second word:

tie	tying
sigh	sighing
lie	lying
buy	buying
shy	shying (away)

Words

ice	fight	high
eyes	bike	fly
I	side	tie
I'm	style	sigh
I'd	night	my
I've	wide	rye
aisle	mile	fly
eye	guide	buy
idle	disguise	rely
idea	decide	apply
ire	outside	defy
iris	Friday	July
iron	divide	
island	combine	
Ireland	arrive	
Ivan	surprise	

Sentences

1 I tried to dial the hotline with a dime.
2 Ice cream and apple pie are my favorite nightly snacks.
3 Items were priced too high at the island market.
4 Dire straits forced Michael to write a bad check.
5 Why must Iris try to drive on the icy street?
6 You can buy fried rice at the Chinese shop.
7 The scientist isolated the virus that caused hepatitis.

8 Iron ore may be mined at the hillside site.
9 I'll write my memoirs as soon as it becomes light.
10 Finally, I filed all the citations for the publication.

SOUND: /aʊ/

PMTL Features: low/central/lax/unrounded to high/back/lax/rounded
Correct Production

The tongue begins at the floor of the mouth in a relaxed position. It then moves to a high, back, relaxed, rounded position.

Pronunciation Errors

1 Substitution of /æʊ/ or /ɛʊ/ for /aʊ/ (dialectal)

Improvement Objectives

1 Change your production of /æʊ/ or /ɛʊ/ to /aʊ/ by opening your mouth wider and by lowering your tongue at the beginning of the diphthong.

Practice Materials
Words

out	round	thou
ouch	mouse	now
owl	ground	how
out	crown	bow
hours	pounce	sow
oust	house	cow
	crowd	bough
	pound	plow
outside	flower	allow
outer	carouse	meow
ourselves	thousand	avow
hour	amount	
output	without	
	shower	
	mountain	
	power	

Sentences

1. I will not allow you to count that hour toward your wage earnings.
2. We must go downtown to shop for a couch and a shower curtain.
3. The farmer plowed the ground around the power plant.
4. Our county bell tower has been invaded by a mouse.
5. Mr. Lauter furrowed his brow at the amount of waste.
6. The South is now known for its generous educational allowance.
7. Out of the corner came the cat to pounce on the wolfhound.
8. Our time has come to mount a campaign for an accounting of government waste.

SOUND: /ɔɪ/

PMTL Features: mid/back/lax/rounded to high/front/lax/unrounded
Correct Production

The tongue is raised in the back to the midposition and glides to the high-front position where it remains relaxed and becomes unrounded.

Articulation Errors

1. Substitution of /ɛɪ/ or /əɪ/ for /ɔɪ/

Improvement Objectives

1. Avoid producing /ɛɪ/ or /əɪ/ for /ɔɪ/ by making sure to lip-round at the beginning of the diphthong.

Practice Materials
Objective 1

Practice these words, rounding your lips at the beginning of each word:

coy	coin	coil
boy	boil	broil
toy	toil	toys
joy	join	joins

Words

oil	join	toy
oink	soil	boy
	voice	soy
	moist	coy
	point	joy
	void	Roy
	foil	Troy
	coin	
oyster	royal	enjoy
oily	poison	decoy
ointment	avoid	destroy
	poignant	alloy
	Detroit	convoy
	soybeans	annoy
	pointed	buoy
	enjoin	employ

Sentences

1. Lloyd pointed out that the pot was about to boil over.
2. Joyce raised her voice in annoyance over his choice of toys.
3. That alloy of nickel can be poison when boiled.
4. Roy enjoys his fried oysters moist and not dry.
5. That moist soil is best for growing soybeans.
6. The doily was spoiled by some oil and vinegar dressing.
7. Freud enjoyed his voyage to Detroit.
8. It was the choice of the royal family to have the gargoyles sculpted.
9. Join us in learning about Doyle's coins.
10. Royce was annoyed that he had to toil in the soil.

PASSAGES FOR PRACTICE

STOPS

/p/ /b/

Blank is the book of his bounty beholden of old, and its binding is
    blacker than bluer:
Out of blue into black is the scheme of the skies, and their dews are
    the wine of the bloodshed of things . . .

        Algernon Charles Swinburne, "Nephelidia"

Piping down the valleys wild,
Piping songs of pleasant glee,
On a cloud I saw a child,
And he laughing said to me:

'Pipe a song about a Lamb!'
So I piped with merry cheer.
'Piper, pipe that song again.'
So I piped: he wept to hear.

        William Blake, "Piping Down the Valleys Wild"

A Book of Verses underneath the Bough,
A Jug of Wine, a Loaf of Bread–and Thou
Beside me singing in the Wilderness—
O, Wilderness were Paradise enow!

Some for the Glories of This World; and some
Sigh for the Prophet's Paradise to come. . .

        Edward Fitzgerald, *The Rubiyat of Omar Khayyam*

There is a pleasure in the pathless woods,
There is a rapture on the lonely shore,
There is society, where none intrudes,
By the deep sea, and music in its roar:

        Lord Byron, *Childe Harold's Pilgrimage,* Canto IV

CHAPTER 10

248

/t/ /d/

Finish every day and be done with it. You have done what you could. Some blunders and absurdities no doubt crept in; forget them as soon as you can. Tomorrow is a new day; begin it well and serenely and with too high a spirit to be cumbered with your old nonsense. This day is all that is good and fair. It is too dear, with its hopes and invitations, to waste a moment on the yesterdays.

Ralph Waldo Emerson, "One Day At A Time"

Come away, come away, death,
And in sad cypress let me be laid.
Fly away, fly away, breath;
I am slain by a fair cruel maid.
My shroud of white, stuck all with yew,
O! prepare it.
My part of death, no one so true
Did share it.

William Shakespeare, "Twelfth Night"

/k/ /g/

Crises there will continue to be. In meeting them, whether foreign or domestic, great or small, there is a recurring temptation to feel that some spectacular and costly action could become the miraculous solution to all current difficulties. A huge increase in newer elements of our defenses; development of unrealistic programs to cure every ill in agriculture; a dramatic expansion in basic and applied research—these and many other possibilities, each possibly promising in itself, may be suggested as the only way to the road we wish to travel.

Dwight D. Eisenhower, "Farewell Address to the Nation"

'Twas brillig, and the slithy toves
   Did gyre and gimble in the wabe:
All mimsy were the borogoves,
   And the mome raths outgrabe.

Lewis Carroll, "Jabberwocky"

He clasps the crag with crooked hands:
Close to the sun in lonely lands,
Ringed with the azure world, he stands.

Alfred, Lord Tennyson, "The Eagle"

249
FRICATIVES

/f/ /v/

What was it—I paused to think—what was it that so unnerved me in the contemplation of the House of Usher? It was a mystery all insoluble; nor could I grapple with the shadowy fancies that crowded upon me as I pondered. I was forced to fall back upon the unsatisfactory conclusion, that while, beyond doubt, there *are* combinations of very simple natural objects which have the power of thus affecting us, still the analysis of this power lies among considerations beyond our depth.

Edgar Allan Poe, "The Fall of the House of Usher"

What a triumph of life these battered cities is over the worst that fire and bomb can do! What a vindication of the civilized and decent way of living we have been trying to work for and work toward in our island! What a proof of the virtues of free institutions! What a test of the quality of our local authorities and of customs and societies so steadily built!

Winston Churchill, April 27, 1941

A noiseless patient spider,
I mark'd where on a little promontory it stood isolated,
Mark'd how to explore the vacant vast surrounding,
It launch'd forth filament, filament, filament, out of itself,
Ever unreeling them, ever tirelessly speeding them.

Walt Whitman, "A Noiseless Patient Spider"

/θ/ /ð/

I think this is the most extraordinary collection of talent, of human knowledge, that has ever been gathered together at the White House—with the possible exception of when Thomas Jefferson dined alone.

John F. Kennedy

They sought it with thimbles, they sought it with care;
    They pursued it with forks and hope.
They threatened its life with a railway share;
    They charmed it with smiles and soap.

Lewis Carroll, "The Hunting of the Snark"

Brother, listen to what we say. There was a time when our forefathers owned this great island. Their seats extended from the rising to the setting sun. The Great Spirit had made it for the use of Indians. He had created the buffalo, the deer, and other animals for food. He had made the bear and the beaver. Their skins served us for clothing. He had scattered them over the country and taught us how to take them. He had caused the earth to produce corn for bread. All this He had done for his red children because He loved them. If we had some disputes about our hunting-ground they were generally settled without the shedding of much blood.

Red Jacket, 1905

/s/ /z/

You do not know what life means when all the difficulties are removed! I am simply smothered and sickened with advantages. It is like eating a sweet dessert the first thing in the morning.

Jane Addams, *Twenty Years At Hull House*

At Christmas I no more desire a rose
Than wish a snow in May's new-fangled mirth;
But like of each thing that in season grows.

William Shakespeare, "Love's Labour's Lost"

Feb. 3. A mild morning, the windows open at breakfast, the red-breasts singing in the garden. Walked with Coleridge over the hills. The sea at first obscured by vapour; that vapour afterwards slid in one mighty mass along the sea-shore; the islands and one point of land clear beyond it. The distant country (which was purple in the clear dull air), overhung by straggling clouds that sailed over it, appeared like the darker clouds, which are often seen at a great distance apparently motionless, while the nearer ones pass quickly over them, driven by the lower winds. I never saw such a union of earth, sky, and sea.

Dorothy Wordsworth, *The Alfoxden Journal*

I celebrate myself, and sing myself,
And what I assume you shall assume,
For every atom belonging to me as good belongs to you.
I loaf and invite my soul,
I lean and loaf at my ease observing a spear of summer grass.

Walt Whitman, "Song of Myself"

Thou sawest, in thine old singing season, brother,
Secrets and sorrows unbeheld of us:
Fierce loves, and lovely leaf-buds poisonous . . .

> Algernon Charles Swinburne, "In Memory of Charles Baudelaire"

When to the sessions of sweet silent thought
I summon up remembrance of things past,
I sigh the lack of many a thing I sought,
And with old woes new wail my dear times' waste.

> William Shakespeare, "Sonnet XXX"

/ʃ/ /ʒ/

I believe in an America where the separation of church and state is absolute—where no Catholic prelate would tell the President (should he be a Catholic) how to act, and no Protestant minister would tell his parishioners for whom to vote . . .

> John F. Kennedy, Houston, Texas, September, 1959

In Xanadu did Kubla Khan
   A stately pleasure-dome decree:
Where Alph, the sacred river, ran
Through caverns measureless to man

> Samuel Taylor Coleridge, "Kubla Khan"

/h/

My heart's in the Highlands, my heart is not here;
My heart's in the Highlands a-chasing the deer;
Chasing the wild deer, and following the roe,
My heart's in the Highlands, wherever I go.

> Robert Burns, "My Heart's In the Highlands"

If Hitler invaded Hell, I would make at least a favorable reference to the devil in the House of Commons.

> Winston Churchill

CHAPTER 10

His impetuous spirit had now a fixed purpose and motive of action, and he turned the light foot of his country towards the wilds, through which he knew, by Mr. Ireby's report, that Morrison was advancing. His mind was wholly engrossed by the sense of injury—injury sustained from a friend; and by the desire of vengeance on one whom he now accounted his most bitter enemy. The treasured ideas of self-importance and self-opinion—of ideal birth and quality, had become more precious to him, like the hoard to the miser, because he could only enjoy them in secret. But that hoard was pillaged, the idols which he had secretly worshipped had been desecrated and profaned.

Sir Walter Scott, "The Two Drovers"

AFFRICATES

/tʃ/ /dʒ/

The most stringent protection of free speech would not protect a man in falsely shouting fire in a theatre and causing a panic. The question in every case is whether the words used are used in such circumstances and are of such a nature as to create a clear and present danger that they will bring about the substantive evils that Congress has a right to prevent.

Oliver Wendell Holmes, Schenk v. U.S., 1919

Just an ivy-covered cottage with a brooklet running near,
Just an aged couple seated in the door . . .

Anonymous, "All That Glitters is Not Gold"

The giraffe, in their queer, inimitable, vegetating gracefulness, as if it were not a herd of animals but a family of rare, long-stemmed, speckled gigantic flowers slowly advancing.

Isak Dinesen, *Out of Africa*, Pt. I, Chap. 1

Bacchus' blessings are a treasure;
Drinking is the soldier's pleasure;
Rich the treasure,
Sweet the pleasure;
Sweet is pleasure after pain.

John Dryden, "Alexander's Feast"

The unpurged images of day recede;
The Emperor's drunken soldiery are abed;

W.B. Yeats, "Byzantium"

NASALS

/m/ /n/ /ŋ/

It was a highly respectable street, where all the houses were exactly alike, and where business men of moderate means begot and reared large families of children, all of whom went to sabbath-school and learned the shorter catechism, and were interested in arithmetic; all of whom were as exactly alike as their homes, and of a piece with the monotony in which they lived.

Willa Cather, "Paul's Case"

The music of Midsummer-madness
Shall sting him with many a bite,
Till, in rapture of rollicking sadness,
He shall groan with a gloomy delight:
He shall swathe him, like mists of the morning,
in platitudes luscious and limp,
Such as deck, with a deathless adorning,
The Song of the Shrimp!

Lewis Carroll, "The Manlet"

Where the domed and daring palace shot its spires
    Up like fires
O'er the hundred-gated circuit of a wall
    Bounding all,
Made of marble, men might march on nor be pressed,
    Twelve abreast.

Robert Browning, "Love among the Ruins"

It was many and many a year ago,
In a kingdom by the sea,
That a maiden there lived whom you may know
By the name of Annabel Lee;—
And this maiden she lived with no other thought
Than to love and be loved by me.

Edgar Allan Poe, "Annabel Lee"

O mistress mine, where are you roaming?
O stay and hear, your true love's coming
That can sing both high and low.
Trip no further, pretty sweeting;
Journeys end in lovers meeting,
Every wise man's son doth know.

William Shakespeare, "Twelfth Night"

Here and there with dimes on the eyes walking,
To feed the greed of the belly the brains liberally spooning,
Tickets buying, taking, selling, but into the feast never once going,
Many sweating, plowing, thrashing, and then the chaff for payment receiving,
A few idly owning, and they the wheat continually claiming.

Walt Whitman, "Song of Myself"

GLIDES

/j/

We ask our daily bread, and God never says, You should have come yesterday. He never says, You must come again tomorrow. But "today if you will hear His voice," today He will hear you.

John Donne, "All Times Are His Seasons"

Are you the new person drawn toward me?
To begin with take warning, I am surely far different from what you suppose;
Do you suppose you will find in me your ideal?
Do you think it is so easy to have me become your lover?
Do you think the friendship of me would be unalloy'd satisfaction?
Do you think I am trusty and faithful?

Walt Whitman, "Are You The New Person Drawn Toward Me?"

/w/

Once upon a midnight dreary, while I pondered, weak and weary,
Over many a quaint and curious volume of forgotten lore—
While I nodded, nearly napping, suddenly there came a tapping,
As of someone gently rapping, rapping at my chamber door.

Edgar Allan Poe, "The Raven"

Weed their hearts of weariness,
Scatter every care
Down a wake of angel-wings
Winnowing the air.

                James Whitcomb Riley, "Dear Lord, Kind Lord"

I wake and feel the fell of dark, not day.
What hours, O what black hours we have spent
This night! what sights you, heart, saw; ways you went!

                Gerard Manley Hopkins, "I Wake and Feel the Fell of Dark"

/r/

Tiger! Tiger! burning bright
In the forests of the night,
What immortal hand or eye
Could frame thy fearful symmetry?

                William Blake, "The Tiger"

There is a river clear and fair,
'Tis neither broad nor narrow;
It winds a little here and there—

It winds about like any hare;
And then it holds as straight a course
As, on the turnpike road, a horse,
Or, through the air, an arrow.

                Catherine Maria Fanshawe, "Fragments"

The years shall run like rabbits,
For in my arms I hold
The Flower of the Ages,
And the first love of the world.

                W. H. Auden, "As I Walked Out One Evening"

CHAPTER 10

> From his shoulder Hiawatha
> Took the camera of rosewood,
> Made of sliding, folding rosewood;
> Neatly put it all together.
> In its case it lay compactly,
> Folded into nearly nothing . . .
>
> Lewis Carroll, "Hiawatha's Photographing"

> The object of this Essay is to explain as clearly as I am able, the grounds of an opinion which I have held from the very earliest period when I had formed an opinion at all on social or political matters, and which, instead of being weakened or modified, has been constantly growing stronger by the progress of reflection and the experience of life: That the principle which regulates the existing social relations between the two sexes—the legal subordination of one sex to the other—is wrong in itself, and now one of the chief hindrances to human improvement; and that it ought to be replaced by a principle of perfect equality, admitting no power or privilege on one side, nor disability on the other.
>
> John Stuart Mill, "The Subjection of Women"

> "Courage!" he said, and pointed toward the land,
> "This mounting wave will role us shoreward soon."
> In the afternoon they came unto a land
> In which it seemed always afternoon.
> All round the coast the languid air did swoon,
> Breathing like one that hath a weary dream.
> Full-faced above the valley stood the moon;
> And, like a downward smoke, the slender stream
> Along the cliff to fall and pause and fall did seem.
>
> Alfred, Lord Tennyson, "The Lotos-Eaters"

FRONT VOWELS

/i/

> In placid hours well-pleased we dream
> Of many a brave unbodied scheme.
> But Form to lend, pulsed life create,
> What unlike things must meet and mate:
>
> Herman Melville, "Art"

ARTICULATION AND PRONUNCIATION

/ɪ/

Imagination! imagination! I put it first years ago, when I was asked what qualities I thought necessary for success upon the stage. And I am still of the same opinion. Imagination, industry, and intelligence—"the three I's"—are all indispensable to the actress, but of these three the greatest is, without any doubt, imagination.

Ellen Terry, The Story of My Life

Music when soft voices die,
Vibrates in the memory—
Odours, when sweet violets sicken,
Live within the sense they quicken.

Percy Bysshe Shelley, "Music, When Soft Voices Die"

/e/

How vainly men themselves amaze
To win the palm, the oak, or bays,
And their uncessant labours see
Crowned from some single herb or tree,
Whose short and narrow-verged shade
Does prudently their toils upbraid

Andrew Marvell, "The Garden"

They were busy much of the day with preparation and rehearsal, and at dinner, that evening, the concourse of guests was such that a place among them for Miss Prime failed to find itself marked. At the time the company rose she was therefore along in the schoolroom, where, towards eleven o'clock, she received a visit from Mrs. Guy. This lady's white shoulders heaved, under the pearls, with an emotion that the very red lips which formed, as if for the full effect, the happiest opposition of color, were not slow to translate. "My dear, you should have seen the sensation—they've had a success!"

Henry James, "Paste"

/ɛ/

"You seem very clever at explaining words, Sir," said Alice. "Would you kindly tell me the meaning of the poem *Jabberwocky*?"

"Let's hear it," said Humpty Dumpty. "I can explain all the poems that ever were invented—and a good many that haven't been invented just yet."

Lewis Carroll, Through the Looking Glass

> The time is not remote when I
> Must by the course of nature die:
> When I foresee my special friends
> Will try to find their private ends:
>
> Jonathan Swift, "Verses on the Death of Doctor Swift"

/æ/

> Alice never could quite make out, in thinking it over afterwards, how it was that they began; all she remembers is that they were running hand in hand, and the Queen went so fast that it was all she could do to keep up with her; and still the Queen kept crying "Faster! Faster!" but Alice felt she could not go faster, though she had no breath left to say so.
>
> Lewis Carroll, *Alice In Wonderland*

CENTRAL VOWELS

/ə/ /ʌ/

> The sun was only ten degrees above the horizon, while the earth turned through nearly a full day during our stay, the sun at Tranquillity Base rose barely eleven degrees—a small fraction of the month-long lunar day. There was a peculiar sensation of the duality of time—the swift rush of events that characterizes all our lives—and the ponderous parade which makes the aging of the universe.
>
> Neil A. Armstrong, Address to Congress, September 16, 1969

/ɝ/ /ɚ/

> Hot sun, cool fire, tempered with sweet air,
> Black shade, fair nurse, shadow my white hair,
> Shine, sun, burn, fire, breathe, air, and ease me,
> Black shade, fair nurse, shroud me and please me;
> Shadow, my sweet nurse, keep me from burning,
> Make not my glad cause, cause of mourning.
>   Let not my beauty's fire
>   Inflame unstaid desire,
>   Nor pierce any bright eye
>   That wandereth lightly.
>
> George Peele, "Bethsabe's Song"

Tender-handed stroke a nettle
    And it stings you for your pains;
Grasp it like a man of mettle
    And it soft as silk remains.
'Tis the same with common natures:
    Use them kindly, they rebel;
But be rough as nutmeg-graters
    And the rogues obey you well.

                    Aaron Hill, "Written on a Window"

BACK VOWELS

/ɑ/

I wander through each chartered street,
Near where the chartered Thames does flow,
And mark in every face I meet
Marks of weakness, marks of woe.

                    William Blake, "London"

/ɔ/

The lady lay in her bed,
    Her couch so warm and soft,
But her sleep was restless and broken still;
    For turning often and oft
From side to side, she mutter'd and moan'd.
    And toss'd her arms aloft.

At last she startled up,
    And gaz'd on the vacant air,
With a look of awe, as if she saw
    Some dreadful phantom there—
And then in the pillow she buried her face
    From vision ill to bear.

                    Thomas Hood, "The Lady's Dream"

Over the land freckled with snow half-thawed
The speculating rooks at their nests cawed
And saw from elm-tops, delicate as flower of grass,
What we below could not see, Winter pass.

                    Edward Thomas, "Thaw"

260

/o/

> The greatest poem ever known
> Is one all poets have outgrown;
> The poetry, innate, untold,
> Of being only four years old.
>
> Christopher Morley, "To a Child"

/ʊ/

> 'Tis as I should entreat you to wear your gloves,
> Or feed on nourishing dishes, or keep you warm,
> Or sue to you to do a peculiar profit
> To your own person: nay, when I have a suit
> Wherein I mean to touch your love indeed,
> It shall be full of poise and difficult weight,
> And fearful to be granted.
>
> William Shakespeare, "Othello"

/u/

> There was a lady lived in a hall,
> Large of her eyes and slim and tall;
> And ever she sung from noon to noon,
> Two red roses across the moon.
>
> William Morris, "Two Red Roses across the Moon"

DIPHTHONGS

/aɪ/

> I became tired and sick,
> Till rising and gliding out I wandered off by myself,
> In the mystical moist night air,
>   and from time to time
> Looked up in perfect silence at the stars.
>
> Walt Whitman, "When I Heard the Learn'd Astronomer"

/aʊ/

> Take this kiss upon the brow!
> And, in parting from you now,
> Thus much let me avow . . .
>
> Edgar Allan Poe, "A Dream Within a Dream"

Ask me no more: the moon may draw the sea;
The cloud may stoop from heaven and take shape,
With fold to fold, of mountain or of cape;
But O too fond, when have I answer'd thee?
Ask me no more.

Alfred, Lord Tennyson, "Ask Me No More"

/ɔɪ/

She makes no noise, but stilly seizeth on
    The flower or herb appointed for her food,
The which she quietly doth feed upon,
    While others range, and gare, but find no good.

John Bunyan, "Upon the Snail"

When that I was and a little tiny boy,
    With hey, ho, the wind and the rain,
A foolish thing was but a toy,
    For the rain it raineth every day.

William Shakespeare, "Twelfth Night"

/ju/

Known and unknown, human, divine;
Sweet human hand and lips and eye;

Alfred, Lord Tennyson, "In Memoriam"

PRONUNCIATION LISTS

The following section contains words that are mispronounced frequently. Words are grouped according to the type of pronunciation error commonly made: phoneme substitution, phoneme omission, phoneme addition, incorrect stress placement, and syllable reduction/deletion. We recommend that you read through *all* lists, checking your pronunciation against correct IPA transcription. Note the words that you miss, and use them as practice materials for your improvement objectives. You will be helped even more if you can use a partner *or* a tape recorder to help you monitor your pronunciation.

SUBSTITUTION

	Standard Pronunciation	Nonstandard Pronunciation
agile	/ædʒəl/	/ædʒaɪl/
beige	/beʒ/	/biʒ/
cache	/kæʃ/	/kætʃ/
censure	/sɛnʃɚ/	/sɛnsɚ/
chagrin	/ʃəgrɪn/	/tʃəgrɪn/
chameleon	/kəmiliən/	/tʃəmiliən/
chassis	/ʃæsi/	/tʃæsi/
chef	/ʃɛf/	/tʃɛf/
children	/tʃɪldrɪn/	/tʃɪldɚn/
chore	/tʃor/	/ʃor/
coma	/komə/	/kɑmə/
conjecture	/kəndʒɛktʃɚ/	/kəndʒɛktɚ/
crux	/krʌks/	/krʊks/
deaf	/dɛf/	/dif/
demise	/dɪmaɪz/	/dɪmiz/
diphthong	/dɪfθɔŋ/	/dɪpθɔŋ/
docile	/dɔsəl/	/dɔsaɪl/
et cetera	/ɛtsɛtərə/	/ɛksɛtərə/
facile	/fæ' sɪl/	/fəsɪ'l/
faux pas	/fo pɑ/	/foks pɑs/
fungi	/fʌndʒaɪ/	/fʌngaɪ/
genuine	/dʒɛnuɪn/	/dʒɛnjuwaɪn/
gist	/dʒɪst/	/gɪst/
handkerchief	/hæŋkɚtʃəf/	/hændkɚtʃəf/
height	/haɪt/	/haɪθ/
homage	/hɔmədʒ/	/homədʒ/
Italian	/ɪtælyən/	/aɪtælyən/
lingerie	/lɑnʒɚre/	/lɪnʒɚre/
macho	/mɑtʃo/	/mɑko/
malignant	/məlɪgnənt/	/məlɪnjənt/

ARTICULATION AND PRONUNCIATION

memento	/məmɛnto/	/momɛnto/
microscopic	/maɪkrəskɑpɪk/	/maɪkrəskɑpɪk/
pathos	/peθos/	/pɑθos/
pitcher	/pɪtʃɚ/	/pɪktʃɚ/
placard	/plækɑrd/	/plekɑrd/
poignant	/pɔɪnjənt/	/pɔɪgnənt/

OMISSION

	Standard Pronunciation	Nonstandard Pronunciation
accessory	/æksɛsɚi/	/əsɛsɚi/
Arctic	/ɑrktɪk/	/ɑrtɪk/
berserk	/bɚzɝk/	/bəzɝk/
champion	/tʃæmpiən/	/tʃæmpin/
dormitory	/dɔrmətɔri/	/dɔmətɔri/
environment	/ənvaɪrnmənt/	/ənvaɪrmənt/
facsimile	/fæksɪməli/	/fæsɪməli/
February	/fɛbrueri/	/fɛbueri/
figure	/fɪgyɚ/	/fɪgɚ/
length	/lɛŋkθ/	/lɛnθ/
library	/laɪbrɛri/	/laɪbɛri/
particularly	/pɚtɪkjulɚli/	/pɚtɪkjɚli/
picture	/pɪktʃɚ/	/pɪtʃɚ/
poem	/poəm/	/pom/
recognize	/rɛkəgnaɪz/	/rɛkənaɪz/
regular	/rɛgyəlɚ/	/rɛglɚ/
scrupulous	/srkrupyələs/	/skrupələs/
strength	/strɛŋkθ/	/strɛnθ/
surprise	/sɚpraɪz/	/səpraɪz/
temperature	/tɛmpɚətʃɚ/	/tɛmpətʃɚ/
terrible	/tɛrɪbəl/	/tɛəbəl/
wouldn't	/wʊdənt/	/wʊnt/

ADDITION

	Standard Pronunciation	Nonstandard Pronunciation
accompanist	/əkʌmpənɪst/	/əkʌmpniəst/
across	/əkrɔs/	/əkrɔst/
aluminum	/əlumənəm/	/əlumniəm/
athlete	/æθlit/	/æθəlit/
athletics	/æθlɛtɪks/	/æθəlɛtɪks/
burglar	/bɝglɚ/	/bɝgəlɚ/
business	/bɪznɪs/	/bɪzənɪs/
chimney	/tʃɪmni/	/tʃɪməni/

corps	/kor/	/korps/
disastrous	/dɪzæstrəs/	/dɪzæstɚəs/
drowned	/draʊnd/	/draʊndəd/
electoral	/ɪlɛktɚəl/	/ɪlɛktɚɪəl/
escape	/ɛskep/	/ɛkskep/
evening	/ivnɪŋ/	/ivənɪŋ/
film	/fɪlm/	/fɪləm/
grievous	/grivəs/	/grivɪəs/
heir	/ɛr/	/hɛr/
herb	/ɝb/	/hɝb/
hors d'oeuvres	/or dɝvz/	/hors də vorz/
hurricane	/hɝəken/	/hyɝəken/
laundry	/lɑndrɪ/	/lɑndərɪ/
monstrous	/mɑnstrəs/	/mɑnstərəs/
often	/ɔfən/	/ɔftən/
once	/wʌns/	/wʌnst/
positively	/pɑsətɪvlɪ/	/pɑsətɪvəlɪ/
psalm	/sɑm/	/psɑm/
salmon	/sæmən/	/sælmən/
statistics	/stətɪstɪks/	/stəstɪstɪks/
subtle	/sʌtəl/	/sʌbtəl/
sword	/sord/	/sword/
veterinarian	/vɛtɚənɝɪən/	/vɛntɚənɝɪən/
wash	/wɑʃ/	/wɔrʃ/
Worcestershire	/wustɚʃɪr/	/worsɛstɚʃɪr/

INCORRECT STRESS PLACEMENT

	Standard Pronunciation	*Nonstandard Pronunciation*
abyss	/ə bɪs'/	/æ' bɪs/
admirable	/æd' mɚ ə bəl/	/əd maɪr' ə bəl/
alias	/e' lɪ əs/	/ə li' əs/
alienate	/el' jə net/	/ə laɪ' ə net/
auspices	/ɔ' spɪʃ səz/	/ɔ spɪʃ' əs/
barbarous	/bɑr bɚ əs/	/bɑr bɛr' i əs/
bravado	/brə vɑ' do/	/brɑ' və do/
brochure	/bro ʃɝ'/	/bro' ʃɚ/
comparable	/kɑm' pɚ ə bəl/	/kəm pɛr' ə bəl/
deluge	/dɛl' juʒ/	/də luʒ'/
epitome	/ə pɪ' tə mi/	/ɛp' ə tom/
guitar	/gə tɑr'/	/gi' tɑr/
ignominious	/ɪg' nə mɪn' ɪ əs/	/ɪg nɑm' ə nəs/
indolence	/ɪn' də ləns/	/ɪn do' ləns/
infamous	/ɪn' fə məs/	/ɪn fem' əs/
maintenance	/men' tə nəns/	/men ten' əns/
maniacal	/mə naɪ' ə kəl/	/men' ɪ æ kəl/

perseverance	/pɚ sə vir′ əns/	/pɚ sɛv′ ɚ əns/
preferable	/prɛf′ ɚ ə bəl/	/prə fɝ′ ə bəl/
superfluous	/su pɝ′ flu əs/	/su pɚ flu′ əs/
theater	/θi′ ə tɚ/	/θi e′ tɚ/
vehement	/vi′ ə mənt/	/və hi′ mənt/

SYLLABLE REDUCTION/DELETION

	Standard Pronunciation	Nonstandard Pronunciation
asphyxiate	/əsfɪksiet/	/əfɪksiet/
bakery	/bekɚɪ/	/bekrɪ/
battery	/bætɚɪ/	/bætrɪ/
boundary	/baʊndɚɪ/	/baʊndrɪ/
camera	/kæmɚə/	/kæmrə/
casualty	/kæʒuəltɪ/	/kæʒəltɪ/
celery	/sɛlɚɪ/	/sɛlrɪ/
correct	/kərɛkt/	/krɛkt/
couldn't	/kʊdənt/	/kʊdnt/
delivery	/dɪlɪvɚɪ/	/dɪlɪvrɪ/
different	/dɪfɚənt/	/dɪfrɪnt/
family	/fæməlɪ/	/fæmlɪ/
federal	/fɛdɚəl/	/fɛdrəl/
geography	/dʒiɑgrəfɪ/	/dʒɑgrəfɪ/
grocery	/grosɚɪ/	/grosrɪ/
history	/hɪstɚɪ/	/hɪstrɪ/
liberal	/lɪbɚəl/	/lɪbrəl/
memory	/mɛmɚɪ/	/mɛmrɪ/
orange	/ɔrɪndʒ/	/ɔrndʒ/
probably	/prɑbəblɪ/	/prɑblɪ/
salary	/sælɚɪ/	/sælrɪ/
temperamental	/tɛmpɚəmɛntəl/	/tɛmprəmɛntəl/
traveling	/trævəlɪŋ/	/trɑvlɪŋ/
veteran	/vɛtɚən/	/vɛtrən/
victory	/vɪktɚɪ/	/vɪktrɪ/

Part Five

Appendices—Reading for Voice Improvement

Appendix 1

Phrases and Sentences Graduated in Length

TWO-SYLLABLE PHRASES AND SENTENCES

		Pitch Inflection	Loudness Stress	
I am.	I will.	You can!	all right	Get up.
You are.	Oh, no.	I'm fine.	King me.	black eye
He is.	Do it.	Look out!	Call me.	Cast off.
We are.	Don't go.	They're gone!	lost time	down here
You are.	What time?	Try it.	My, my.	eat out
They are.	I'll try.	Why not?	No good	free up
Come in.	Stop it.	no time	Oh, my.	gee whiz
Get out.	Catch up.	too bad	part time	hot time
Keep out.	Watch out.	Get lost.	Guess what?	I'm fine.
Get up.	Thank you.	tea time	right now	last night
So long.	Go home.	Buy now!	Start up.	my mom
Stand up.	Strike out.	Come back!	too much	next time
Sit down.	Turn right.	Don't go.	used up	on top
Jump up.	first base	end run	Vote now.	post card
How much?	home plate	fast food	Where to?	rest stop
Push it.	Wake up.	great big	uptown	run down
Why not?	You bet.	grown up	yes, sir	Step down.
Help me.	Good night.	Have some.	yes, mam	Sew up.
Prove it.	Goodbye.	I was!	Act now.	Where to?
Tell me.	too much	Just so.	Be good.	May I?

269

APPENDIX 1

THREE-SYLLABLE PHRASES AND SENTENCES

		Pitch Inflection	Loudness Stress
Pick it up.	Is that so?	Put that back.	See you soon.
Put it down.	Bake a pie.	Make salad.	Catch the ball.
Bring it here.	Ride the horse.	Fly away.	I said no.
I don't know.	Close the door.	Wear a tie.	more or less
Why not go?	Sweep the floor.	Go downtown.	Clean the tub.
Come over.	Start the game.	Race the car.	Wash dishes.
Go away.	Set the clock.	down the road	Fly the kite.
Here we are.	That's all right.	back by five	Build a house.
Good morning.	Go to town.	I found it.	Light the lamp.
Can you go?	not so fast	Run it down.	Wind your watch.
Do it now.	Hit the ball.	Hurry up.	Don't touch it.
How are you?	Sleep all night.	Come back soon.	There she is.
Help me, please.	Ring the bell.	It's snowing.	I'm sorry.
Is it time?	Don't do it.	like old times	Don't buy that.
I'm on time.	That's not true.	pretty eyes	Write a book.
Am I late?	Come back here.	far away	buy and sell
I told you.	Start a fire.	Go to sleep.	Look around.
over there	Mop the floor.	Call me soon.	Share the toy.
what about	Go to school.	You look good.	Push and pull.
Should we go?	Write a check.	I feel fine.	a red light

FOUR-SYLLABLE PHRASES AND SENTENCES

	Pitch Inflection	Loudness Stress
It's very hot.	What could I do?	Give it to me.
Fry the bacon.	Will you be there?	Please say something.
Am I on time?	You should say so.	Is that enough?
Are you ready?	Am I early?	Write a letter.
I didn't know.	Where do you sit?	Answer the phone.
Pick the apples.	I told you so.	When do we go?
a baby boy	That's not my fault.	Was I correct?
Feed the kitten.	How do you feel?	Do it again.
Don't wait for me.	Show it to me.	They all have jobs.
Can we go now?	Let's wait for them.	Open your eyes.

PHRASES AND SENTENCES GRADUATED IN LENGTH

I don't know why.	What time is it?	We must go now.
How are you now?	What have you done?	Did you know that?
Bring some money.	They are so slow.	How do you do?
over the top	Where do you live?	Tell me the truth.
I like ice cream.	Turn to the left.	Did you hear me?
Open the door.	Fill the bird bath.	Keep on trying.
Bake apple pie.	Turn on the light.	Put it away.
I don't like that.	Walk down the hall.	It stopped snowing.
Should we go now?	Let's go swimming.	Type the letter.
Is that your car?	Play volleyball.	Let's go downtown.

FIVE-SYLLABLE SENTENCES

	Pitch Inflection	Loudness Stress
Give it to me now.	The rain was welcome.	I wouldn't do that.
You are a good dog.	We designed our house.	Did he say maybe?
Come back when you can.	She burst the balloon.	Stop, look, and listen.
He has a nice car.	Speak clearly to them.	Bring a keg of beer.
How much do you want?	He is very shy.	Answer the question.
There's not enough room.	There's not enough time.	I'm moving forward.
The wind blew all day.	They've sold their horses.	Use a safety pin.
Do it before noon.	The crowd was pushed back.	Are you running now?
Do you want to go?	He planted sweet corn.	How did the race go?
Go to the bookstore.	The weather was cold.	The light bulb burned out.
I want some pizza.	Who pulled the alarm?	Why don't you like it?
Do you have a dime?	Bring a stronger rope.	You made a mistake.
I'll come back today.	The dogs were barking.	Where did you grow up?
Have you talked to them?	We picked the berries.	Can you believe it?
Don't give it to me.	Let's watch some TV.	Open the window.
It's not all my fault.	We rode the rapids.	Keep on working hard.
I don't want to talk.	That's a better one.	I missed the last class.
They are very nice.	Is she your sister?	Let's play basketball.
You shouldn't do that.	We went to the bank.	The room was noisy.
They played in the sand.	Please open the door.	I was so nervous.

SIX-SYLLABLE SENTENCES

Mike was cutting the grass.	What's not right must be wrong.
The player broke his arm.	Go to the store with me.

APPENDIX 1

All the girls were laughing.
Get there before they close.
Did you hear what she said?
Come in and close the door.
Are you going tonight?
Put everything away.
Come whenever you can.
We heard that yesterday.
The player broke his leg.
The children went swimming.
It's time to go to class.
Please open the window.
Hit the ball to shortstop.
Don't wait till it's too late.
Meet me at the courthouse.
Feed the dog his supper.
What's on TV tonight?

The fields were very dry.
Did you find your notebook?
Let's go skiing today.
Do you like your new job?
Promise that you won't tell.
May I borrow that too?
How are you this morning?
Beth was washing her clothes.
The flags blew in the wind.
He slept under the tree.
We don't want it to rain.
He couldn't start the fire.
Do you think he's happy?
When should we come around?
Let's go to a movie.
How much rent do you pay?
Who's on the telephone?

SEVEN- AND EIGHT-SYLLABLE SENTENCES

What movie would you like to see?
There's plenty of room in my house.
Sometimes I think you're very wrong.
Would you come by about seven?
May I have another piece?
I was raised in the Midwest.
Were you able to hear him speak?
The fisherman caught a large fish.
We grew roses on the back fence.
Show me how it should be done.
Yesterday he bought a new car.
I have too much to do today.
What do you want on your pie?
We ran a match race yesterday.
Come over this afternoon.

Please make sure your hands are clean.
The snow was a welcome sight.
All the fences were jumped with ease.
What's your favorite music?
I need to go to the bank.
Let's not take too much time here.
Why are there only seven?
The clock stopped at four thirty-nine.
Put it back where you found it.
The boy found it by the cooler.
We went skiing on the lake.
I eat breakfast every day.
Do you think we should start that now?
The trip was very exciting.
Make sure you turn off the printer.

NINE- AND TEN-SYLLABLE SENTENCES

We need to go to the grocery store.
I scored one hundred percent on the test.

Let's go scuba diving this summer.
She had an interview this afternoon.

She has five brothers and four sisters.
Two of her brothers are in college.
That was the best time I ever ran.
Let's go to the ball game on Saturday.
I couldn't believe how many were there.
She went to Florida during spring break.
Would you hold the door open for me?
I'm very happy that you could come.
He ordered a hamburger for lunch.
The snow melted before we could ride sleds.
We went fishing in Lake Superior.
I'm tired of cafeteria food.
What good movies have you seen lately?

I studied all night long for this test.
The marching band practiced before the game.
I'm going home for the holidays.
Do you have to work after class today?
There wasn't one parking space to be found.
Sometimes it's hard to keep up with the news.
You look absolutely marvelous.
What time do you think we should leave today?
The party was over by one-thirty.
I should be finished in time to leave then.
Why don't you take a fifteen-minute break?
Who was it that called on the telephone?
It's your turn to wash the dishes tonight.

ELEVEN- TO FIFTEEN-SYLLABLE SENTENCES

The instructor was rigid in his opinion.

With any luck, this course shouldn't be too difficult.

American History is my favorite class.

I would have helped you with that problem if you had only asked.

I want to jog for an hour before I begin to study.

My parents are coming to visit for the weekend.

How many more tests do you have this semester?

It's important that you listen closely in his class.

I wrote for so long that my hand began to cramp.

What was in the package that you received this afternoon?

Most people wouldn't even consider doing that.

We stood in line for two hours to buy the tickets.

I just can't seem to get this program to run.

There were eight hundred people in the psychology class.

My pen ran out of ink in the middle of the test.

Most of this information can be found in the library.

Were you able to finish your project on time?

I was happy when classes were cancelled because of snow.

Everyone was shocked when he announced the surprise test.

The professor wouldn't start before she had her coffee.

Two students from Taiwan were in my physics class.

We are going on a picnic if it doesn't rain.

My tape recorder couldn't pick up his voice.

What time do you want to leave for the basketball game?

Our dormitory had a false alarm last night.

I can't wait until the Christmas holidays.

I swam ten laps this morning before eight o'clock.
Someone left his coat in the biology lab.
Make sure that you have all of the facts and then proceed.
The library was so quiet, you could hear your heartbeat.

SIXTEEN- TO TWENTY-SYLLABLE SENTENCES

The proposal was opposed by everyone who was eligible to vote.
How many times must we listen to the same thing over and over again?
I had steak, fried potatoes, and a tossed salad for dinner last night.
We knew as soon as we entered the room that someone had been here before us.
He posed the most important question that we would have to consider.
If I can raise the money, I'm going to fly to California.
Though we had been there only for a week, it seemed more like a month.
Let me know if there's anything I can do to help you get ready.
Since the building didn't have air conditioning, the class was unbearable.
Nobody noticed when he entered the room a half-hour late.
Did you hear about the plans to renovate the stadium for next year?
How many people do you think it will take to permit us to break even?
The runner developed a blister on his foot halfway through the race.
Students were caught painting victory signs on the railroad overpass.
How many months do you think it will take us to finish this project?
We should be able to afford it if six of us rent the apartment.
He commuted to the university every day for five years.
She had already learned many of the skills in her co-op job.
I have eighteen more hours to complete for graduation.
The referee had obviously made a serious error in judgment.
The smoke was so thick in the lab that the sprinklers suddenly came on.
We carefully placed the project on the table for the instructor's inspection.
Someone threw an aerosol can on the fire, causing a loud explosion.
Would you rather take a written or an oral examination?
If you wait too long then you're going to miss a great opportunity.
I've been invited to go on vacation with my best friend's family.
It's impossible to measure the knowledge gained from this seminar.
Most people would not have the imagination to create such a thing.
Stop at the store on your way home and pick up a gallon of milk.
We can't decide whether or not to participate in formal graduation.

Appendix 2

Paragraph Readings

PASSAGE 1

For the most wild yet the most homely narrative which I am about to pen,/ I neither expect nor solicit belief./ Mad indeed would I be to expect it,/ in a case where my very senses reject their own evidence./ Yet, mad am I not—/ and very surely do I not dream./ But tomorrow I die, and today I would unburden my soul./ My immediate purpose is to place before the world,/ plainly, succinctly, and without comment,/ a series of mere household events./ In their consequences, these events have terrified—/ have tortured—have destroyed me./ Yet I will not attempt to expound them./ To me, they have presented little but horror—/to many they will seem less terrible than baroques./ Hereafter, perhaps, some intellect may be found which will reduce my phantasm to the commonplace—/ some intellect more calm, more logical, and far less excitable than my own,/ which will perceive, in the circumstances I detail with awe,/ nothing more than an ordinary succession of very natural causes and effects.

Edgar Allen Poe
from *The Black Cat*

PASSAGE 2

Mr. President and Gentlemen of the Convention:/ If we could first know where we are, and whither we are tending,/ we could better judge what to do, and how to do it./ We are now far into the fifth year since a policy was initiated/ with the avowed object, and confident promise, of putting an end to slavery agitation./ Under the operation of that policy, that agitation not only has not ceased,/ but has constantly augmented./ In my opinion,/ it will not cease until a crisis shall have been reached and passed./ "A house divided against itself cannot stand."/ I believe this government cannot endure permanently, half slave and half free./ I do not expect the Union to be dissolved;/ I do not expect the house to fall;/ But I do expect that it will cease to be divided./ It will become all one thing or all the other./

Either the opponents of slavery will arrest the further spread of it,/ and place it where the public mind shall rest in the belief that it is in the course of ultimate extinction;/ or its advocates will push it forward till it shall become alike lawful in all the States,/ old as well as new,/ North as well as South. . . .

Abraham Lincoln

PASSAGE 3

The wrath of God is like great waters that are dammed for the present;/ they increase more and more, and rise higher and higher, till an outlet is given;/ and the longer the stream is stopped, the more rapid and mighty is its course,/ when once it is let loose./ 'Tis true, that judgement against your evil work has not been executed hitherto;/ the floods of God's vengeance have been withheld;/ but your guilt in the meantime is constantly increasing,/ and you are every day treasuring up more wrath;/ the waters are continually rising, and waxing more and more mighty;/ and there is nothing but the mere pleasure of God that holds the waters back,/ that are unwilling to be stopped, and press hard to go forward./

If God should only withdraw his hand from the floodgate, it would immediately fly open,/ and the fiery floods and the fierceness and the wrath of God would rush forth with inconceivable fury/ and would come upon you with omnipotent power;/ and if your strength were ten thousand times greater than it is,/ yea, ten thousand times greater than the strength of the stoutest, sturdiest devil in hell,/ it would be nothing to withstand or endure it./

The bow of God's wrath is bent, and the arrow made ready on the string,/ and justice bends the arrow at your heart, and strains the bow,/ and it is nothing but the mere pleasure of God,/ and that of an angry God, without any promise or obligation at all,/ that keeps the arrow one moment from being made drunk by your blood.

Jonathan Edwards

PASSAGE 4

In the long history of the world,/ only a few generations have been granted the role in defending freedom in its hour of maximum danger./ I do not shrink from this responsibility;/ I welcome it./ I do not believe that any of us would exchange places with any other people or any other generation./ The energy, the faith, the devotion which we bring to this endeavor/ will light our country and all that serve it,/ and the glow from that fire can truly light the world./

And so, my fellow Americans,/ ask not what your country can do for you;/ ask what you can do for your country./

My fellow citizens of the world,/ ask not what America will do for you,/ but what together we can do for the freedom of man.

Finally, whether you are citizens of America or citizens of the world,/ ask of us here the same high standards of strength and sacrifice which we ask of you./ With a good conscience our only sure reward,/ with history the final judge of our deeds,/ let us go forth to lead the land we love,/ asking His blessing and His help,/ but knowing that here on earth God's work must truly be our own.

John F. Kennedy

PASSAGE 5

While I was in San Francisco, I enjoyed my first earthquake. It was one which was long called the "great" earthquake, and is doubtless so distinguished till this day. It was just after noon, on a bright October day. I was coming down Third street. The only objects in motion anywhere in sight in the thickly built and populace quarter, were a man in a buggy behind me, and a streetcar wending slowly up a cross street. Otherwise, all was solitude and a Sabbath stillness. As I turned the corner, around a frame house, there was a great rattle and jar, and it occurred to me that here was an item!—no doubt a fight in that house. Before I could turn and seek the door, there came a really terrific shock; the ground seemed to roll under me in waves, interrupted by a violent joggling up and down, and there was a heavy grinding noise as of brick houses rubbing together. I fell up against the frame house and hurt my elbow. I knew what it was, now, and from mere reportorial instinct, nothing else, took out my watch and noted the time of day; at that moment a third and still severer shock came, and as I reeled about on the pavement trying to keep my footing, I saw a sight! The entire front of a tall four-story brick building in Third street sprung outward like a door and fell sprawling across the street, raising a dust like a great volume of smoke! And here came the buggy—overboard went the man, and in less time than I can tell it the vehicle was distributed in small fragments along three hundred yards of the street. One could have fancied that someone had fired a charge of chair-rounds and rags down the thoroughfare. The streetcar had stopped, the horses were rearing and plunging, the passengers were pouring out of both ends, and one fat man had crashed half way through a glass window on one side of the car, got wedged fast and was squirming and screaming like an impaled madman. Every door of every house, as far as the eye could reach, was vomiting a stream of human beings; and almost before one could execute a wink and begin another, there was a massed multitude of people stretching in endless procession down every street my position commanded. Never was solemn solitude turned into teeming life quicker.

Mark Twain
from *The San Francisco Earthquake*

PASSAGE 6

They tell us, sir, that we are weak; unable to cope with so formidable an adversary. But when shall we be stronger? Will it be the next week, or the next year? Will it be when we are totally disarmed, and when a British guard shall be stationed in every house? Shall we gather strength by irresolution and inaction? Shall we acquire the means of effectual resistance, by lying supinely on our backs, and hugging the delusive phantom of hope, until our enemies should have bound us hand and foot? Sir we are not weak, if we make proper use of the means which the God of nature hath placed in our power. Three millions of people, armed in the holy cause of liberty, and in such a country as that which we possess, are invincible by any force which our enemy can send against us. Besides, sir, we shall not fight our battles alone. There is a just God who presides over the destinies of nations; and who will raise up friends to fight our battles for us. The battle, sir, is not to the strong alone; it is to the vigilant, the active, the brave. Besides, sire, we have no election. If we were base enough to desire it, it is now too late to retire from the contest. There is no retreat, but in submission and slavery! Our chains are forged! Their clanking may be heard on the plains of Boston! The war is inevitable—and let it come! I repeat it, sir, let it come!

It is in vain, sir, to extenuate the matter. Gentlemen may cry peace, peace—but there is no peace. The war is actually begun! The next gale that sweeps from the north will bring to our ears the clash of resounding arms! Our brethren are already in the field! Why stand we here idle? What is it that gentlemen wish? What would they have? Is life so dear, or peace so sweet, as to be purchased at the price of chains and slavery? Forbid it, Almighty God! I know not what course others may take; but as for me, give me liberty, or give me death!

Patrick Henry

PASSAGE 7

Friends and fellow-citizens: I stand before you tonight under the indictment for the alleged crime of having voted at the last Presidential election, without having the lawful right to vote. It shall be my work this evening to prove to you that in thus voting, I not only committed no crime, but, instead, simply exercised my citizen's rights, guaranteed to me and all United States citizens by the National Constitution, beyond the power of any State to deny.

The preamble of the Federal Constitution says:

"We, the people of the United States, in order to form a more perfect union, establish justice, insure domestic tranquility, provide for the common defense, promote the general welfare, and secure the blessings of liberty to ourselves and our posterity, do ordain and establish this Constitution for the United States of America."

It was we, the people; not we, the white male citizens; nor yet we, the male citizens; but we, the whole people, who formed the Union. And we formed it, not to give the blessings of liberty, but to secure them; not to the half of ourselves and the half of our posterity, but to the whole people—women as well as men. And it is a downright mockery to talk to women of their enjoyment of the blessings of liberty while they are denied the use of their only means of securing them provided by this democratic-republican government—the ballot.

For any State to make a sex qualification that must ever result in the disfranchisement of one entire half of the people is to pass a bill of attainder, or an ex post facto law, and is therefore a violation of the supreme law of the land. By it the blessings of liberty are forever withheld from women and their female posterity. To them this government has no just powers derived from the consent of the governed. To them this government is not a democracy. It is not a republic. It is an odious aristocracy; a hateful oligarchy of sex; the most hateful aristocracy ever established on the face of the globe; an oligarchy of wealth, where the rich govern the poor. An oligarchy of learning, where the educated govern the ignorant, or even an oligarchy of race, where the Saxon rules the African, might be endured; but this oligarchy of sex, which makes fathers, brothers, husbands, sons, the oligarchs over the mothers and sisters, the wives and daughters of every household—which ordains all men sovereigns, all women subjects, carries dissension, discord and rebellion into every home of the nation.

Webster, Worcester and Bouvier all define a citizen to be a person in the United States, entitled to vote and hold office.

The only question to be settled now is: Are women persons? And I hardly believe any of our opponents will have the hardihood to say they are not. Being persons, then, women are citizens; and no State has a right to make any law, or to enforce any old law, that shall abridge their privileges or immunities. Hence, every discrimination against women in the constitutions and laws of the several States is today null and void, precisely as is every one against Negroes.

Susan B. Anthony

PASSAGE 8

It chanced on Sunday, when Mr. Utterson was on his usual walk with Mr. Enfield, that their way lay once again through the by-street; and that when they came in front of the door, both stopped to gaze on it.

"Well," said Enfield, "that story's at an end at least. We shall never see more of Mr. Hyde."

"I hope not," said Utterson, "Did I ever tell you that I once saw him, and shared your feeling of repulsion?"

"It was impossible to do the one without the other," returned Enfield. "And by the way, what an ass you must have thought me, not to know that this was a back way to Dr. Jekyll's! It was partly your own fault that I found it out, even when I did."

"So you found it out, did you?" said Utterson. "But if that be so, we may step into the court and take a look at the windows. To tell you the truth, I am uneasy about poor Jekyll; and even outside, I feel as if the presence of a friend might do him good."

The court was very cool and a little damp, and full of premature twilight, although the sky, high up overhead, was still bright with sunset. The middle one of the three windows was half-way open; and sitting close beside it, taking the air with an infinite sadness of mien, like some deconsolate prisoner, Utterson saw Dr. Jekyll.

"What! Jekyll!" he cried. "I trust you are better."

"I am very low, Utterson," replied the doctor drearily, "very low. It will not last long, thank God."

"You stay too much indoors," said the lawyer. "You should be out, whipping up the circulation like Mr. Enfield and me. (This is my cousin-Mr. Enfield-Dr. Jekyll.) Come now; get your hat and take a quick turn with us."

"You are very good," sighed the other. "I should like to very much; but no, no, no, it is quite impossible; I dare not. But indeed, Utterson, I am very glad to see you; this is really a great pleasure; I would ask you and Mr. Enfield up, but the place is really not fit."

"Why then", said the lawyer, good-naturedly, "the best thing we can do is to stay down here and speak with you from where we are."

"That is just what I was about to venture to propose," returned the doctor with a smile. But the words were hardly uttered, before the smile was struck out of his face and succeeded by an expression of such abject terror and despair, as froze the very blood of the two gentlemen below. They saw it but for a glimpse for the window was instantly thrust down but that glimpse had been sufficient, and they turned and left the court without word. In silence, too, they traversed the by-street; and it was not until they had come into a neighbouring thoroughfare, where even upon a Sunday there were still some stirrings of life, that Mr. Utterson at last turned and looked at his companion. They were both pale; and there was an answering horror in their eyes.

"God forgive us, God forgive us," said Mr. Utterson.

But Mr. Enfield only nodded his head very seriously, and walked on once more in silence.

Robert Louis Stevenson
from *Dr. Jekyll and Mr. Hyde*

Appendix 3
Poetry Readings

PASSAGE 1

Annabel Lee

It was many and many a year ago,
In a kingdom by the sea,
That a maiden there lived whom you may know
By the name of Annabel Lee;—
And this maiden she lived with no other thought
Than to love and be loved by me.

She was a child and I was a child,
In this kingdom by the sea,
But we loved with a love that was more than love—
I and my Annabel Lee—
With a love that the winged seraphs of Heaven
Coveted her and me.

And this was the reason that, long ago,
In this kingdom by the sea,
A wind blew out of a cloud, by night
Chilling my Annabel Lee;
So that her highborn kinsmen came
And bore her away from me,
To shut her up in a sepulchre
In this kingdom by the sea.

The angels, not half so happy in Heaven,
Went envying her and me;
Yes! that was the reason (as all men know,
In this kingdom by the sea)
That the wind came out of the cloud, chilling
And killing my Annabel Lee.

But out love it was stronger by far than the love
Of those who were older than we—
Of many far wiser than we—
And neither the angels in Heaven above
Nor the demons down under the sea,
Can ever dissever my soul from the soul
Of the beautiful Annabel Lee;—

For the moon never beams without bringing me dreams
Of the beautiful Annabel Lee;
And the stars never rise but I see the bright eyes
Of the beautiful Annabel Lee;
And so, all the night-tide, I lie down by the side
Of my darling, my darling, my life and my bride,
In her sepulchre there by the sea—
In her tomb by the sounding sea.

Edgar Allan Poe

PASSAGE 2

The Wife of Usher's Well

There lived a wife at Usher's Well,
And a wealthy wife was she;
She had three stout and stalwart sons,
And sent them o'er the sea.

They hadna been a week from her,
A week but barely ane,
Whan word came to the carline wife
That her three sons were gane.

They hadna been a week from her,
A week but barely three,
Whan word came to the carline wife
That her sons she'd never see.

"I wish the wind may never cease,
Nor fashes in the flood,
Till my three sons come hame to me,
In earthly flesh and blood."

It fell about the Martinmass,
When nights are lang and mirk,
The carline wife's three sons came hame,
And their hats were o the birk.

It neither grew in syke nor ditch,
Nor yet in ony sheugh;
But at the gates o Paradise,
That birk grew fair eneugh.

"Blow up the fire, my maidens,
Bring water from the well;
For a' my house shall feast this night,
Since my three sons are well."

And she has made to them a bed,
She's made it large and wide,
And she's taen her mantle her about,
Sat down at the bed-side.

Up then crew the red, red cock,
And up and crew the gray;
The eldest to the youngest said,
"Tis time we were away."

The cock he hadna crawd but once,
And clapped his wings at a',
When the youngest to the eldest said,
"Brother, we must awa.

"The cock doth craw, the day doth daw,
The channerin worm doth chide;
Gin we be mist out o our place,
A sair pain we maun bide.

"Fare ye weel, my mother dear!
Fareweel to barn and byre!
And fare ye weel, the bonny lass
That kindles my mother's fire!"

Unknown

PASSAGE 3

Bonny Barbara Allan

In Scarlet town, where I was born,
There was a fair maid dwelling,
Made every youth cry Well-a-away!
Her name was Barbara Allan.

All in the merry month of May,
When green buds they were swelling,
Young Jemmy Grove on his death-bed lay,
For love of Barbara Allan.

O slowly, slowly rose she up,
To the place where he was lying,
And when she drew the curtain by,
"Young man, I think you're dying."

O 'tis I'm sick, and very, very, very sick,
And 'tis a' for Barbara Allan";
"O the better for me ye's never be,
Tho your heart's blood were spilling,

"O dinna ye mind, young man," said she,
"When ye was in the tavern drinking,
That ye made the healths go round and round,
And slighted Barbara Allan?"

He turned his face unto the wall,
And death was with him dealing:
"Adieu, Adieu, my dear friends all,
And be kind to Barbara Allan."

And slowly, slowly rose she up,
And slowly, slowly left him,
And sighing said she could not stay,
Since death of life had reft him.

She had not gane a mile but twa,
When she heard the dead-bell knelling,
And every jow that the dead-bell gave
Cried, "Woe to Barbara Allan!"

"O mother, mother, make my bed!
O make it saft and narrow!
Since my love died for me today,
I'll die for him tomorrow."

Unknown

PASSAGE 4

The Old Cloak

This winter's weather it waxeth cold,
And frost it freezeth on every hill,
And Boreas blows his blast so bold
That all our cattle are like to spill.
Bell, my wife, she loves no strife;
She said unto me quietly,
"Rise up, and save cow Crumbock's life!"
Man, put thine old cloak about thee!"

HE

O Bell my wife, why dost thou flyte?
Thou kens my cloak is very thin:
It is so bare and over worn,
A cricket cannot creep therein.
Then I'll no longer borrow nor lend;
For once I'll new apparell'd be;
To-morow I'll to town and spend;
For I'll have a new cloak about me.

SHE

Cow Crumbock is a very good cow:
She has been always true to the pail;
She has help'd us to butter and cheese, I trow
And other things she will not fail.
I would be loth to see her pine.
Good husband, counsel take of me:
It is not for us to go so fine—
Man, take thine old cloak about thee!

HE

My cloak it was a very good cloak,
It hath been always true to the wear;
But now it is not worth a groat:
I have had it four and forty year.
Sometime it was of cloth in grain:
'Tis now but a sieve, as you may see:
It will neither hold out wind nor rain;
And I'll have a new cloak about me.

SHE

It is four and forty years ago
Since the one of us the other did ken;
And we have had, betwixt us two,
Of children either nine or ten:
We have brought them up to women and men:
In the fear of God I trow they be:
And why wilt thou thyself misken?
Man, take thine old cloak about thee!

HE

O Bell my wife, why dost thou flyte?
Now is now, and then was then:
Seek now all the world throughout,
Thou kens not clowns from gentlemen:
They are clad in black, green, yellow and blue,
So far above their own degree.
Once in my life I'll take a view;
For I'll have a new cloak about me.

SHE

King Stephen was a worthy peer;
His breeches cost him but a crown;
He held them sixpence all too dear,
Therefore he called the tailor 'lown.'
He was a king and wore the crown,
And thou'se but of a low degree:
It's pride that puts this country down:
Man, take thine old cloak about thee!

HE

Bell my wife, she loves not strife,
Yet she will lead me, if she can:
And to maintain an easy life
I oft must yield, though I'm good-man.
It's not for a man with a woman to threap,
Unless he first give o'ver the plea:
As we began, so will we keep,
And I'll take my old cloak about me.

Unknown

PASSAGE 5

By-low, My Babe

By-low, my babe, lie still and sleep;
It grieves me sore to see thee weep.
If thou wert quiet I'd be glad;
Thou mourning makes my sorrow sad.
By-low, my boy, thy mother's joy,
Thy father breeds me great annoy—
By-low, lie low.

When he began to court my love,
And me with sugared words to move,
His feignings false and flattering cheer
To me that time did not appear.
But now I see most cruelly
He cares not for my babe nor me—
By-low, lie low.

Lie still, my darling, sleep awhile,
And when thou wak'st thou'llt sweetly smile;
But smile not as thy father did,
To cozen maids-nay, God forbid!
But yet I fear thou wilt grow near
Thy father's heart and face to bear—
By-low, lie low.

I cannot choose, but ever will
Be loving to thy father still;
Where'er he stay, where'er he ride
My love with him doth still abide.
In weal or woe, where'er he go,
My heart shall not forsake him; so
By-low, lie low.

Unknown

References

Blood, G., Mahan, B. and Hyman, M. (1979), Judging personality and appearance from voice disorders, *Journal of Communication Disorders*, 12, 63–67.

Boone, D. (1979), *The Voice and Voice Therapy*, Englewood Cliffs, N.J.: Prentice-Hall.

Chomsky, N. (1965), *Aspects of the theory of syntax*, Cambridge, Mass.: MIT Press.

Fairbanks, G. (1960), *Voice and Articulation Drill Book*, New York: Harper and Brothers.

Hall, E. T. (1966), *The hidden dimension*, Garden City, N.Y.: Doubleday.

Harper, R. G., Wiens, A. N., and Matarazzo, J. D. (1978), *Nonverbal communication*, New York: Wiley.

Lindfors, J. W. (1987), *Children's Language and Learning*, 2nd ed., Englewood Cliffs, N.J.: Prentice-Hall.

Mackay, I. (1987), *Phonetics: the Science of Speech Production*, 2nd ed., Boston: Little, Brown.

Stemple, J., and Forner, L., *Quick-Screen For Voice Effectiveness*, United Publishers, Inc.: in Press.

Vandenberg, J. (1958), Myoelastic-aerodynamic theory of voice production, *Journal of Speech and Hearing Research*, 1, 227–224.

Wolfram, W., and Johnson, R. (1982), *Phonological Analysis: Focus on American English*, Washington, D.C.: Center for Applied Linguistics.

Appendix 4

Student Pronunciation/Articulation Test (SPAT)

WORD LIST

police	valuable	smooth	wife	seems
bag	thief	alias	year	building
Tom	the	wise	rope	bracelet
diamond	safe	cash	last	guest
camera	zipper	prestige	away	ask
gathering	shadow	chief	lawyer	early
apparent	hotel	jewel	arrive	were
hobby	effort	reaching	nylon	such
September	discover	adjust	hole	amount
hidden	pathetic	wretch	through	jewel
record	leather	huge	street	would
began	inside	money	prison	only
cop	amazed	night	creep	autumn
grab	convention	famous	spite	promise
theft	illusion	window	stone	you
had	bellhop	finger	scale	while
luck	life	dumb	sleep	out
rogue	glove	down	black	Roy
fact	month	long	fled	

PARAGRAPH READING

It seems so long ago, but in fact you know it was only last year. The month was September and promise of an early autumn was in the air. A huge gathering of famous lawyers and their wives had arrived for a convention. Roy Stone, the hotel's chief bellhop, was amazed by the amount of jewels, valuables, and money stored in the hotel safe. One night, while the guests were sleeping, a thief scaled the building with a nylon rope, crept in through a hole in an eighth-story window and discovered the safe. With little effort, the rogue began to pry open the door and, reaching inside with a glove, scooped the cash and jewels into a zippered leather bag. He fled away undetected through the lobby and down the street. The next day, the theft was apparent when Mrs. Black asked for her diamond bracelet. The police were summoned to solve the crime, but it was the hidden camera that fingered the pathetic thief. Tom Wise, alias the Shadow, was out of luck. In spite of his long record, the dumb wretch had been under the illusion that no cop would ever grab such a smooth operator. Now he must adjust to prison life—no adventure, no prestige.

PRONUNCIATION

lapel	figure	coma
preferable	statistics	height
infamous	chimney	avenue
library	burglar	yellow
regular	brochure	criminal

SCORING KEY

Word Position

Phoneme	Initial			Medial			Final		
		Word	Paragraph		Word	Paragraph		Word	Paragraph

STOPS

Phoneme	Initial	Medial	Final
p	*p*olice	a*p*parent	co*p*
b	*b*ag	ho*bb*y	gra*b*
t	*t*om	Sep*t*ember	thef*t*
d	*d*iamond	hi*dd*en	ha*d*
k	*c*amera	re*c*ord	lu*ck*
g	*g*athering	be*g*an	ro*gue*

FRICATIVES

Phoneme	Initial	Medial	Final
f	*f*act	e*ff*ort	li*fe*
v	*v*aluable	disco*v*er	glo*ve*
θ	*th*ief	pa*th*etic	mon*th*
ð	*th*e	lea*th*er	smoo*th*
s	*s*afe	in*s*ide	alia*s*
z	*z*ipper	ama*z*ed	wi*se*
ʃ	*sh*adow	conven*ti*on	ca*sh*
ʒ		illu*si*on	presti*ge*
h	*h*otel	bell*h*op	

AFFRICATES

Phoneme	Initial	Medial	Final
tʃ	*ch*ief	rea*ch*ing	wret*ch*
dʒ	*j*ewel	a*dj*ust	hu*ge*

NASALS

Phoneme	Initial	Medial	Final
m	*m*oney	fa*m*ous	du*mb*
n	*n*ight	wi*n*dow	dow*n*
ŋ		fi*ng*er	lo*ng*

GLIDES

Phoneme	Initial	Medial	Final
w	*w*ife	a*w*ay	
j	*y*ear	law*y*er	
r	*r*ope	ar*r*ive	
l	*l*ast	ny*l*on	ho*le*

			□□□□□□□□	□□□□□□□□
BLENDS	θr str pr kr sp st sk sl bl fl	*th*rough *str*eet *pr*ison *cr*eep *sp*ite *st*one *sc*ale *sl*eep *bl*ack *fl*ed		
VOWELS	i ɪ e ɛ æ ɝ ɚ ʌ ə u ʊ o ɔ ɑ	s*ee*ms b*ui*lding br*a*celet g*ue*st *a*sk *ear*ly w*ere* s*u*ch *a*mount j*e*wel w*ou*ld *o*nly *au*tumn pr*o*mise	□□□□□□□□□□□□□□	□□□□□□□□□□□□□□
DIPHTHONGS	ju aɪ aʊ ɔɪ	*you* *whi*le *ou*t *Roy*	□□□□	□□□□

*Scoring Key:
S = substitution
O = omission
D = distortion
A = addition
Articulation: Mark errors with appropriate symbol (S, O, D, or A)
Pronunciation: Circle mispronounced words.

STUDENT PRONUNCIATION/ARTICULATION TEST (SPAT)

295

Inappropriate stress:	lap él	pré ferable	iń famous
Omission:	lib*r*ary	reg*u*lar	fig*u*re
Addition:	statistics	chimney	burglar
Substitution:	bro*ch*ure	*c*oma	heigh*t*
Syllable reduction/ deletion	a*v*enue	yell*ow*	crim*i*nal

PARAGRAPH READING

As paragraph is read, circle errors as they are produced. Note above each circled error what type of error it was: S (substitution), O (omission), D (distortion), A (addition). When you have finished, return to word list and mark appropriate errors in paragraph column for each word.

It *s*eems so long ago, but in *f*act *you* know it was *o*nly *l*ast *y*ear. *Th*e mon*th* was *S*eptember and the *p*romise of an *e*arly *au*tumn was in the air. A hu*g*e *g*athering of fa*m*ous la*wy*ers and their *w*ives had a*rr*ived for a con*v*en*t*ion. *R*oy *S*tone, the hotel's *ch*ief bell*h*op, was amazed by the *a*mount of *j*ewels, *v*aluables, and *m*oney stored in the *h*otel safe. One *n*ight, while the *g*uests were *s*leeping, a *th*ief *s*caled the bui*l*ding with a ny*l*on *r*ope, *c*rept in *th*rough a ho*l*e in an eighth-story wi*n*dow and disco*v*ered the safe. With little eff*o*rt, the rogue began to pry open the door and, rea*ch*ing inside with a glove, scooped the ca*sh* and *j*ewels into a *z*ippered lea*th*er *b*ag. He *f*led a*w*ay undetected through the lo*bb*y and dow*n* the *s*treet. The next day, the theft was a*p*parent when Mrs. *B*lack *a*sked for her *d*iamond br*a*celet. The *p*olice w*e*re summoned to solve the crime, but it was the hi*dd*en *c*amera that fi*n*gered the pa*th*etic thief. Tom Wise, alia*s* the *Sh*adow, was *o*ut of lu*ck*. In *sp*ite of his lo*ng* record, the du*mb* wret*ch* had been under the illu*s*ion that no co*p* would ever gra*b* su*c*h a smoo*th* operator. Now he must a*d*just to *p*rison life—no adventure, no prestige.

Glossary

Abdomen The part of the torso below the diaphragm; contains major organs such as the liver, gallbladder, spleen, and intestines.

Abduction A term used to describe the separation or opening of the vocal folds.

Abnormal voice Voice that occurs when the quality, pitch, or loudness differ from those of persons of similar age, sex, cultural background, or geographic location.

Adduction A term used to describe the approximation or closing of the vocal folds.

Allophone A variation of a phoneme that does not change the meaning of a word. The different *l* sounds in *"light"* and *"dull"* are allophones of the phoneme /l/.

Alveolar ridge The bony part of the hard palate just behind the upper teeth. It is the place of articulation for sounds such as /s/, /t/, and /d/.

Articulation The process of producing the sounds of language.

Articulators The movable and immovable parts of the oral cavity used to produce speech.

Articulatory phonetics The study of how the speech mechanism is used to produce sounds.

Aryepiglottic fold The top rim of the larynx; forms a sphincter muscle that contracts when we swallow to protect the airway.

Arytenoid cartilages Small pyramid-shaped cartilages to which the vocal folds are attached on their posterior end. These cartilages sit on the cricoid cartilage and are made to swivel and slide by various laryngeal muscles, thus separating and approximating the vocal folds.

Aspiration The inspiration of foreign material (food, water, etc.) into the trachea and lungs.

Assimilative nasality A nasal resonance that occurs when the sounds adjacent to the three nasal consonants /m/, /n/, and /ng/ are nasalized along with these sounds.

Bernoulli effect The approximation of the vocal folds created by air rushing between the folds.

Breath support The appropriate increase of air pressure below the vocal folds needed for the production of voice.

Breathy phonation An airy voice produced when the vocal folds are not approximated tightly enough to prevent an unusual escape of air.

Central nervous system The part of the nervous system consisting of the brain, brainstem, and spinal cord.

Cerebration A term used in this text to describe the nervous system contribution to speech production.

Channel The medium by which a message is sent or received. Channels can be through hearing or vision.

Coarticulation The process by which neighboring sounds influence the production of each. Compare the position of the tip of your tongue for the words *deep—duke*.

Communication The process of exchanging information and ideas.

Consonants A group of phonemes that are produced by some tightening or closing of the vocal tract.

Corniculate cartilages Small laryngeal cartilages located at the top of both arytenoid cartilages.

Cranial nerves Twelve paired nerves that send and receive both sensory and motor impulses to and from the brain. Cranial nerves directly contribute to speech and voice production.

Cricoid cartilage The base cartilage of the larynx; attaches to the first tracheal ring.

Cricothyroid muscle Paired intrinsic laryngeal muscles responsible for stretching the vocal folds to permit the production of higher pitches.

Cul de sac nasality The nasal resonation of all sounds without the presence of a great deal of nasal emission.

Cuneiform cartilages Laryngeal cartilages that are embedded in supporting laryngeal tissues just lateral to and above the arytenoid cartilages.

Decibel (db) The unit of measurement for intensity or loudness.

Decoding The process of extracting meaning from a message.

Deep structure The abstract representation of a sentence in transformational grammar.

Denasality See hyponasality.

Dialect A variety of a language that may differ in sounds, words, or syntax.

Diaphragm Arch-shaped muscular sheath located at the bottom of the thoracic cavity.

Diphthong A combination of two vowels that sound like one vowel when produced together.

Distinctive features Characteristics used to describe sounds, such as voiceless, nasal, back, and fricative.

Edema A medical term that means swelling.

Encoding Putting thoughts into symbols such as words or facial expressions.

Environmental stress A term used to describe the many occurrences in human life that can cause emotional and psychological stresses that may affect voice production.

Epiglottis A leaf-shaped laryngeal cartilage.

Erythema A medical term that means tissue irritation causing redness.

Esophagus The foodpipe.

Exhalation The outward exchange of air from the lungs while breathing and speaking.

Feedback A verbal or nonverbal response from a listener.

First tracheal ring The most superior circular band of cartilage; provides support for the trachea (windpipe) and serves as the foundation for the larynx.

Frequency The physical correlate of pitch.

Fricative A consonant produced by constricting the vocal tract and allowing the airstream to flow turbulently in a continuous fashion; *s*, *f*, and *sh* are fricatives.

Fundamental frequency Average pitch level of an individual speaking or singing voice.

Glides Consonants that have no consistent place of articulation. Vowels move toward or away from glides, and glides always have many characteristics of the vowels.

Glottal fry A low-pitched growl-like sound.

Glottis The space between the abducted (separated) vocal folds.

Habitual pitch The pitch level most often used by an individual.

Hard glottal attack Initiation of phonation by forcing the vocal folds tightly together, building too great subglottic air pressure and sharply releasing the sound.

Hearing The process of receiving sounds and completing some preliminary processing.

Hertz (Hz) The unit of measurement for frequency or pitch.

Hoarseness Aperiodic vibration of the vocal folds causing an inappropriate voice quality.

Hypernasality A nasal resonance that occurs when excessive nasal emission is present during speech production.

Hyoid bone A small, nonarticulated bone located in the neck; serves as the supporter for the larynx.

Hyponasality A nasal resonance that occurs when the normal nasal consonants, /m/, /n/, /ng/, are not permitted to be produced through the nasal cavity during speech.

Inappropriate voice components   Respiration, phonation, resonation, pitch, and loudness are all voicing components that may be used inappropriately.

Inflection   Variations in pitch and loudness used in conversational speech.

Inhalation   The intake of air into the lungs during breathing and speech production.

Inner ear   The portion of the ear from the oval window to the auditory nerve. This structure (cochlea) also contains the sense organ for balance.

Intensity   The physical correlate of loudness.

IPA—International Phonetic Alphabet   A pronunciation alphabet in which every speech sound is represented by a symbol.

Language   A system of symbols for communicating thoughts and feelings.

Language competence   A speaker's knowledge about the components, phonology, semantics, syntax, and pragmatics of a language.

Language performance   How a speaker uses his or her language in daily situations.

Laryngeal ventricle   The space in the larynx located between the ventricular folds (false vocal folds) and the true vocal folds.

Laryngeal vestibule   The space in the larynx located between the aryepiglottic folds and the ventricular folds (false vocal folds).

Larynx   Valved structure located between the pharynx and the trachea; responsible for protecting the trachea and windpipe from foreign material; also provides vibratory structure for voice production.

Lateral   A manner of articulation in which the air escapes between the teeth and the sides of the tongue. /l/ is the lateral in English.

Lateral cricoarytenoid muscles   Paired laryngeal muscles that aid in the adduction (approximation) of the vocal folds.

Letters   The symbols of the alphabet used for spelling. A letter or combination of letters can represent several different sounds. *th* can be pronounced /ð/ or /θ/ as in *this* or *thought; gh* can stand for /f/ in *tough* or be silent as in *though*.

Loudness   The psychological correlate of intensity.

Lung   The paired organ of respiration responsible for gas exchange with the circulatory system.

Lung capacity   The total amount of air that may be inhaled into the lungs measured in a unit of milliliters of water.

Manner   The amount of constriction in the vocal tract and the way in which air is released from the vocal tract. *Stops* require complete closure of the vocal tract; *fricatives* allow constant, turbulent airflow.

Melody   When related to voice, refers to the variations in rhythm, rate, and inflection which provide expression, intent, and mood to our spoken thoughts.

Message   A collection of ideas and feelings communicated by a source.

Middle ear The air-filled space from the tympanic membrane to the round and oval windows. This compartment contains three small bones—malleus, incus, and stapes.

Monotone The production of voice without the use of pitch and loudness variation; a flat monotonous voice production.

Nasal cavity The portion of the upper respiratory system that extends from the tip of the nose to the pharynx. The nasal cavity is one entrance and exit of air for respiration and also serves as a major resonator.

Noise A distraction, internal or external, that interferes with communication.

Nonphonemic diphthongs Diphthongs that do not change word meaning. Nonphonemic diphthongs are often used in syllables that receive stress. *Row* often will be pronounced /rou/ but the same syllable in "furrow" would be pronounced /ro/.

Nonstandard dialect A dialect that differs from a standard dialect in grammatical rules. A nonstandard dialect is considered acceptable by a subgroup of the speech community.

Nonverbal communication The exchange of thoughts and ideas through eye contact, facial expression, gesture, and distance between speakers.

Oblique arytenoid muscles Paired laryngeal muscles that cross between the arytenoid muscles in an X configuration; aid in the adduction of the vocal folds.

Optimum pitch The pitch level most effective for each individual for voice production.

Oral cavity The portion of the upper respiratory system that extends from the lips to the pharynx. The oral cavity is one entrance and exit of air for respiration and also serves as a major resonator. The oral cavity also contains the major structures responsible for articulation.

Orthography The system of spelling for any language where a letter represents a sound or number of sounds. English orthography does not accurately portray the English language as much as Spanish orthography represents the Spanish language.

Outer ear The portion of the hearing mechanism from the ear canal to the tympanic membrane.

Paralanguage The set of vocal qualities, such as stress, intonation, and speech rate, that adds meaning to speech.

Peripheral nervous system The part of the nervous system consisting of both motor and sensory nerves, which arise from the brain stem and the spinal cord.

Pharynx A part of the upper respiratory system that extends from the conjunction of the nasal and oral cavities to the level of the larynx. The pharynx serves as a major resonator.

Phonation The production of sound created through the vibration of the vocal folds.

Phoneme A family of sounds, a sound that makes a difference, and a bundle of distinctive features.

Phonemic diphthong Diphthong that changes a word when used. /baɪ/—*buy* and /bɔɪ/—*boy* are examples of words with phonemic diphthongs.

Phonetics The study of the sounds of a language.

Phonetic transcription Using a phonetic alphabet, the process of writing out the pronunciation of a word. /ræt/ is the phonetic transcription for *rat*.

Phonics A method of teaching reading by associating sounds with letter symbols.

Phonology The system of rules for combining sounds into words.

Pitch The psychological correlate of frequency; refers to how high or low our voices are perceived by others.

Pitch breaks Sudden, uncontrolled, inappropriate change in pitch during speech production.

Pitch inflection The variability in pitch levels used during conversational speech.

Pitch range The total range from high to low that an individual voice is able to achieve.

Place The area of primary constriction in the vocal tract for consonant and vowel production.

Posterior cricoarytenoid muscle Paired laryngeal muscles; the only muscles that abduct or separate the vocal folds.

Pragmatics The system of rules that determines the appropriate use of language in contextual situations, such as conversations or lectures.

Proxemics The study of the use of space or distance between participants in a conversation.

Rate The speed at which speech is produced; may be measured by dividing the number of spoken words by the elapsed time.

Receiver The listener or intended audience for a message.

Recurrent laryngeal nerve A branch of the tenth cranial nerve; provides motor and sensory fibers to all of the laryngeal muscles except cricothyroid.

Residual air The volume of air left in the lungs that may be forcefully expelled following a normal exhalation.

Resonation The enhancing and damping of sound by structures that are sympathetic to or that absorb all or part of the sound waves.

Respiration The exchange of gases into and out of the bloodstream through tiny capillaries in the lungs.

Rhythm Regularity of the rate of speech production.

Semantics The system of rules for word meaning.

Servosystem A system in which a speech sound is produced and a feedback loop monitors that production and makes adjustments as necessary.

Source The person or persons who originate and send a message.

Spectrum A complex tone made up of many frequencies that give the tone its distinctive quality.

Speech The expression of language by sound production.

Speech perception The process of discriminating and analyzing speech sounds as a part of deriving meaning from speech.

Standard dialect A dialect spoken by persons in positions of social, political, and economic power. A standard dialect is often considered "acceptable" by a speech community.

Stress The relative emphasis placed on word syllables. Vowels that receive more stress are longer and produced with more tension than unstressed vowels.

Superior laryngeal nerve A branch of the tenth cranial nerve; provides motor and sensory fibers to the cricothyroid laryngeal muscles.

Surface structure The form of a sentence as it is intended to be produced.

Syntax The set of rules used to combine words into sentences.

Thorax The part of the trunk of the body located between the base of the neck and the diaphragm.

Thyroarytenoid muscles Paired laryngeal muscles which when combined with the vocalis muscles make up the vocal folds.

Thyroid cartilage The laryngeal cartilage that makes up the main body of the laryngeal frame. It articulates inferiorly with the cricoid cartilage and superiorly with the hyoid bone.

Trachea Windpipe.

Transformational rules The set of rules that rearrange the components from deep structure to surface structure.

Transverse arytenoid muscle An unpaired laryngeal muscle that crosses from one arytenoid cartilage to the other. Contraction aids in the adduction of the vocal folds.

Vagus nerve The tenth cranial nerve, which gives off both the recurrent and superior laryngeal nerves that provide motor and sensory fibers to the laryngeal muscles.

Velum The part of the palate, or roof of the mouth, that extends beyond the hard palate. Also called the soft palate. The velum is raised for nasal sounds /m/, /n/, and /ŋ/ and lowered for all other sounds in English.

Ventricular folds The false vocal folds.

Verbal communication The exchange of thoughts and ideas that occurs through the medium of speech.

Vital capacity The maximum inhalation and subsequent exhalation continued until all possible air is forced from the lungs.

Vocal folds Folds of muscular tissue that contract to protect the airway from foreign substances and vibrate for the production of speech.

Vocalis muscles Paired laryngeal muscles which when combined with the thyroarytenoid muscles make up the vocal folds.

Voice The major element of speech that provides the speaker with the vibration signal upon which speech is carried.

Voice abuse Abuse that occurs when the vocal folds are forced to adduct too vigorously such as through shouting, coughing, making unusual vocal noises, and so on.

Voice misuse Misuse that occurs when the voice is used incorrectly either through voice abuse or the use of inappropriate voice components: pitch, loudness, phonation, and so on.

Voice quality The final voice product produced by an individual once the vibratory signal from the larynx has passed through and been influenced by the entire vocal tract.

Vowels Sounds that are produced with a relatively open vocal tract, are voiced, and form the nucleus or center of a syllable.

Index

Abdomen, 32
  bladder, 32
  breathing, 73–74
  gall bladder, 32
  intestines, 32
  liver, 32
  pancreas, 32
  spleen, 32
  stomach, 32
Abdominal cavity, 31
Abdominal wall, 32
Abductors, 45–46, 48
  posterior cricoarytenoid muscles, 46
Abnormal voice, 55
Acoustic signal, 24
Addams, Jane, 250
Addition errors, 158–160, 167, 170, 177, 208, 212, 214, 217, 227, 238–239, 241, 263–264
  pronunciation, 159–160, 263–264
    consonants, 167, 170, 177, 208, 212, 214, 217
    vowels, 227, 238–239, 241
Adduction, 45–48
  lateral cricoarytenoid muscles, 46
  oblique arytenoid muscles, 46–47
  transverse arytenoid muscles, 46–47
Affricates, 125–127
  practice, 200, 202, 252–253
Airflow, 110, 112, 114, 118, 122, 124–127, 129, 194, 197–198, 200, 202, 204, 206
Airstream, 115–117, 119, 121, 123, 130, 170, 177, 179, 181, 185, 187, 189, 192, 194, 196, 208, 217
"Alexander's Feast," 252
Alfoxden Journal, The, 250
Alice in Wonderland, 258
Allophones, 18, 185
"All That Glitters Is Not Gold," 252
"All Times Are His Seasons," 254
Alveolar, 100, 111–112, 119, 121, 127, 129, 135, 172, 174, 189, 192, 204, 206, 217
Alveolar ridge, 96–97, 99, 111–112, 119, 121–123, 125–126, 128–129, 132–133, 135, 172, 174, 189–190, 192, 194, 196, 206, 212, 217
American Sign Language (ASL), 17
American Speech-Language Hearing Association (ASHA), 166

Amplitude, 49
Anatomy of larynx. *See* Larynx, anatomy
"Annabel Lee," 253, 281–282
Anthony, Susan B., 278–279
Anvil. *See* Incus
Aorta, 48
Aperiodic vibration, 59
Aphonia, 64
Appalachian English, 22
Arbitrary symbols. *See* Language
"Are You the New Person Drawn Toward Me?," 254
Armstrong, Neil A., 258
"Art," 256
Articulation, 36–37, 91, 107–108, 162, 166–167
  assessment, 157–164
  disorders, 159
  errors, 137–156, 158–159
    addition, 158–159
    consonants, 109–126, 128–135, 162, 167, 170, 172, 174, 177, 179, 185, 187, 190, 192, 194, 196, 200, 202, 204, 214, 217
    distortion, 158–159
    omission, 158–159
    substitution, 158–159
    vowels, 137–156, 229, 231–232, 234, 239, 245
  imprecision, 159
  improvement, 163–164, 165
  phonemes, 91–94, 98–104
  phonetics, 91–92, 94–95
  structures, 36–37, 96–97
Articulators, 92
  hard palate, 92
  jaw, 92
  lips, 92
  soft palate, 92
  teeth, 92
  tongue, 36, 92
Aryepiglottic folds, 42–43
Arytenoid cartilage, 43–44, 46–47
  muscles, 46–47
    oblique, 46–47
    transverse, 46–47
"As I Walked Out One Evening," 255
"Ask Me No More," 261
Aspiration, 41, 167, 170, 172, 211

305

INDEX

Assimilative nasality, 59–60, 78–79
Auden, W. H., 255
Auditory cortex, 23–24
Auditory nerve, 23
Auditory pathway, 23
Auditory processing, 28

Bernoulli effect, 48
"Bethsabe's Song," 258
Bilabial, 99–100, 108, 110, 129, 131, 167, 170, 204, 206, 210
Black Cat, The, 275
Black English, 22, 111, 117, 119
Bladder, 32
Blake, William, 247, 255, 259
Blood, G., 53
Body movement, 25
"Bonny Barbara Allen," 284
Boone, D., 58
Brain stem, 23, 29
   cranial nerves, 29, 47
Breakdown, 13, 30, 51
   cerebration, 30
   communication, 13
   voice production, 51
Breath stream, 58
Breath support, 56–57, 58, 62, 66, 75, 77–78
   clavicular, 57
   diaphramatic, 57
   thoracic, 57
Breathy phonation, 59, 67–68
Broca's area, 28
Bronchial tubes, 30-31
   bronchioles, 31
   left primary, 31
   right primary, 31
Bronchioles, 31
Browning, Robert, 253
Bunyan, John, 261
Burns, Robert, 251
"By-Low, My Babe," 287
Byron, Lord, 247
"Byzantium," 253

Carroll, Lewis, 248–249, 253, 256–258
Carruth, G., 95
Cartilage, 41, 43–44, 46–47
   arytenoid, 43–44, 46–47
   corniculate, 43–44
   cricoid, 43, 46–47
   cuniform, 43–44
   larynx, 41
   thyroid, 43
Cather, Willa, 253
Central nervous system, 24–25, 27–30
   cerebrum, 28–29
   major lobes, 28–29
   meninges, 27–30
Central vowels, 227–234, 236–239, 258–259
   practice, 227–241
Cerebral palsy, 159
Cerebration, 27–30
   breakdown, 30
Cerebrum, 27
Channel, 12
Chest cavity. *See* Thoracic cavity
Childe Harold's Pilgrimage, Canto IV, 274
Chomsky, Norm, 19–20
Churchill, Winston, 249, 251
Clavicular breathing, 57
Cleft palate, 166
Closed box, 57
Closed syllable, 100–101
Coarticulation errors, 99, 161
Cognates, 99

Coleridge, Samuel Taylor, 251
Communication, 12–17
   breakdown, 13
   model, 12–13
   modifying, 13
   monitoring, 13
   nonverbal, 14
   pragmatics, 17
   process, 12–13
      channel, 12
      feedback, 12–13
      message, 12
      noise, 12–13
      receiver, 12
      source, 12–13
   verbal, 14
Confusion errors, 167, 183, 217, 239
   consonants, 167, 183, 217
      fricatives, 183
      glides, 217
   vowels, 239
Consonants, 15, 24, 37, 58, 60, 91, 97, 161
   affricate practice, 252–253
   airflow, 104, 107
   combined with vowel, 104, 107
   errors, 167, 170, 177, 208, 212, 214, 217
      addition, 167, 170, 177, 208, 212, 214, 217
      confusion, 167
      distortion, 172, 174, 177, 179
   fricative practice, 249–252
   fricatives, 99
   glide practice, 254–256
   glides, 99
   glottal, 99
   improvement, 181–220
      affricates, 200–204
      fricatives, 181–200
      glides, 211–219
      nasals, 204–210
      stops, 168–181
   laterals, 99
   manner, 99
   nasal practice, 253–254
   nasals, 99
   place, 99
   PMV, 104, 107
   stops, 98–99, 108–115
   stops practice, 247–248
   velum, 104, 107
   vocal tract constriction, 104, 107
   voice, 104, 107
      unvoiced, 98–100
      voiced, 98–100
Conversation regulators, 14–15
   eye contact, 14
   facial expression, 14
   gestures, 14–15
   use of space, 14–15
Cool Hand Luke, 11
Corniculate cartilage, 43–44
Cranial nerves, 29, 47
   accessory, 29
   acoustic, 29
   facial, 29
   glossopharyngeal, 29
   hypoglossal, 29
   trigeminal, 29
   vagus, 29
Cricoarytenoid muscles, 46
Cricoid cartilage, 43, 46–47
Cricothyroid muscles, 46–48
   lateral, 46
   pars oblique, 47–48
   pars rectus, 47–48
Cross-cultural differences, 14–15, 21

INDEX

Cul de sac nasality, 59–60, 78–79
Cuniform cartilage, 43–44

"Dear Lord, Kind Lord," 255
Decoding, 12, 14, 20, 23
   hearing perception, 23–25
Deep structure, 19–20
Deletion, 159–160
Denasality, 59–60, 68–69
Dialects, 21, 25, 51–53
   major areas, 21–22
      subdivisions, 21
   nonstandard, 22, 107, 161
      Appalachian English, 22
      Black English, 22, 111, 117, 119
      Eastern English, 144–145, 147
      Native Spanish, 138
      Oriental English, 135, 217
      Scandinavian English, 133, 212
      Southern White English, 22, 139, 144–145, 154, 208
      Spanish, 116, 118–119, 124, 194
   standard, 21–22, 107, 130, 135, 161
      consonants, 109–135
      vowels, 137–156
Diaphram, 31–33, 57, 73–74
Dinesen, Isak, 252
Diphthongs, 98, 103–104, 107, 124, 139, 145, 159, 219, 225, 236, 239, 241–242, 244–245
   nonphonemic, 104, 149
   phonemic, 104, 153–156
   practice, 241–246, 260–261
   quadrilateral, 103
Distortion errors, 158
   consonants, 172, 174, 177, 179
      affricates, 200, 202
      fricatives, 181, 190, 192, 194, 196, 198
Donne, John, 254
"Dream Within a Dream, A," 260
Dr. Jekyll and Mr. Hyde, 279–280
Dryden, John, 252
Dysphonias, 64
Dysphonic, 75

"Eagle, The," 248
Ear, 23
   anatomy, 23
      inner ear, 23
      middle ear, 23
      outer ear, 23
      auditory cortex, 23
Eardrum. *See* Tympanic membrane
Eastern dialect, 144–145, 147
Edwards, Jonathan, 276
Ehrlich, E., 95
Eisenhower, Dwight D., 248
Emerson, Ralph Waldo, 248
Encoding, 12, 20, 23. *See also* Messages
English, 107
   nonstandard, 107
      phonemes, 37, 92–94
   standard, 107
Environmental stress, 63
Epiglottis, 43, 45, 96
Esophagus, 41–42, 96
Etiology of voice disorders, 56
   medical, 63
   personality related, 63–64
   voice misuse, 56
Exhalation, 30, 33–34, 73–74
Expiration, 58
External intercostal muscles, 30
Eye contact, 14, 25

Facial expression, 14–15, 25
   cues, 14
   indicators of emotion, 14
   innate, 14
"Fall of the House of Usher, The," 249
False vocal folds. *See* Ventricular folds
Fanshawe, Catherine Maria, 255
"Farewell Address to the Nation," 248
Feedback, 12–15, 25, 82
   nonverbal, 12
   verbal, 12
First tracheal ring, 43
Fitzgerald, Edward, 247
Flexner, S. B., 95
Food pipe. *See* Esophagus
"Fragments," 255
Frequency, 23, 33–34. *See also* Pitch
Fricatives, 99, 158, 162, 170
   consonants, 110, 114–125, 181, 183, 185, 187, 189, 192, 194, 196, 198
   practice, 181–200, 249–252
Frontal lobe, 28
   Broca's area, 28
Front vowels, 219, 221–225, 241–242, 245
   practice, 219–226, 256–258
Fundamental frequency, 34

Gall bladder, 32
"Garden, The," 257
Gestures, 14–15
Glides, 99, 131–136, 210, 212, 214, 217
   practice, 211–219, 254–256
Glottal, 100, 124, 198
   consonants, 99
Glottal attacks, 67
   hard, 58–59, 75–77
Glottal fry phonation, 59, 67–68, 75, 78
Glottis, 43, 46
Grammar. *See* Syntax
Greek dialect, 124

Hall, E. T., 15
Hammer. *See* Malleus
Hard glottal attacks, 58–59, 75–77
   vocal folds, 58
Hard palate, 36, 92, 96–98, 122, 137, 142, 219, 236
   alveolar ridge, 97
Hawkins, J. M., 95
Hearing, 29
   anatomy, 23
Hearing loss, 25
Hebrew dialect, 124
Henry, Patrick, 278
Hertz, 34
"Hiawatha's Photographing," 256
High-oral cavity, 137–138, 150–151, 153–156, 219, 221, 237, 239, 241–242, 244–245
Hill, Aaron, 259
Hoarseness, 15, 56, 59, 67–68, 75, 78
Holmes, Oliver Wendell, 252
Hood, Thomas, 259
Hopkins, Gerard Manley, 255
"Hunting of the Snark, The," 249
Hyoid bone, 43
Hypernasality, 59–60, 68, 78–81

Identity conflicts, 64
Immovable articulators, 96
   hard palate, 96
   teeth, 96
Immovable structures, 96–97
Inappropriate voice, 15
Incorrect stress placement, 264–265
   pronunciation, 264–265
Incus, 23

INDEX

Infectious laryngitis, 56
Inflection, 51–52, 57, 69–70, 83. *See also* Pitch; Loudness
Inhalation, 30, 32–34, 41, 57, 73
"In Memory of Charles Baudelaire," 251
Inner ear, 23
  receptor cells, 23
Intensity, 33–34, 49, 62. *See also* Loudness
  variations, 49
Intercostal muscles, 30
  external, 30
  internal, 30
Interdental lisp, 120, 122
Internal intercostal muscles, 30
International Phonetic Alphabet (IPA), 94–95
Intestines, 32
Intonation, 15
Intrinsic laryngeal muscles, 45–48
  lateral cricoarytenoid, 46
  oblique arytenoid, 46–47
  transverse arytenoid, 46–47
"I Wake and Feel the Fall of Dark," 255

"Jabberwocky," 248
James, Henry, 257
Japanese dialect, 124
Jaw, 80–81, 96–97, 124, 137, 146

Kennedy, John F., 249, 251, 276–277
"Kubla Khan," 251
Kurath, Hans, 21

Labiodental, 100, 115–116, 118, 181, 183
"Lady's Dream, The," 259
Language, 15–20, 23–25
  competence, 15–17, 19
  performance, 15–17
  phonology, 17–19
    phonemes, 17
  pragmatics, 19
  processing, 20
    model, 19–20
  production, 20
    speech components, 23–25
  semantics, 18–19
    lexicon, 18
  syntax, 18–19
Language Development: An Introduction, 19
Laryngeal, 25, 55
  anatomy, 81
  framework, 43–45
    arytenoid cartilage, 43–44
    corniculate cartilage, 43
    cricoid cartilage, 43
    cuniform cartilage, 43–44
    epiglottis, 43, 45
    first tracheal ring, 443
    hyoid bone, 43
    thyroid cartilage, 443
  muscles, 45
    abductors, 45
    adductors, 45
    intrinsic laryngeal muscles, 45
    vocal fold, stretchers, 45
    vocal folds, 45
  pathology, 75, 78
  ventricle, 43
  vestibule, 43
Laryngitis, 78
Larynx, 23, 29–30, 34, 41–48, 60, 78–81, 96
  anatomy, 41–48
    aryepiglottic folds, 42–43
    cartilages, 41
    connective tissues, 41
    esophagus, 42
    glottis, 43
    laryngeal framework, 43–45
    laryngeal muscles, 45–48
    muscles, 41
    ventricular folds, 42–43
  physiology, 48–50
  vagus, 29
  vocal folds, 34
  voice production, 50
Lateral cricoarytenoid muscles, 46
Lateral lisp, 120–122, 190, 192, 194, 196
Laterals, 99
Lax tongue, 221, 223, 225, 227–228, 232, 234, 237, 242, 244–245
Left hemisphere, 23
  specialized area, 23
Left inferior frontal gyrus. *See* Broca's area
Left primary bronchi, 30–31
Lexicon, 18
Lincoln, Abraham, 276
Lindfors, J. W., 16
Linguadental, 100, 117, 185, 187
Linguistic Atlas of the United States, The, 21
Lips, 25, 36, 91–92, 96, 101, 108, 110, 115–116, 124, 127, 131, 167, 170, 181, 183, 204
  rounded, 101–102, 144–146, 148–151, 153, 155–156, 210, 229, 231, 234, 236–237, 239, 241, 244–245
  unrounded, 137–143, 146, 153–156, 219, 221–223, 225, 227–228, 232, 241–242, 244–245
Lisp, 157, 200
Listening skills, 166
Liver, 32
"London," 259
"Lotos-Eaters, The," 256
Loudness, 15, 33–34, 52–54, 56–57, 62, 70–72, 77, 79. *See also* Intensity
  assessment, 70–71
  exercises, 84–85
  improvement, 84–85
  variability, 70
"Love Among the Ruins," 253
"Love's Labour's Lost," 250
Lower jaw, 29
Low-oral cavity, 141, 146–147, 154–155, 225, 232, 234, 242, 244
Lungs, 23, 30–31, 33–34, 41–43, 48, 57–58, 66, 73–75

Major American English speech varieties, 22
Major lobes, 28–29
  frontal, 28–29
    Broca's area,, 28–29
  occipital, 28–29
  parietal, 28–29
  sense integrators, 28
  temporal, 28–29
Malleus, 23
Mandible, 36
"Manlet, The," 253
Manner, 99, 101–102, 107
Marvell, Andrew, 257
Medical diagnoses, 63, 75, 78
Melody, 51, 54, 87
Melville, Herman, 256
Meninges, 27
Messages, 12–15
  decoding, 13
  encoding, 12
Mid-cental oral cavity, 222–223, 227–229, 231, 236, 245
Middle ear, 23
  incus, 23
  malleus, 23
  stapes, 23
Mid-oral cavity, 139–140, 142–145, 149, 156
Mill, John Stuart, 256

INDEX

Misuse of voice, 56–63
Model of communication. *See* Communication, model
Modifying communication, 13
Monitoring communication, 13, 15
Monotone pitch, 62, 81–83, 85
Mood, 87
Morley, Christopher, 260
Motor nerves, 29
Movable articulators, 96
  jaw, 96
  lips, 96
  soft palate, 96
  tongue, 96
  velum, 96
Muscular movements for speech, 23–24
  larynx, 41
"Music, When Soft Voices Die," 257
Muteness, 64
"My Heart's in the Highlands," 251
Myoelastic aerodynamic theory, 48
  Bernoulli effect, 48

Nasal cavity, 23, 35, 42, 60, 78, 80, 91, 96, 129–130
  resonance, 35, 53
  soft palate, 35
  sounds, 35
Nasals, 99, 162
  consonants, 78–79, 127–131, 204, 206, 208
  practice, 204–210, 253–254
  resonance, 35, 53
Native Spanish dialect, 138
"Nephelidia," 247
Nerve supply, 47
  auditory, 23
  recurrent laryngeal, 47
  superior laryngeal, 47
Newman, Paul, 11
New York dialect, 144–145
Nist, J., 22
Noise, 15
"Noiseless Patient Spider, A" 249
Nonphonemic diphthongs, 104
Nonstandard English dialects, 22, 161
  Appalachian English, 22
  Black English, 22, 111, 117, 119
  Oriental English, 135, 217
  Southern White, 22
Nonverbal communication, 14, 25
  conversation regulators, 14–15
    eye contact, 14
    facial expression, 14
    gestures, 14–15
    use of space, 14–15
Normal voice, 52, 54, 73, 78
  resonance, 52
  voice quality, 52

Oblique arytenoid muscles, 46–47
Occipital lobe, 28
"Old Clock, The," 285–286
Omission errors, 158–160, 263
  consonants, 167, 172, 174, 177, 179, 185, 198, 204, 217
  vowels, 227
"One Day at a Time," 248
Open syllables, 100–101
Optimum pitch, 69
Oral cavity, 23, 35–36, 42, 78, 80, 91, 96–97, 101, 108, 114, 130, 139, 167, 189, 192, 222–223
  anatomy, 36
    hard palate, 36
    lips, 36
    mandible, 36
    soft palate, 36
    teeth, 36
  articulation, 36
  hard palate, 36
  resonance, 36
Oral tract, 127
Oriental English dialect, 135, 217
"Othello," 260
Otolaryngologist, 56, 78
Outer ear, 23
Out of Africa, 252
Owens, R. E., Jr., 19, 100

Palatal, 100, 122–123, 131–133, 194, 196, 212, 214
  pharyngeal, 79–80
    closure, 79
    opening, 80
Palatal damage, 60
Palato-alveolar, 125–126, 200, 202
Pancreas, 32
Paralanguage, 14
Parietal lobe, 28
"Paste," 257
"Paul's Case," 253
Peele, George, 258
Perception, 53
  speech, 23–24
Performance, 15–17, 19
  language, 15–17, 19
Peripheral nervous system, 27, 30
  motor nerves, 29
  sensory nerves, 29
Personal distance. *See* Use of space
Personality-related causes, 63–64
  aphonia, 64
  dysphonias, 64
  environmental stress, 63
  identity conflicts, 64
  muteness, 64
  psychological stress, 63
Personal voice assessment, 65–72, 75, 78, 81, 84–86
  loudness, 70–71
  phonation, 67–68
  pitch, 69–70
  rate, 71–72
  resonance, 68–69
  respiration assessment, 66–67
  results, 72
Pharyngeal, 29
  glossopharyngeal, 29
Pharyngeal damage, 60
Pharynx, 23, 29, 35, 41–42, 60, 78–79, 96, 101, 198
Phonation, 33–34, 41, 48–49, 56, 72
  assessment, 67-68
    breathy, 67
    glottal attacks, 67
    glottal fry, 67
    hoarseness, 67
  breathy, 59
  glottal fry, 59
  hard glottal attacks, 58–59
  hoarseness, 59
  improvement, 75–78
    exercises, 75–79
  myoelastic areodynamic theory, 48
  vocal folds, 33, 48
Phonemes, 17–18, 91, 130, 157–159, 162
  allophones, 18
  anatomy/physiology of production, 94
  classification, 98–104
    coarticulation, 99
    consonants, 98–99
    constriction, 99–100
    vowels, 98, 100–104

Phonemes (cont'd.)
  consonants, 37
  English, 37, 92–94, 107
    diphthongs, 93–94
    vowels, 37, 93–94
  production, 165
  transcription, 94
Phonemic diphthongs, 104
Phonetic alphabet, 94–95
  International Phonetic Alphabet, 94–95
Phonetics, 91
Phonology, 17–19, 21–22, 91
  phonemes, 17–18, 91
"Piping Down the Valleys Wild," 247
Pitch, 33–34, 47–49, 52–54, 56–57, 60–62, 69, 72, 75, 78, 81. See also Frequency
  assessment, 69
    breaks, 69–70
    habitual, 69
    inflection, 69–70
    optimum, 69
    range, 69
  breaks, 62
  habitual, 61
  hertz, 34
  improvement, 81
    exercises, 82–83
  inappropriate, 60
  inflection, 61–62
  monotone, 62
  optimum, 61
  range, 60–61, 81–83
  sex differences, 48–49
Place, 99, 101–102, 107
PMTL, 102, 166. See also Lips; Manner; Place; Tension
  vowels, 137–156
    central, 227–234, 236–239
    diphthongs, 153–156, 241–242, 244–245
    front, 219, 221–225
PMV, 99, 108, 110–119, 121–127, 129–133, 166. See also Manner; Place; Voice
  consonants, 181–217
    affricates, 200, 202
    fricates, 181, 183, 185, 187, 189, 192, 194, 196, 198
    glides, 210, 212, 214, 217
    nasals, 204, 206, 208
    stops, 167, 170, 172, 174, 177, 179
Poe, Edgar Allen, 249, 253–254, 260, 275, 281–282
Posterior cricoarytenoid muscles, 46
Pragmatics, 19, 21, 23
Presentation vocal, 86–87
Primary sensory control area, See Pariental lobe
Processing, 24
Pronunciation, 15, 137–265
  assessment, 157–164
  consonants, 109–126, 128–135, 167, 170, 172, 174, 177, 179, 181, 183, 185, 187, 190, 192, 194, 196, 198, 200, 204, 206, 208, 210, 212, 214, 217
  errors, 166–167
    addition, 159–160, 263–264
    inappropriate stress, 159–160, 264–265
    omission, 159–160, 263
    substitution, 159–160, 262–263
    syllable reduction/deletion, 159–160, 265
  improvement, 163–165
  vowels, 137–156, 219, 221, 224–225, 227–229, 231, 234, 236, 238–239, 241–242, 244
Psychological/emotional causes, 75, 78
Psychological stress, 63

Quadrilateral, 102–103
  vowels, 102
    diphthongs, 103
Quality, 33–34, 52, 54, 56. See also Spectrum

Rate, 53, 56, 62–63, 72
  assessment, 71–72
    rhythm, 71–72
    variability, 71–72
  improvement, 86
"Raven, The," 254
Receiver, 12–13, 15, 25
  decoding, 12
Receptor cells, 23
Recurrent laryngeal nerve, 47–48
Red Jacket, 250
Reduction errors, 241
Residual air, 58, 73–74
Resonance, 35–36, 52–53, 78–79, 81, 127
  nasal, 35, 52–53, 78–79, 81, 127
  oral, 35–36
Resonation, 34–36, 72
  assessment, 68–69
    denasality, 68–69
    hypernasality, 68
  improvement exercises, 78–81
  inappropriate, 56, 59
  spectral components, 35
  vocal sound resonators, 34–36
    nasal cavity, 35
    oral cavity, 36
    pharynx, 35
Resonators, 35–36
  coupling, 60
  nasal cavity, 35
  oral cavity, 36
  pharynx, 35
Respiration, 25, 56, 58–59, 72, 75, 78
  abdomen, 32
  assessment, 66–67
  breath support, 30, 36, 56
  exhalation, 30
  improvement exercises, 73–75
  inhalation, 30
  residual air, 58–59
  speech, 32–33
  thoracic cavity, 30–33
    spinal vertebrae, 30
Respiratory passages, 30–31
  bronchial tubes, 30–31
  lungs, 30–31
  tranchea, 30
Rhythm, 51–54, 87
Rib cage, 32
Ribs, 30, 33
Right primary bronchi, 30–31
Riley, James Whitcomb, 225
Roof of mouth. See Hard palate
Rubiyat of Omar Khayyam, The, 247

San Francisco Earthquake, The, 278
Scandinavian English dialect, 133, 212
Schenk vs. United States, 252
Scott, Sir Walter, 252
Semantics, 18–19, 21–22
  cultural differences, 21
  lexicon, 18
Sensory cells, 25
Sensory channels, 15
Sensory nerves, 29
Sentence, 19–20
  deep structure, 19–20
  surface structure, 19–20
  transformation rules, 19–20
Servosystem, 24–25
Severity levels, 65
Shakespeare, William, 21, 248, 250–251, 254, 260–261
Shelley, Percy Blake, 257

INDEX

Simple vowels, 98, 100–103
Soft glottal attack, 76
Soft palate, 29, 35–36, 60, 92, 96, 113–114, 177, 179
"Song of Myself," 250, 254
"Sonnet XXX," 251
Sound confusion, 159–160
Sound production and improvement, 104
Source, 12–13, 15, 25
Southern White nonstandard English, 22, 144–145, 154, 208
Spanish dialect, 116, 118–119, 124, 194
Spectral components, 33–36
Spectrum, 33–34, *see also* quality
Speech, 21–25, 28, 32–34, 36–37
  articulation, 36–37
  breathing, 32–33
    thoracic, 33–34
  cultural differences, 21–22
  dialects, 21–22
  hearing, 23
  musculature, 23, 28
  perception, 23–24
  production components, 23–25
Speech pathologist, 55–56, 78, 159, 166
Speech therapist, *see* Speech pathologist
Spinal cord, 23
Spinal vertebrae, 30
  ribs, 30
  sternum, 30
Spleen, 32
Standard dialects, 21
  Southern Standard English, 21
  Standard English, 21
Standard English, 22, 130, 135, 161
Stapes, 23
Sternum, 30, 32
Stevenson, Robert Louis, 279–280
Stirrup, *see* Stapes
Stomach, 32
Stops, 108, 110–114, 162
  improvement, 167, 170, 172, 174, 177, 179
  practice, 247, 168–172
Story of My Life, The, 257
Stress, inappropriate, 159–160
Structural History of English, A, 22
Student Pronunciation/Articulation Test (SPAT), 162–163
  procedure, 162
  results, 162–163
Subclavian artery, 48
Subcostal muscles, 30
Subglottic air pressure, 75, 77
"Subjection of Women, The," 256
Substitution errors, 158–160, 262–263
  consonants, 172, 183, 185, 187, 190, 192, 194, 196, 200, 204, 206, 208, 212, 214, 217
  vowels, 219, 221, 224–225, 228–229, 231–232, 234, 236, 238, 242, 244–245
Subsystems of sounds. *See* Phonology
Superior laryngeal nerve, 47–48
Surface structure of speech, 19–20
Swift, Jonathan, 258
Swinburne, Algernon Charles, 247, 251
Syllables, 37, 124
  reduction errors, 159–160, 265
  stressed, 103, 151, 159–160, 238–239
  unstressed, 142, 149, 153, 160, 198, 236
Syntactic cultural differences, 22
Syntax, 19, 21

Target sounds, 162
Teeth, 36, 96, 111–112, 115–119, 122–123, 125, 133, 144, 172, 174, 181, 183, 185, 187
Temporal lobe, 28
Tennyson, Alfred Lord, 261, 248, 256

Tense tongue, 219, 223, 229, 231, 236, 239, 241
Tension, 101–102, 107
Terry, Ellen, 257
"Thaw," 259
Thomas, Edward, 259
Thoracic breathing, 33–34, 57
Thoracic cavity, 30–33, 57
  intercostal muscles, 30–32
    external, 30–32
    internal, 30–32
  respiratory passages, 30
    bronchial tubes, 30–31
    lungs, 30–31
    trachea, 30
  spinal vertbrae, 30
    ribs, 30
    sternum, 30
  subcostal muscles, 30–32
Throat. *See* Pharynx
Through the Looking Glass, 257
Thyroarytenoid muscles, 45
Thyroid cartilage, 43, 47
Thyroid gland, 48
"Tiger, The," 255
Tissues, 41
  larynx, 41
"To a Child," 260
Tone, 34
Tongue, 29, 36, 42, 60, 80–81, 91–92, 96–97, 101–103, 111–114, 124, 128, 130–133, 177, 187, 198, 208, 210
  back, 97, 146–147, 149–151, 153, 155–156, 232, 234, 236–237, 239, 241, 244–245
  blade, 97, 111–112, 119, 121–123, 125–126, 129, 132, 172, 174, 189–190, 192, 194, 196, 206, 212
  center, 97, 142–145, 154–155
  front, 97, 137–141, 153–154, 156
  glossopharyngeal, 29
  tension, 101, 107
    lax, 138, 140–143, 146–147, 150, 154–156
    tense, 137, 139, 144–145, 149, 151, 153
  tip, 97, 111–112, 122, 125–126, 129, 132, 135, 144, 172, 174, 185, 194, 196, 206, 212, 214–215, 217
Trachea, 23, 30, 32–34, 41–42, 57, 96
Transcription, 165
  nonstandard, 165
  standard, 165
Transformational rules, 19–20
Transverse arytenoid muscles, 46–47
Triphthong, 139
True vocal folds, 43
Twain, Mark, 277–278
"Twelfth Night," 248, 261, 254
Twenty Years at Hull House, 250
"Two Red Roses Across the Moon," 260
Tympanic membrane, 23

"Upon the Snail," 261
Urdang, L., 95
Use of space, 14–15
  proxemics, 15

Vagus nerve, 47
  recurrent laryngeal, 47
  superior laryngeal, 47
Vandenberg, J., 48
Velar, 100, 113–114, 129–130, 177, 179, 206, 208
Velum, 36, 96–97, 99, 101, 124, 127, 129–130, 204, 206, 208. *See also* Soft palate
Ventricular folds, 42–43
Verbal communication, 14, 25
  paralanguage, 14
"Verses on the Death of Doctor Swift," 258

INDEX

Vibratory pattern, 33–34
  frequency, 33–34
  intensity, 33–34
  spectrum, 33–34
Vital capacity, 58
Vocal abuse, 62–63, 75
Vocal components, 53, 56
Vocal cords, 73
Vocal folds, 41, 58, 96, 99, 124, 198
  adduction, 45
  approximators, *see* adductors
  closure, 75, 77
  musculature, 34
  separators. *See* Abductors
  stretchers, 45–47
    cricothyroid muscles, 47
  thyroary muscles, 45
  variations, 34
  vibration, 33–34, 56–59, 74, 77–78
Vocal misuse, 56
Vocal tract, 42, 55, 78, 98–99, 104, 107
Voice
  box. *See* Larynx
  components, 65, 72, 75
  disorders, 55–64
    abnormal voice, 55
    etiology, 56–64
    infectious laryngitis, 56
    severity levels, 55
  improvement, 72–73
  melody, 51
  muscles, 45
  normal, 52–53
  personality, 53
  placement, 35
  production, 50–54
    breakdown, 51
    inflection, 51–52
    melody, 51
    normal, 52–53
    rate, 51
    rhythm, 51–52
  quality, 86–87
  sound resonators, 35–36
  nasal cavity, 35
  oral cavity, 36
  pharynx, 35
  unvoiced, 108, 110–111, 113, 115, 117, 119, 122, 124–125, 167, 170, 172, 177, 181, 185, 189, 194, 198, 200
  voiced, 112, 114, 116, 118, 121, 123, 126, 129, 174, 179, 183, 187, 192, 196, 202, 204, 206, 208, 210, 212, 214, 217
Voicing components, 36, 99–100
Vowels, 24, 37, 58–59, 86, 91, 97, 107, 161
  airflow, 104
  articulation, 104
  central, 227–234, 236–239
  diphthongs, 98, 153–156, 241–242, 244–245, 260–261
    phonemic, 153–156
  errors, 137–156
  front, 219, 221–225, 256–258
  lip rounding, 101–102
  manner, 101–102
  place, 101–102
  PMTL, 107, 137–156
  practice, 219–246, 256–261
    central, 227–241, 258–259
    diphthongs, 241–246, 260–261
    front, 219–226, 256–258
  quadrilateral, 102
  simple, 98–103
  syllable, 100–101
  tension, 101–102
  velum, 104
  vocal tract, 104

"When I Heard the Learn'd Astronomer," 260
Whistling, 120–121, 190, 192
Whitman, Walt, 249–250, 254, 260
"Wife of Usher's Well, The," 282–283
Windpipe, *see* trachea
Word meanings. *See* Semantics
Wordsworth, Dorothy, 250
"Written on a Window," 257

Yeats, W. B., 253